# Female performance practice on the fin-de-siècle popular stages of London and Paris

MANCHESTER
1824

Manchester University Press

# WOMEN, THEATRE
# AND PERFORMANCE

Series editors
Maggie B. Gale and Viv Gardner

Already published

# FEMALE PERFORMANCE PRACTICE ON THE FIN-DE-SIÈCLE POPULAR STAGES OF LONDON AND PARIS

## Experiment and advertisement

CATHERINE HINDSON

Manchester University Press
Manchester and New York

*distributed exclusively in the USA by Palgrave*

Copyright © Catherine Hindson 2007

The right of Catherine Hindson to be identified as the author of this work
has been asserted by her in accordance with the Copyright, Designs and
Patents Act 1988.

*Published by* Manchester University Press
Oxford Road, Manchester M13 9NR, UK
and Room 400, 175 Fifth Avenue, New York, NY 10010, USA
www.manchesteruniversitypress.co.uk

*Distributed exclusively in the USA by*
Palgrave, 175 Fifth Avenue, New York,
NY 10010, USA

*Distributed exclusively in Canada by*
UBC Press, University of British Columbia, 2029 West Mall,
Vancouver, BC, Canada V6T 1Z2

*British Library Cataloguing-in-Publication Data*
A catalogue record for this book is available from the British Library

*Library of Congress Cataloging-in-Publication Data applied for*

ISBN    978 0 7190 7485 1 hardback

First published 2007

16  15  14  13  12  11  10  09  08  07        10  9  8  7  6  5  4  3  2  1

Typeset by
Servis Filmsetting Limited, Manchester
Printed in Great Britain
by Biddles Ltd, King's Lynn

# Contents

# SERIES EDITORS' FOREWORD

This series, *Women, Theatre and Performance*, has its origins in the work of a number of feminist theatre academics from the 1980s and 1990s – a period when interest burgeoned in the part that women have played in theatre over the centuries. That interest was in its turn the daughter of the 'Second Wave' women's movement, the women's theatre movement and the women's history movement from the previous two decades. It was with some delight that women theatre workers, spectators and scholars alike discovered that women *did* have a significant history in perform-ance, and these women – and some men – have continued to investigate, interrogate and work with their histories. Feminist performance analysis and women's theatre history have now become an established part of per-formance practice and theatre studies at both a university and a more popular level.

In the 1990s, the journal *Women and Theatre Occasional Papers* became the host for the documentation and dissemination of contem-porary research and innovation in theatre practice and scholarship in Britain. The emphasis on history and historiography was a considered decision. It was felt that at that time no consistent outlet existed for all the work that carried on the feminist retrieval project of the 1980s which was emerging from theatre and drama departments in Britain and else-where. This emphasis on history did not – and does not – preclude engagement with contemporary practice. On the contrary, it was felt that our history was very much part of our present and that the two could, and should, be studied side by side. This series seeks to continue that original project and to make the research and debate available on a more than 'occasional' basis. The series will consist of themed volumes that consider theatre as part of a wider nexus of social and cultural prac-tices. Women's contribution to all areas and types of theatre and per-formance will be included, from opera and acrobatics to management and dramaturgy. Continuities and consistencies will not be sought, though they may be found within the transhistorical and transcultural organisation of the material.

The series is designed for students at all levels, teachers and prac-titioners, as well as the interested enthusiast who wishes simply to 'fill in the blanks' where women have been hitherto 'hidden' in theatre histories.

Maggie B. Gale
Viv Gardner

# ILLUSTRATIONS

# Acknowledgements

A significant amount of the archival research for this volume was enabled by an AHRC Small Grant in the Creative and Performing Arts, which funded research periods at New York Public Library and the Museum of Montmartre. The completion of this project has been made possible by an award made by HEFCE and The University of Birmingham made under their Emerging Researcher Scheme, for which I am grateful.

I would also like to thank the numerous archivists and librarians at the National Art Library, London, the Dance Archive in Toronto, the Performing Arts Division of New York Public Library, the Theatre Museum, London, the Museum of Montmartre, the Mander and Mitchenson collection, London, the Site Richelieu of the Bibliothèque Nationale de France and the National Art Library, London who have been enthusiastic about this project, and aided its research.

Preparing this book for publication has been a simultaneously pleasurable and agonising experience, and many people have supported it – and its author – along the way. They all know who they are, and how grateful I am. Nonetheless, particular thanks are owed to Maggie Gale and Viv Gardner, who have been tirelessly enthusiastic and encouraging about this project from its early (if slightly incomprehensible) stages, through to the finished product. I am also indebted to the readers for Manchester University Press who raised pertinent questions that forced me to interrogate my approach, to its benefit.

To colleagues in the School of Theatre, Performance and Cultural Policy studies at the University of Warwick and in the Department of Drama and Theatre Arts at the University of Birmingham, who have commented on various versions of these ideas, I also offer my thanks. I would also like to record my gratitude to all the students who have enthusiastically followed my undergraduate course on Parisian cabaret performers over the last five years.

Thanks are also due to my mum, and to the other friends and family members – my own and extended – and my closest friend Kerry who have listened, read, commented and sympathised, as required. Finally, however, my complete gratitude is offered to Phil, for everything. It is to him, and our daughter Grace, that I dedicate this volume, with love.

'Our stars are women who bring us in money, and we live on them'.
(Charles Zidler, co-owner of the Moulin Rouge, Paris)

# INTRODUCTION

Our impressions of the modern city continue to be influenced by the popular legacies of late nineteenth- and early twentieth-century London and Paris. Historicisations of the period have linked the two metropolitan centres with the leisure and pleasure of commodity culture. Certainly many of the products that we associate with the period, including posters, novels, fashion and architecture, encapsulate the fantasies of glamour and spectacle that were created in and by new city environments and the social practices they engendered.

The entertainment industry is located at the core of many of these projected visions of urban utopias. Inherited images of fashionable venues, spectacular shows and international celebrities have established a romanticised, mythical vision of the fin de siècle's leisure activities. Entertainment mirrored and advertised the spectacular visual culture of the city. On stage, the rapidly changing fashions and trends, and the technological developments and social changes that identify the modern metropolis, supplied the material for a significant proportion of the plays and the acts that were presented to the period's large audiences. But this was also the fin de siècle: a time when atmospheres of optimism and anxiety became inseparable.[1] As Walter Laquer has stated:

> Fin de siècle has meant and still means a great variety of things. In France it signified to be fashionable, modern, up to date, recherché, sophisticated. It has also been a synonym for morbidity, decline, decadence, cultural pessimism.[2]

Co-existing with the energy of the belle époque, a time that celebrated and clothed itself in new forces and ideas, was the darker side of modernity. Change was exciting, but it was also unsettling. For many, this was a time when all that was solid appeared to 'melt into air'.[3] Social, technological, geographical and cultural transitions exacerbated existing anxieties, and provoked new ones. New phenomena, including the widespread use of electricity, more affordable worldwide travel, developing communication networks, increased mass production and sprawling conurbations, coupled with older questions concerning housing, poverty, health, drug and alcohol abuse and sex, sparked debate and anxiety. Amidst a changing world, concerns about the degeneration of the human race, gender, sexuality, class, psychology and spirituality bubbled to the surface.

In spite of their diverse sources, these concerns were primarily experienced and expressed in sociological terms. They prompted and fuelled extended debates about humanity and civilisation: debates that rapidly became apparent across the period's cultural products. In spite of the glamorous image of the popular stage that we have inherited, the entertainment industry was neither exempt nor removed from the fin de siècle's concerns. Its themes, performers and motifs were embedded in the modern experience of the city.

Programmes, venues, performers and audiences were in a state of flux in the late nineteenth- and early twentieth-century city. In response to a growing public demand for entertainment, the spectacles offered to audiences increased in number and scale, as the classes, genders and nationalities of performers and spectators diversified. The entertainment industry's dependence on the new technologies of electricity and print culture to create its spaces, produce its spectacular stage effects and to promote them changed the nature of its output further. As Sally Ledger and Scott McCracken have noted, 'one of the most significant reasons for the disorientation felt in [this] period' can be discovered in the 'new experience of mass culture' that was offered by the modern city. Its unfamiliarity 'threw all previous definitions into confusion': this was new territory.[4]

The popular stages of London and Paris were spaces where social changes were enacted in front of large bodies of individuals. Drawing on the conventions and codes of the modern urban experience, they acted as sites that not only reflected fin-de-siècle society's most evident anxieties and changes, but also contributed to them. A fusion of the spectacle, energy and pessimism characteristic of the period is evident in its venues, stars and products and it requires a new way of approaching the fin de siècle. An approach that counteracts the tendency of historians to 'describe the end of the nineteenth century as either beleaguered or belle', and to instead acknowledge a dialectic relationship between energy and pessimism: an interaction that created both the period's cultural moment and its cultural products.[5] In the case of the popular stage, to dissect the fin-de-siècle experience and present it as either beleaguered or belle is to fail to understand its products, its significance and its cultural role.

The female star performer emerged out of this changing entertainment industry, materialising as an international cultural phenomenon of the fin de siècle. Although widespread celebrity culture has generally been identified as a result of the rapid growth in mass culture that occurred after the end of the First World War, the growth of metropolitan centres and the development of an international network of cultural communications at the fin de siècle had established and fuelled a specific model of celebrity culture. Recognising this earlier manifestation of a celebrity culture supplies relatively new terrain for both performance scholars and cultural historians.[6] Largely predating the glamour of the film star, it centres on the popular stage and on the stage favourites of the day.

Lenard R. Berlanstein has emphasised the importance of the celebrity to historical understandings of culture. Any society, he argues, will inevitably project 'reigning myths about self-fulfilment and personal uniqueness' on to its stars.[7] During a period when ideas about gender were contested and challenged, the high-profile female celebrity performer – simultaneously a product of and a contributor to commodity culture – became a significant and powerful figure. In her on- and off-stage performances contemporary ideas and concerns about gender and society were reflected, refracted and resisted. Playing with, and amidst, the fluctuating conventions of the entertainment industry and the international network of fame, the female performer's presence on the popular stage could interrogate and destabilise contemporary ideological values and aesthetic ideas.

This study explores the connections between popular entertainment and experimental performance between 1880 and 1910. It focuses on seven women who used the fin de siècle's popular stage as a space to develop their experimental performance practices: acts that won them international fame and critical acclaim. The diverse entertainment careers of Maud Allan (1873–1956), Jane Avril (1868–1943), Loïe Fuller (1868–1926), Sylvia Grey (1866–1958), Yvette Guilbert (1867–1944), Letty Lind (1862–1923) and Cissie (Cecilia) Loftus (1876–1943) encompassed song, dance, impersonation and acting. In accounts, reviews, autobiographical writings, interviews and other cultural products associated with them it is clear that individual female celebrities understood their work as creative, professional and original performance practice.

It is undeniable that these women's lives were fascinating. Nonetheless, this volume does not aspire to tell their stories. Rather it is motivated by an acknowledgement that the focus needs to be shifted away from the pervasive biographical interest that has shaped a significant amount of writing about popular performers. Fuelled by a romanticised vision of the belle époque, earlier biographical works (particularly those dating from the mid-twentieth century) established a model of the famous women of the fin de siècle, through their embrace of the glamour and spectacle associated with the period. Its legacy can be discovered in the repeated presentation of popular performers as signifiers of a spectacular culture, rather than as autonomous creative figures.

Reconsidering and reinterpreting the connections between early celebrity culture, historiography and dominant understanding of fin-de-siècle performance demands an interdisciplinary approach. The dynamic interactions between social, cultural and historical ideas that shaped the modern city simultaneously created the entertainment industry. They carved out the terrain on which the performer, the act and the spectator's experience occurred. Audiences watched a performer, but never in a cultural vacuum. Spectators were also the market for press interviews, merchandise and promotional posters, whilst the programmes and interiors of entertainment venues were designed for their consumption.

Unpacking the multi-layered ideas and the numerous forces that were contained within the entertainment industry of the fin de siècle necessitates a consideration of the environment that it was in dialogue with. To organise the complicated and interwoven urban geographies, cultural networks and multiple performances that created the celebrity act, at the same time as maintaining a clear emphasis on the connections between them, the volume is divided into four sections. 'The terrain', 'Spaces', 'Image' and 'Intersections' offer areas of investigation that draw together performers, performances and their contexts.

'The terrain' considers the geographical and ideological environments against which female celebrity performances occurred. Chapter one focuses on the importance of London and Paris as metropolitan spaces used by the fin-de-siècle celebrity performer, whilst Chapter two explores questions of gender and corporeality in relation to the on-stage female body. Together, they demonstrate the ways in which popular female performance practice challenges historical understandings of performance in the modern city.

'Spaces' is devoted to discussions of two specific sites in London and Paris. The iconographies associated with the Gaiety Theatre (Chapter three) and the Salpêtrière hospital (Chapter four) frame an exploration of the identities and creative processes developed by popular female performers. Advertising, self-promotion and celebrity identity form the focus of 'Image'. Chapter five investigates the role of the fin de siècle's new print-culture industries in the entertainment industry, questioning how the lithograph, the interview and the autobiography were strategically employed by performers to establish and disseminate strong on- and off-stage images.

In Chapter six the emergence of impersonation as a popular entertainment form and the rise of the female mimic draw on and develop the ideas concerning identity raised in the preceding chapter. The volume concludes with 'Intersections', two chapters that illustrate the fusion of ideas about popular and experimental performance that were revealed in the work of individual fin-de-siècle female celebrities. Chapter seven traces the appearance of Symbolist aesthetics on the dance-hall stage and Naturalist practices in the café-concert. In Chapter eight the figure of Salome, a popular choice of role for popular stage performers, is aligned and compared with the construct of the female celebrity.

Examples of female experimental performances in fin-de-siècle cities can be easily aligned with the contemporary demand for spectacle, distraction and glamour. Generally they occurred on a grander scale, and in a less diverse range of spaces, than the work offered by their bohemian contemporaries. Nonetheless, the popular acts of Maud Allan, Jane Avril, Loïe Fuller, Sylvia Grey, Yvette Guilbert, Letty Lind and Cissie Loftus shaped the cultural terrain of the fin de siècle. Their performances blurred divisions between the popular and the experimental, and brought new ideas to capacity houses filled with a diverse mix of spectators. Working within the modern entertainment industry, the celebrity female variety performer engaged with the fantasies of pleasure that were projected by the modern city. On stage, her performing body acted as a signifier, adopted by herself, and by others, to represent current questions and anxieties about gender and mass audiences.

The exclusion of the creative work of these seven women from established narratives of fin-de-siècle performance practice has been founded on hierarchical approaches to cultural environments, to gender and to physical, non-scripted performance. The 'high' and 'low' cultural divisions that these have instilled demand to be interrogated for, in the tendency that David Savran has identified for scholars of performance to routinely dismiss the 'kinds of theatrical practice that have held millions spellbound', evidence about crucial intersections between performance practice, the entertainment industry and gender is lost.[8] For the audiences, managers and performers of the fin de siècle the areas that have been retrospectively separated were symbiotic and co-dependent. The strikingly different, original performance practices of Maud Allan, Jane Avril, Loïe Fuller, Sylvia Grey, Yvette Guilbert, Letty Lind and Cissie Loftus fused styles, motifs and ideas that would now be understood as distinctly popular or experimental.

Witnessed by hundreds of thousands of spectators, the acts created by these female performers were the products of the specific social, historical and cultural conditions of the late nineteenth and early twentieth centuries. Reviewing them as nexus of popular forms, fashionable images, experimental performance and aesthetic debate enables us to question the extent to which female celebrity could employ the popular stage space to challenge and to appropriate current ideas about gender and performance. In so doing, this volume seeks to account for, and to begin to amend, the significant gap in the history of female experimental performance that their exclusion has created.

## Notes

1 Although fin de siècle literally translates as end of century, this was not an experience that was to end on 1 January 1900. Indeed many would argue that the fin de siècle's close came only with the outbreak of the First World War in 1914.
2 Walter Laquer, 'Fin de Siècle: Once More with Feeling', *Journal of Contemporary History* 31:1, January 1996, pp. 5–47 (5).
3 See Marshall Berman, *All that is Solid Melts into Air: The Experience of Modernity* (London and New York: Penguin, 1988).
4 Sally Ledger and Scott McCracken (eds), *Cultural Politics at the Fin de Siècle* (Cambridge: Cambridge University Press, 1995), p. 8.
5 Mary Louise Roberts, *Disruptive Acts: The New Woman in Fin-de-Siècle France* (Chicago and London: University of Chicago Press, 2002), p. 2.
6 Lenard R. Berlanstein, 'Historicizing and Gendering Celebrity Culture: Famous Women in Nineteenth-Century France', *Journal of Woman's History* 16:4, 2004, pp. 65–91 (67). See also Berlanstein, *Daughters of Eve: A Cultural History of French Theater Women from the Old Regime to the Fin de Siècle* (Cambridge, MA: Harvard University Press, 2001). Since the appearance of Berlanstein's article, essays by Sos Eltis, Peter Raby and Maggie B. Gale in Mary Luckhurst and Jane Moody (eds), *Theatre and Celebrity in Britain, 1660-2000* (Basingstoke and New York: Palgrave Macmillan, 2005) have approached questions about the late nineteenth century and celebrity.
7 Berlanstein, 'Historicizing and Gendering Celebrity Culture: Famous Women in Nineteenth-Century France', p. 67.
8 David Savran, 'Towards a Historiography of the Popular', *Theatre Survey* 45:2, 2004, pp. 211–17 (212).

# Part I

## THE TERRAIN

'I wanted to go to a city where, as I had been told, educated people would like my dancing and would accord it a place in the realm of art.' (Loïe Fuller)

# 1

# THE THEATRE OF THE CITY: URBANISATION, PERFORMANCE AND SPECTATORSHIP IN FIN-DE-SIÈCLE LONDON AND PARIS

During the late nineteenth and early twentieth centuries, leisure and tourist industries flourished in London and Paris. Department stores, restaurants, museums, monuments, galleries, exhibitions and entertainment venues attracted visitors and consumers from home and from abroad to these two modern European cities. In London's West End the Palace Theatre of Varieties and the Gaiety Theatre offered two of the capital's most fashionable nights out. In Paris, the Folies-Bergère, on the rue Richer, and Montmartre's Moulin Rouge became familiar worldwide as signifiers of the fin de siècle's capital of pleasure. In these four popular and fashionable metropolitan sites the spectacle and spirit of a new entertainment industry were encapsulated. From their stages and their auditoriums ideas about entertainment, spectacle and celebrity were transmitted to international audiences. Each of the performers discussed in this volume appeared on the stage or the dance floor of at least one of these representative fin-de-siècle entertainment venues.

Comprehending the significance of these metropolitan performance spaces, and the key role that they played in the identities created and the performances offered by female celebrities, depends upon a wider consideration of the city environments and the entertainment industries from which they emerged. To a large extent, the geographical and cultural locations occupied by these venues, and their audiences, governed their output. Rapid urbanisation and population growth made the city a powerful force and signifier of the fin de siècle and, as a result of this, modern metropolises became sites where current ideas about performance, spectatorship and identity were realised: not only on the stage, but also on the streets.

The recurrent appearance of the city as a trope and a stimulus of modernist art, literature and the movements of the avant-garde has been widely noted. Edward Timms has commented on a new dynamic that was

produced by the modern city, a dynamic that 'generated new forms of
expression which accentuated its energy and turmoil' and rendered 'conventional modes of representation . . . no longer adequate'.[1] Similarly,
Raymond Williams identified a clear link between 'the practices and ideas
of the avant-garde movements of the [early] twentieth century and the
specific conditions and relationships of the twentieth-century metropolis'.[2] Timms refers to painting, poetry and the novel, whilst Williams
focuses primarily on the avant-garde. Nonetheless, both of their arguments are equally applicable to examples of popular performance from
the late nineteenth and early twentieth centuries.

Although the modes of representation that are associated with the
popular stage may immediately appear to have been more conventional,
or less experimental, than those of modernist art or literature, there was,
arguably, an even closer connection between the city and the performance
innovations that occurred on its popular stages. In these expanding metropolitan spaces large crowds of people came together: bodies of individuals, a new set of spectators, that moved through the same spaces, and
visited and looked at the same sights. The modern metropolis was preoccupied with display; its sites, sights and day-to-day life depended upon
and fostered the theatrical and the spectacular.[3] Alongside other European
and American cities, London and Paris were the sources of influential and
pervasive ideas about spectacle: it is logical that performance – a form that
is inseparable from current ideas about display – engaged with and
reflected this crux of the modern metropolitan experience. Amidst the
urban geographies of these two fashionable European capitals, constructs
of female celebrity were established, played with and played out.

Large audiences were both a product and a feature of London and
Paris at the fin de siècle. Contemporary street maps from guides to
London and Paris reveal the leisure zones established in the modern city.
The separate identification of numerous venues (including the Gaiety
Theatre and the Moulin Rouge) illustrates the centrality of the entertainment industry to the new urban economy (Figure 1). As John McCormick
has noted, 'what the nineteenth century showed most clearly was the existence of a real and large popular public . . . a huge population requiring
diversion whenever they could afford it or find the leisure to enjoy it'.[4]
Entertainment acts and the plots of popular stage plays frequently drew
on the tropes of modern urban existence. Metropolitan trends and
current affairs became an important source for stage material, whilst
technological developments and popular fashions supplied the stuff of
many spectacular stage effects. However, the interrelationships between

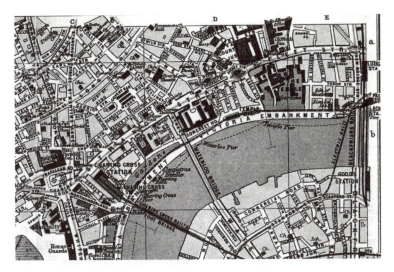

1 London street map, *Pocket Guide to London* (1899)

popular performance and the modern metropolis were greater than those that are revealed by the stage's mirroring of urban life. Cities are never comprised solely of their buildings, their 'glass and bricks'; they also 'live in the bodies, habits and movements of their inhabitants'.[5] The fin-de-siècle music-hall goer, the café-concert audience member, or the play-goer necessarily entered into the metropolis' trends and crowds. For the spectator, visiting an entertainment venue meant immersing her or himself into this theatre of the city, offering their body, habits and movement as part of a wider culture of display.

Arriving at the Palace Theatre of Varieties, the Gaiety Theatre, the Folies-Bergère or the Moulin Rouge was a performance in itself: a performance whose conventions were shaped by its immediate socio-historical context. By choosing to visit a fashionable venue, or to attend a performance by a particular celebrity, a spectator made a visual statement about their cultural awareness, their fashionable status and their social knowledge. Each evening, each spectatorial choice that was made in London and Paris represented a response to the interconnected industries of marketing, fashion and the media, as well as a response to current ideas about performance. This new 'real and large' popular public out in search of entertainment itself invested in, and formed an important element of, metropolitan spectacle and performance.

## Fin-de-siècle London and Paris

France and Britain had been political adversaries since the middle ages, and the difficult relationship between the two countries continued during France's Third Republic (1870–1940) and Britain's Victorian (1837–1901) and Edwardian eras (1901–10). This ongoing acrimony was not only the domain of politics and current affairs; it also formed familiar subject matter for newspaper, journal and novel readers, and for theatre and music-hall goers. Having celebrated Paris as the perfect location for the American, male tourist, one journal went on to explain that visiting the French capital was infinitely more problematic for the English, male tourist who had been brought up to believe that, 'one Englishman can [and by implication in the text, should] thrash three Frenchmen'.[6]

Eventually the most severe of the Franco-British disputes of the late nineteenth and early twentieth centuries brought about a treaty to secure peace. The entente cordiale of 1904 aimed to resolve long-standing dis-agreements over the two nations' colonial outposts, its signing signalling a closer political alliance between them.[7] Yet before this early Edwardian diplomatic breakthrough, the products and the processes of an interna-tional commodity culture had closely connected the two countries, in spite of their political differences. In 1860, the Cobden-Chevalier treaty's reduc-tion of import duties and abolition of French embargoes on British prod-ucts had increased trade between the nations. Improved commerce resulted in strong links developing between the two countries' tastes and cultures, particularly in the areas of fashion, entertainment and the visual arts.

Contemporary publications make it clear that the cultures, fashions and trends that emerged in London and Paris were of interest to the other city. Information about them was widely available to the British or French fin-de-siècle consumer. On vacation, or living in Paris, the English reader could easily access *The Times* and *The Saturday Review*, whilst the French visitor or resident could purchase *Le Figaro* in London. Both coun-tries also published bi-national journals: in England, *Paris-London: An Illustrated Review of News and Current Events,* and in Paris, *Le Courrier de Londres et de Paris: politiques, literatures et commerce.* In the fashion and entertainment industries, these interests and influences are particularly clear.

By the 1890s, the designs of the House of Worth and Paquin had cemented Paris' reputation as the world-capital of chic. Details of Parisian fashion houses, their new collections and off-the-peg replicas formed the frequent subject of the British press, and of specialist journals that included *The Latest Paris Fashions: A Monthly Journal for English and American Ladies, The Paris Mode* and the *Englishwoman's Domestic Magazine*. Parisian couture was available in London's shops, and the city's leading department store, the Bon Marché, deliberately targeted the British market with extensive catalogues, seeing overseas mail order sales as holding the potential for much revenue.[8] Meanwhile, London department stores launched sites in Paris: Maison Liberty, a fabric and clothing arm of the London company, opened a store in the French capital in 1889.[9]

Fashion created a shared language between London and Paris, but the leisure industries of the fin de siècle also played an instrumental role in fostering cross-Channel trends. Newspaper entertainment listings, guidebooks and reviews from the 1890s reveal that London and Paris offered their audiences comparable entertainment venues and performance styles. French and British variety acts, popular performers and theatre companies frequently toured around Europe, attracting large audiences. Translated plays from the Parisian boulevard theatres often bolstered British theatrical programmes, whilst British plays added to the repertoires of Paris' boulevard theatres.[10] Popular entertainment even engaged with the shifting political relationship between the two nations. In June 1908, four years after the signing of the treaty, London's Alhambra Theatre staged a ballet created to celebrate the entente cordiale. *The Two Flags: A Franco-British Divertissement* featured representative 'national' figures, including France's emblematic warrior Marianne and Britain's Union-Jack clad John Bull, amongst its characters.[11] An industry that had fostered cultural links between France and Britain now staged a version of their recent diplomatic history in front of large and enthusiastic audiences.

Walter Benjamin's much cited 1935 description of Paris as the 'capital of the nineteenth century' reiterated the way that people had thought about the French capital since the late nineteenth century.[12] Forty years earlier, in 1895, *Harper's New Monthly Magazine* had stated that whilst 'Americans go to London for social triumph or to float railroad shares, to Rome for art's sake, and to Berlin to study music and economize', they go to Paris simply 'to enjoy themselves'.[13] At the fin de siècle Paris meant pleasure. Tourist guides to the city published in England, France and America all devote significant amounts of space to the entertainments that were on offer in the city. Paris' café-concerts, music halls, dancing gardens and theatres were considered by these editors, and their projected readers, to be of as much interest to the fin-de-siècle visitor as the city's famous museums, galleries and architecture.[14] A visit to the city was incomplete without them. By the 1890s, Paris' role as the modern world's capital of pleasure and spectacle was firmly established, and had been self-consciously adopted by the city, and by many of its inhabitants.

## Paris' spectacular theatre of the city

Paris' reputation for a love of display became a widely identified characteristic of the city's inhabitants and visitors, as well as of its entertainment industry. At the fin de siècle, 'Paris' meant more than its buildings and its street maps; the city's name also signified the spectacle associated with its day-to-day events and its public spaces. The eyes of the world watched Paris, and, whether visiting the theatre, going out to dinner, to the department store or riding through the city's streets and parks, stepping out in public in the French capital was inherently connected with being on display. As the English publication *John Bull's Trip to Paris* recorded in 1900, '[t]he talent for acting comes more readily to a Frenchman than to an Englishman. Every Frenchman is more or less of a born actor.'[15]

Contemporary images and ideas about Paris were articulated in a language of spectacle, a language that was inseparable from ideas about performance and display. It is no coincidence, therefore, that the two commercial sectors that were at the core of Paris' renown as the capital of fin-de-siècle spectacle – the fashion and entertainment industries – depended upon and developed a prioritisation of the visual.[16] Both fashion and entertainment reflected and extended the aesthetic of display that characterised and advertised the city.

Paris' entertainment industry peaked during the late nineteenth century. In the city's popular performers and venues we can discover both an integral element of this pervasive aesthetic of spectacle, and a metaphor and representation of it. Following the 1864 revocation of the restrictions imposed by Napoleon I on the number of theatres allowed in the French capital, a steady stream of new venues had opened. Audiences also grew, by the 1880s and 1890s more than a half a million Parisians went to the theatre once a week and more than a million went once a month.[17] By 1896 the recorded population of Paris was 2, 536, 834: 40 per cent of this body of people as regular theatre-goers is a significant audience.[18] Moreover, these figures only provide evidence of the recorded box office sales for the city's main theatres; they do not include the spectators that visited its variety venues, café-concerts and dance halls.

Alongside the programmes of opera, classics, light comedies and operettas offered by the city's state-subsidised venues, the Opéra, Opéra-Comique and Comédie Française, Paris' secondary theatres offered well-made plays, operettas and the stage spectacles of féerie, magic plays, historical pageants, vaudeville and melodrama.[19] This was a theatre, an entertainment industry, with a need, and an aim, to entertain. Rarely did the programmes of these theatres reflect the economic and cultural diversity of the city's audiences and population. Its offerings projected a fantasy vision of life in Paris, a belle époque whose legacy remains with us today. As John Henderson has stated:

> The theatre in the nineteenth century was a reflection of the society in which it flourished. The age of economic expansion which followed the Industrial Revolution favoured the growth of a mercantile middle class, and this class demanded for its entertainment a theatre in which it saw an idealized picture of its own qualities, a theatre that was moral, comfortable and thoroughly predictable.[20]

The nineteenth-century French theatre staged the 'capital of the nineteenth century'. However, it would be incorrect to assume that its largely moral, comfortable and predictable programmes meant that Paris' theatre industry was unaffected by the ongoing processes of urbanisation that were impacting on the city: during the second half of the nineteenth century it had undergone major changes. In line with similar shifts across Europe and North America, Parisian audiences, and thus auditoriums, had increased in size. Simultaneously, and in line with urban spectacle and trends, going to the theatre had become progressively more concerned with which venue one went to and what one went to see. The entertainments on offer were diverse and in demand, and Paris' audiences were large and experienced in the amount of performance that they saw.

Amidst this burgeoning and competitive entertainment industry, theatrical celebrities formed one of the major attractions that drew audiences to venues. As a result of star actresses and actors attaining international fame and fan bases, the traditional ensemble companies of the French stage were largely replaced with a 'star system'. Theatres programmed productions that showcased the star performer they had contracted, and long runs of these 'celebrity productions' became central to the industry. Runs that numbered one or two hundred performances financed the significant costs involved in casting stars, and of staging the effects of spectacular productions. Spectacle permeated every level of the entertainment industry, on the stage, in the auditorium, in the performers it hired and in its marketing. Whilst figures like the novelist Emile Zola expressed concerned about the impact that these changes were having on the quality of French theatre and its cultural status and development, their views were in the minority. For audiences at the music hall, the theatre, or the café-concert, the presence of a star performer on the stage in front of them remained an important element of entertainment.[21] Across theatrical and variety entertainment celebrity culture was dominant.

Co-existing, and in dialogue, with this successful commercial entertainment industry, fin-de-siècle Paris was the site of many of the late nineteenth and early twentieth centuries' avant-garde movements. The French capital was identified at the time as 'the outright dominant centre [of modernism] . . . the fount of bohemia, tolerance and the émigré lifestyle', and it has retained this position in later understandings of the fin de siècle's aesthetic innovations and challenges. However, as a new term that emerged for literature and theatre in the 1880s and 1890s, the remit and definition of avant-garde were still being mapped out at this time.[22] Many small, experimental, counter-cultural movements first emerged in Paris' galleries, artistic cabarets, theatres and artistic cafés, but understandings of their significance has largely been retrospective.[23]

Paris was a seedbed for experimental theatrical work: at André Antoine's Théâtre Libre (1887–94), productions reflected current thinking about Naturalism and Symbolism. After this company disbanded, Antoine continued his important stagings of new work and ideas at the Théâtre Antoine between 1897 and 1907. Between 1893 and 1929 Aurélien Lugné-Poe's Théâtre de l'Oeuvre produced successive seasons of challenging new writing: short runs of challenging productions that engaged with emerging ideas about theatre and performance. Paul Fort's company, the Théâtre d'Art (1890–93), took Symbolism into performance, offering some of the most ambitious and radical experiments with the concept of stage synthesis that have been seen up until today. Further innovations in performance styles emerged in the chansons, sketches and shadow-theatre shows of the city's artistic cabarets, most famously the Chat Noir cabaret in Montmartre. Motivated by a belief in the spirit of collaboration, performers, writers and artists came together in cabaret spaces, using popular, small-scale performance forms to push at the boundaries of the theatrical experience and to offer a theatre that both reflected and rejected the associations with the status quo that they saw reflected on the commercial mainstream stage.

In addition to the state-subsidised venues, the boulevard theatres and the small audiences of the avant-garde, Paris' entertainment industry offered further choice. Circuses were hugely popular during the period, with venues that seated up to 8,000 spectators, whilst café-concerts, housed in auditoriums or large gardens, and dance halls attracted many spectators.

The acts at these venues included acrobats, horseback riders, dancers, singers, sketches, musicians, performing animals and comedians. In the same ways as the programmes of the popular stage, these venues and performers reflected the 'values and tastes of the metropolis'.[24] Finances and transport permitting, fin-de-siècle audiences moved freely between these entertainment forms. The contemporary spectator's understanding of entertainment is thus likely to have compounded examples, or images, from all of these choices on offer to them.

### 'Such sights I'd never seen before': fantasy projections of metropolitan London and Paris[25]

Fantasy visions of the modern city were embedded in the products and in the venues of the fin de siècle's international entertainment industry. Soon to make a slight adjustment to his name and become one of the most iconic figures of cinema, Charles Chaplin began his comedy career on the British music-hall stage. His early performances included a song called 'Oui! Tray Bong! or, My Pal Jones', a lyric written by the popular song-writer Norton Atkins that told of a recent trip to Paris taken by the singer and his two friends, Tom and Harry. Out in the French capital, Chaplin informed his audience that:

> We thought we would see the sights of it,
> But we've made some fair old nights of it;
> Still, I can assure you, we've enjoyed ourselves immensely . . .
> My pal Jones, full of cognac, started prancing,
> Then he said, 'Let's go and see the ladies dancing'
> To this place we'd never been before,
> And such sights I'd never seen before.[26]

The use of Paris as the subject of Chaplin's song is in no way unique: lyrics and illustrations from sheet music collections disclose the popularity of the French capital as a recurring theme in music-hall entertainment. Dating from the late 1890s, collections reveal many popular songs concerned with the French capital, including 'Oui, Oui, Oui, or, Going to Paris', 'Gay Paree', 'The Paris Exhibition', 'Paree! Paree!' and 'What they Showed me in Paree'.[27] In these lyrics that were heard by large audiences and reprinted to buy, play and sing at home, Paris' location as a signifier of eroticism and pleasure is secured.

Although late nineteenth- and early twentieth-century London is less regularly associated with a language of spectacle and glamour, in the familiar and influential products of the popular entertainment industry this modern British city also appears as a representative site of pleasure and eroticism. Whilst Paris may have been renowned and historicised as the fin de siècle's capital of pleasure, a love of spectacle also drew the resident and tourist audiences of late Victorian and Edwardian London to the theatre, and on to the streets of the city. Counteracting the enduring prudish image of the Victorian era, work in nineteenth-century studies has uncovered a mainstream metropolitan leisure culture grounded in spectacle and pleasure.[28] London's entertainment industry was at the heart of this British culture of display.

Amongst the celebrity music-hall performer Vesta Tilley's popular repertoire was a song entitled 'When a Fellah has Turned Sixteen', a lyric that humorously debates the most appropriate way for a young Victorian man to celebrate and mark this milestone birthday. His father suggests a visit to Madame Tussaud's display of waxworks. The son refuses, exclaiming, 'What! just to see the stuffed guys? / Come with me to the Palace, the Tableaux Vivants / Are the right sort to open your eyes.'[29] Since 1893, the Palace Theatre of Varieties had presented on-stage living pictures – the tableaux vivants – as a standard part of their programme. Staged within 'a gold frame and accompanied by music', the tableaux vivants showed silent and immobile 'female performers attired in flesh-tinted tights' striking various 'artistic' poses for the audience's pleasure.[30]

The Palace astutely attempted to authorise the apparent, although not actual, visions of female nudity that were central to many of these stagings by offering recreations of respected, 'high' works of art, thus drawing on the acceptable image of the classical nude. Nonetheless, tableaux vivants provoked controversy throughout the late nineteenth century. They were eventually removed from the theatre's programme by a London County Council ban, but not until 1907. For fourteen years the tableaux vivants formed a popular part of the Palace programme, and of the spectacle associated with London's popular stage. The furore that they provoked has been well documented; the positive responses of the hundreds of thousands of spectators who went to the Palace, and expected the tableaux vivants as part of their evening's entertainment, are less easily recoverable, but arguably more central to understanding ideas about female performers at the time.

Paris may dominate contemporary and historical understandings of pleasure and leisure in the late nineteenth and early twentieth centuries, however the scale and the success of London's entertainment industry was a source of celebration and promotion. In the mid-1890s the *Tit-Bits*

*Guide to London* boasted that 'the places of entertainment in London would hold all the inhabitants of Edinburgh, and then there would be several thousand vacant seats'.[31] This was a flourishing industry, and the British capital's venues and performers were internationally renowned. In the eyes of London's entrepreneurs and of many of the city's spectators and visitors, London's leisure industry was not secondary to Paris'; it formed its direct competition.

The fin de siècle's accelerated commodity culture resulted in international patterns and practices of consumerism, and in their designs, their programmes and their consumers London's capital's theatres, department stores and music halls were strikingly similar to those of Paris. Indeed, in 1900, *Cassell's Guide to Paris and the Universal Exhibition* drew a direct comparison between the programmes and the décor of Paris' café-concerts and those of London's music halls.[32] Melodrama, pantomime, magic, spectacular historical reconstructions of Shakespeare's plays and music-hall acts formed the dominant entertainment forms on the British capital's stage. In the late nineteenth and early twentieth centuries, a Londoner visiting Paris, or a Parisian visiting London, would be familiar with the majority of the entertainment forms on offer. The two cities offered spectators facets of an international entertainment culture; their venues and their programmes reflected worldwide trends and fashions and featured touring stars.

In spite of the similarities in their commercial theatre industries, unlike Paris, London was not home to a recognised and highly publicised avant-garde. It was an absence that contemporary British theatre aficionados who were familiar with the Parisian cultural landscape mourned. In January 1896, the influential publication *The Saturday Review* noted that many of London's play-goers 'env[ied] Paris for the multitude of little theatres it possesse[d]'. The presence of these small-scale, 'inexpensive' companies, such as the Théâtre de l'Oeuvre, acted as 'exercise grounds for the dramatic talent of both authors and actors'; a similar presence in London would, this writer claims, result in a 'gayer and more interesting' theatrical scene.[33] Although there was less of a recognised, we might say an established or publicised, avant-garde in the British capital, its stage was a 'radical and influential place' that offered a mixture of popular entertainment and experimental work.[34] During this period London did witness the emergence of its own little theatres and innovative companies, including stagings of the works of Oscar Wilde, Henrik Ibsen and George Bernard Shaw, and productions by J. T. Grein's Independent Theatre and the New Century Theatre.

In both capital cities impassioned and high-profile debates were provoked and sustained by the current status and provision of theatre: debates that spanned the nineteenth and early twentieth centuries. Demands were being made for new theatres, new companies and new forms of entertainment. Diverse groups of creative practitioners were gathering to challenge contemporary understandings of performance in a variety of spaces and forms. History has had a hand both in the prioritisation of Paris as *the* centre of experimental performance, and in the canonisation of the small-scale experiment as the model of theatrical innovation. However significant these works were, new ideas about performance were evident in more spaces than those occupied by avant-garde movements that have been retrospectively canonised.

The similarities and the connections between London and Paris' entertainment industries reveal two modern metropolises concerned with projecting fantasy images of themselves internationally: images that would reassure their citizens and attract visitors and spectators. These idealised visions veiled the simultaneous urban realities of poverty, crime and disease; at the same time they were popular with audiences. It is important to consider the reasons for this, rather than dismiss them for their superficiality, and the fictions that they created and disseminated. Just as ideas about cities do not make sense without their inhabitants, performance cannot exist without its spectators. Histories of popular entertainment demand a consideration of their audiences, in spite of the difficulties in discovering information about them that invariably ensue.

## Fin-de-siècle spectatorship

The new, mass public out seeking entertainment at the fin de siècle was a body composed of many individuals: many of the same individuals that were making and watching the quotidian spectacle of the modern city. This spectatorship was diverse and shifting. Vesta Tilley's, 'Three Young Ladies', an inter-theatrical song that comments on the entertainment industry from its music-hall stages, illustrates the mixed nature of London's audiences at this time. The lyric tells of three women, 'one high born, one of middle class and one of Bryant and May's [the match factory]', who, with their partners, all go to see the same play:

> The first pair in a brougham went, at once to see the play
> The second took an omnibus, a penny all the way,
> The third pair walked along the streets arms round each other twined
> And seated in the 'Gods' they seemed for jollity inclined.[35]

All three of these couples sat in the same auditorium and watched the same entertainment, albeit with sightlines and entrances that differed according to the price that they paid for their admission. Although it cannot be claimed that this was a democratic entertainment industry, as high prices still denied access to some and necessarily made some venues exclusive, this was nevertheless a time of increasingly diverse individuals within a growing public body of consumers.

Changing audiences were not simply the result of the increasing choice between venues and forms and the larger auditoriums that were on offer to the fin-de-siècle spectator. New widespread social and cultural ideas about the mass culture industry also came to the fore during this period. In 1892, *The Saturday Review* devoted much column space to a lively debate on the flaws and the future of London's theatre industry. In these discussions 'theatre' was employed as a relatively fluid term, and included the city's music halls in its remit. This is a different approach to entertainment in the modern city than has been adopted in retrospect, where 'high' and 'low' culture have been differentiated between, and treated primarily as separate cultural products.

In London and Paris during the 1890s, the prevailing sense was that the content and the venues of the popular entertainment industry had greatly improved. One result of this shift that is evident in much of the press from the period was that music-hall and café-concert entertainments and performers could be considered alongside those of the legitimate stage. As one writer noted, 'it is legitimate ground for congratulation that the advance of the music-hall is not confined to its housing, but extends also to the respectability of its *clientèle* and its programme'.[36] Fuelled by this shift in status, and the concomitant increase in 'respectable' audiences, entertainment managers introduced the matinee as a regular feature; beginning an afternoon theatre-going trend. A daylight sojourn to the theatre enhanced the growing respectability of the institution: spectators could visit without venturing into the night-time world of the city. Afternoon performances made day trips to see a performance easy for suburban visitors, as well as encouraging family trips: they were to prove central to the fame and success of the period's female celebrities.

In contrast to the diverse and changing spectatorship created by these transformations in the entertainment industry, the frontispiece illustration of Richard O'Monroy's *La Soirée parisienne*, published in 1890 (Figure 2), conveys a rather different idea of the fin-de-siècle audience. In this line drawing a representative male, middle-class spectator closely studies a dancing girl on the stage in front of him. The spectator's use of

2 Frontispiece, Richard O'Monroy, *La Soirée parisienne* (1890)

binoculars, in spite of his front-row seat, suggests that it is the dancer's form, rather than her performance skills, that has attracted his interest. Indeed, he seems to have paused in reading the paper that he holds in his left hand, in order to temporarily focus his full attention on the bare-legged dancer before him. O'Monroy was a journalist, a critic and a writer for the stage; *La Soirée parisienne* was a personal, 'critical' guide to the forms of entertainment on offer in Paris. The work consists of a series of short accounts describing his visits to the city's main entertainment sites, and in many ways this image reflects the nature of a work written by a prioritised critic-spectator.

However, the voyeuristic male spectator studying the objectified female performer is also a familiar trope of the late nineteenth and early twentieth centuries. It reflects the figure that springs to mind when the question of looking during this period is raised: the flâneur. The flâneur appears in the poet and critic Charles Baudelaire's 1863 essay, 'The Painter of Modern Life'. As a figure this 'botaniser on the asphalt' was fundamentally connected to the modern city environment. Baudelaire famously identified the crowd as the source of the flâneur's creative energy, stating that, 'the lover of universal life enters into the crowd as though it were an immense reservoir of electrical energy'. What this suggests is a one-way relationship between this privileged spectator and the crowd. The flâneur feeds off the collective visual stimulus and energy that is offered by the crowd, whilst simultaneously retaining his subjectivity and remaining distanced from it. A network of hierarchical presuppositions are at play in this image: the flâneur's privileged position is the result of his gender, and of intellectual, social and aesthetic positions. These presuppositions do not map on to the diverse spectatorship that was active in the modern city, rather they reflect and illustrate one spectatorial position.

By the time that O'Monroy published his collection of accounts of Parisian entertainment, the flâneur as a figure was outdated. He had been replaced by the metropolitan spectator, becoming 'a responsive audience member in a mass-cultural space', rather than occupying an 'isolated corner'.[37] Whilst attempts have been made to dispel the myth of the predominant male flâneur by identifying his female counterpart,[38] it is the cultural historian Vanessa Schwartz's concept of flânerie that proves more useful here. In *Spectacular Realities: Early Mass Culture in Fin-de-Siècle Paris*, Schwartz argues that explorations of the crowds of fin-de-siècle mass culture both demand and offer alternative models of the gaze. One approach is to replace the figure of the flâneur with the historically evident activity of flânerie; substituting the privileged individual spectator with a society of individuals preoccupied with the act of spectating.[39] Schwartz's critical reclamation of this heterogeneous set of spectatorial positions does seem to move nearer to a reflection of the metropolitan conditions of the 1890s. It further enables the gender and class-specific subject represented by the flâneur to be questioned, through the multiplication and complication of contemporary viewing positions.

Schwartz's approach locates spectators, the mass audience, at the core of the commodity culture that defined and supported the entertainment industry in 1890s' Paris: the anonymous and generally unrecorded representative of the masses replaces the privileged, aloof individual. The flâneur is one response, one attempt, to characterise modes of spectatorship in the nineteenth century. This figure is a model, a representative, historical, spectatorial position, not an actual one. To accept and apply it as a working definition of how people watched entertainment at the fin de siècle can only result in a reductive approach to the question of spectatorship. Spectatorship is, after all, important; it is the primary condition of performance. As changes in the entertainment industry have already revealed, spectators were not all male and middle-class. Furthermore, they attended different theatrical events. Some spectators may have seen a production at the Gaiety Theatre on one evening, an Independent Theatre production the following afternoon, visited the Haymarket Theatre at the weekend, and considered them all to be part of their conception of entertainment and the theatrical.

The modern entertainment industry framed the female celebrity performer in its popular 'spaces': a set of real, conceptual and ideological environments that simultaneously created and enabled celebrity identity. The spectatorship of these different spaces encompassed the bodies of people inside venues who came together to watch an individual celebrity performer, as well as the bodies of people who followed a celebrity's off-stage celebrity performances, responding to and funding her self-promotion, and supporting her career. Furthermore, there were crossovers within these spectatorial groups: some fans would not have seen an actual performance, others would have seen the performer perform, and some spectators would have watched the celebrity performer, but not considered themselves as one of her fans. Across the entertainment spaces of the fin de siècle, spectatorship was complex. This complexity blurs and questions the possibility of a firm definition between ideas about the popular and the avant-garde.

## A popular avant-garde?

Paris' artistic cabarets have been identified as laboratories of the avant-garde: authorised as important sites of experimentation in the histories of performance, literature, music and the visual arts. In these small venues, artists, writers, poets and musicians collaborated, sharing, debating and creating new work. It is Montmartre's Chat Noir (Black Cat) cabaret, founded by Rodolphe Salis in 1881, that forms the main focus of many scholarly discussions of these social and cultural groups. Offering *fumiste* entertainment, for a cheap admission price, and offering affordable beverages and snacks, the Chat Noir quickly became famous for its *chansonneurs* and its sketches.[40] For Parisian audiences the Chat Noir represented cabaret.

The Chat Noir was undeniably an important site for the avant-garde, its members included Adolphe Willette, Aristide Bruant, Maurice MacNab, Henri Somm, Jules Jouy, André Gill, Erik Satie and Claude Debussy, but it was not only the members of the cabaret's circle who watched the group's chansons, sketches and shadow-theatre productions. The cabaret's reputation as an exciting and radical venue quickly spread and it became a fashionable metropolitan venue. By 1885 the Chat Noir had become widely known as a venue offering new and exciting entertainment, the number of spectators increased, and the building on the boulevard de Rochechouart became too small to accommodate its audiences. In response to these commercial factors, and marked by a spectacular example of street theatre, in this year the cabaret relocated to a larger venue on the rue Victor Massé. Here a shadow theatre (the Théâtre d'Ombres) was opened, a purpose-built small space used to stage synthetic experiments with light, music, movement, colour and song; it proved another great draw for audiences.[41]

Spectatorship at the Chat Noir was diverse, and it was a diversity that was encouraged. In 1900 several artistic cabarets were listed in *Baedeker's Guide to Paris* as recommended stops on the tourist-trail; the Chat Noir was recommended for its 'clever' offering of 'songs, mystic illusion and shadow-plays'.[42] As Harold Segel noted, 'the circle of artists who made up the cabaret were hardly unaware of the legend of which they were rapidly becoming a part and seldom missed an opportunity to enhance it'.[43] Another tourist guide, *The American Tourist in France* (1900), included a list of the 'leading popular places of entertainment . . . for the benefit of our gentleman travellers'. Featuring on this list were the 'dance halls' the Moulin Rouge and the Folies-Bergère, alongside the Chat Noir, described as a 'concert hall'.[44]

The appearance of the Moulin Rouge, the Folies-Bergère and the Chat Noir on the same list of entertainments, and the labels used to identify them, is interesting. The description of 'concert hall' was not one that would be used today, as thanks to the reclamation of cabaret, artistic cabarets have been 'authorised' and 'legitimised' as experimental spaces. Their 'clever' offerings, 'operating on the interface between high and low culture' are now, quite rightly, studied and taught as a reflection of this cultural terrain.[45] However, this list reveals how fluid these definitions and understandings of performance spaces are: entertainment spaces meant, and mean, different things to different audiences with different objectives.

Paris' fin-de-siècle artistic cabarets were not far removed from the commercial entertainment industry. Lisa Tickner has identified a shift in ideas about cabaret during the 1880s and 1890s, from a form 'rooted in the more or less private and spontaneous exchanges of writers and poets' into an intimate but public entertainment, 'by turns literary, dramatic, satirical, scabrous, sentimental, and demotic'.[46] This transformation was the combined result of entrepreneurial figures like Salis, popular performers like Bruant, and the audiences and leisure industries of the fin de siècle. The cultural intersections at the heart of this later 'intimate but public' cabaret entertainment space have been largely lost to us, but in the performances of Bruant we can rediscover how celebrity performers could bridge the popular and experimental.

Aristide Bruant was a *chansonneur* (singer-songwriter), a café-concert performer who joined the Chat Noir circle in 1883. His realist lyrics were gritty; they dealt with crime, with poverty, with prostitution. On stage he sang of the side of Paris – and the modern metropolitan experience – that was excluded from the city's fantasy projections of itself. The risqué nature of his subjects was coupled with an unusual delivery style, a repetitive melody reminiscent of the singing of psalms in church. Together they quickly secured him a large following amongst both his fellow cabaret artists and larger audiences. When the Chat Noir moved to its second venue Bruant remained at the boulevard de Rochechouart, taking over the lease of the original site, and using the building to open his own cabaret, Le Mirliton (The Reed Pipe). In this 'temple of folly' Bruant featured as both headline performer and cabaret host, and he quickly came renowned for the rudeness and the insults with which he greeted his clientele.[47] Bruant's personality as performer and host became the draw of Le Mirliton; he was a celebrity aware of and dependent on current mechanisms of self-promotion. At Le Mirliton the entire cabaret experience became a performance, one that the audience member had to engage with and enter into.

The chanson was à la mode in the 1880s and 1890s; as well as featuring on cabaret programmes it formed the main feature of many café-concert entertainments.[48] Bruant performed on both the popular and the cabaret stage. Clothed in his trademark black cape, wide-brimmed black hat and bright red scarf, the *chansonneur* remains a familiar figure, immortalised in his presence on some of the most recognisable and frequently reproduced of the posters created by Henri de Toulouse-Lautrec. 'Ambassadeurs: Aristide Bruant dans son cabaret' and 'Eldorado: Aristide Bruant dans son cabaret' were commissioned in 1892 to advertise his forthcoming appearances at the two fashionable music halls. The following year, Toulouse-Lautrec produced another work for the *chansonneur*, 'Bruant au Mirliton', an image designed to advertise his own small cabaret venue.

The Eldorado was one of the 'great music halls [or café-concerts] of the Belle Epoque'.[49] A representative venue of Paris' commercial entertainment industry, it attracted fashionable metropolitan audiences and visitors to the city. Similarly Les Ambassadeurs on the Champs Elysées was internationally renowned as one of 'the best' café-concerts in the city. Appealing to a chic and wealthy clientele, the venue was regularly 'thronged with people' from nine o'clock in the evening until one o'clock in the morning.[50] Both Bruant's performances at the city's fashionable café-concerts and at his cabaret, Le Mirliton, received much press coverage, and the *chansonneur* became a Parisian celebrity in his own right. His identity became so familiar to the public that 'Bruant's' was adopted as an alternative name for Le Mirliton in the press.[51] In 1895 the American writer Richard Harding Davis noted that Bruant was:

> the poet of the people, and more especially of the criminal classes . . . He is the bard of the bully, and of the thief, and of the men who live on the earnings of women. He is unquestionably one of the most picturesque figures in Paris, but his picturesqueness is spoiled in some degree by the evident fact that he is conscious of it. He is a poet, but he is very much more of a poseur.[52]

Harding Davis indicates a familiar tension here, a strain between the construct of the 'poet', the artist, and that of the 'celebrity performer'. His concern was echoed in a complaint published by the journal *La Vie parisienne*, which noted that although 'Bruant is supposed to be an artist', his image was pasted all over Paris.[53] This perceived tension between creativity and popularity has permeated approaches to celebrity performers, shaping how and where they have been considered. There are essential questions contained within Harding Davis' and *La Vie parisienne*'s responses. Did the fact that Bruant performed his chansons at the Eldorado and Les Ambassadeurs, as well as at the Chat Noir and Le Mirliton, make them less experimental? Is it possible that different audiences and spaces could completely change the nature of Bruant's performance, although he was offering similar programmes of material?

A complex relationship between the popular and the experimental is demonstrated in Bruant's performances. The lettering on the two posters designed for the Eldorado and Les Ambassadeurs advertises Bruant *in* his cabaret *at* the cafe-concert. In a contemporary review from *The Era*, this is explained:

> His performance under the trees in the Champs-Elysées [at the Eldorado was] . . . merely a reproduction of that on the outer boulevard. A miniature presentation of his tavern on the small stage, with its piano, the famous door, and an assemblage of customers, enables spectators who have never run the gauntlet of the howling reception to appreciate its unquestionable originality, the vocal talent of its inventor and the atticism of the entire business.[54]

Bruant presented his fashionable café-concert audience with a replica of Le Mirliton: an intimate artistic cabaret on the music-hall stage. At the Eldorado and Les Ambassadeurs the *chansonneur* performed a repertoire of chansons that have been historically identified as experimental and innovative. In this context the 'avant-garde' performance of the artistic cabaret became material for popular entertainment, an inversion of the popular entertainment industry acting as a stimulus for the avant-garde. The *Era*'s review may not have been wholly approving, but admiration for Bruant's originality and skill are at the core of their response. These factors could still be noticed and commented on in the popular entertainment space.

At the fin de siècle, large audiences had access to experimental performance, innovative acts programmed by popular and fashionable venues. Bruant could perform his challenging experimental material and demonstrate his new performance style on the café-concert stage, and be paid well for it. Simultaneously, it was also common for experimental venues to become popular and fashionable metropolitan sites. Bruant's performances at the Eldorado, Le Mirliton, the Chat Noir and the Folies-Bergère illustrate the commercial forces that fed the entertainment industry: forces that operated across large and small, commercial and seemingly non-commercial, performance spaces in the modern city. But this relative freedom available to performers did not apply across the board: the founders and the associates of Paris' artistic cabarets, the writers, performers and artists who emerged out of the experimental spaces that they offered, and the performers whose new work appeared on the popular stage were notably male. Amongst seventy individuals whose biographies are appendixed to Phillip Dennis Cate and Mary Shaw's *The Spirit of Montmartre: Cabarets, Humor, and the Avant Garde, 1875–1905*, just four are women.[55]

The histories of artistic cabarets, aesthetic communities and experimental theatre companies in London and Paris reveal that the admittance of women to these environments as creative figures tended to be the exception, rather than the norm. Whilst male performers could access, and find space and recognition for their experimental work in, the metropolitan spaces associated with both the popular and the experimental, female performers created another route to discover a performance space. Amidst the popular programmes of the fin-de-siècle's entertainment industry, examples of female experimental performance can be discovered on the popular stage. Creative female performers located a potential experimental performance space in the theatre of the city: an experimental performance space that was the result of the mass culture and the urban environment of modernity.

In a study of mid-Victorian London, Lynda Nead offers a useful model of space as an 'active agent of modernity'. Historical sites, physical, geographical or experiential, were 'never a passive backdrop for the formation of historical identities and experiences, but . . . an active constituent of historical consciousness'.[56] In spite of attempts to fix identities through marketing, entertainment spaces were unfixed, changing and morphing. In this context, the spaces historically identified as the birthplaces of experimental performance were always more than theatres, or small cabarets, or music halls, popular or avant-garde. As venues they were also social and ideological constructs: the Chat Noir artistic cabaret no less so than the Moulin Rouge or the Palace Theatre of Varieties.

Whilst some contemporary, and many retrospective, definitions of performances in the modern city have identified them as *either* popular *or* experimental, a reflection of 'the binary division between art and entertainment', it is a complex and symbiotic relationship between the 'popular' and the 'experimental' that is revealed by the performances, performance spaces and spectators of the modern city.[57] All of the venues and the entertainments referred to in this study occurred in one of two cities: on the same terrain, within – and often responding to – the same general social, political and cultural climates. Whilst there were some restrictions from financial or social status, spectators could move between many of these venues. The café-concert and the artistic cabaret, two modern performance spaces that were both products of urbanisation and the metropolitan desire for spectacle, illustrate this complicated relationship. Their programmes, reputations and audiences offer a clear idea of how much less defined the boundaries between entertainments were for a fin-de-siècle spectator in the modern city.

The fin-de-siècle cities of London and Paris supply the geographical terrain on which the female celebrity performances that are considered in this volume occurred. These two metropolises, their entertainment industries and their public spaces shaped the programmes, the careers and the identities of the popular performers that they embraced: they formed active agents in the creation of celebrity. But dominant understandings of these urban spaces have been influenced, and in some cases modified, by the processes of history and by theories about culture. By looking closely at the performances that were taking place within the theatre of the city, and attracting audiences to its venues, some of these issues can be exposed and reconfigured. After all, it was the citizens of, and the visitors to, these spaces that invested in popular trends and secured female performers a performance space and a large audience.

## Notes

1 Edward Timms, 'Unreal City – Theme and Variations', in Edward Timms and David Kelly (eds), *Unreal City: Urban Experience in Modern European Literature and Art* (Manchester: Manchester University Press, 1988), p. 3.

2 Raymond Williams, 'The Metropolis and the Emergence of Modernism', in Timms and Kelly (eds.), *Unreal City: Urban Experience in Modern European Literature and Art*, p. 13.

3 See Vanessa Schwartz, *Spectacular Realities: Early Mass Culture in Fin-de-Siècle Paris* (Berkeley: University of California Press, 1998) and Sally Charnow, *Theatre, Politics and Markets in Fin-de-Siècle Paris: Staging Modernity* (Basingstoke and New York: Palgrave Macmillan, 2005).

4 John McCormick, *Popular Theatres of Nineteenth-Century France* (London: Routledge, 1993), p. 5.

5 Petra Kuppers, 'Moving in the Cityscape: Performance and the Embodied Experience of the *Flâneur*', *New Theatre Quarterly* 60, 1999, pp. 308–17 (308).

6  Richard Harding Davis, 'The Show-Places of Paris: Night', *Harper's New Monthly Magazine* 90, December 1894–May 1895, pp. 125–39 (125).

7  See William R. Keylor, 'Franco-British Relations', in Patrick H. Hutton (ed.), *Historical Dictionary of the Third French Republic, 1870–1940* (Westport, CT: Greenwood Press, 1986).

8  See Michael B. Miller, *The Bon Marché: Bourgeois Culture and the Department Store* (Princeton: Princeton University Press, 1981), pp. 61–2.

9  Victoria and Albert Publications, *Liberty's, 1875–1975* (London: V & A Publications, 1975), p. 5. For further information on the popularity of Worth and Paquin in the late nineteenth century see Cheryl Buckley and Hilary Fawcett, *Fashioning the Feminine: Representation and Women's Fashion from the Fin de Siècle to the Present* (London and New York: I. B. Taurus, 2002), p. 18 onwards.

10 It is important to note that there were also differences between London and Paris. In the British capital the National Vigilance Society's campaign against the entertainment industry's immoral output was higher profile than corresponding French movements that aimed at 'cleaning up' mass culture. For an example of this see Joseph Donohue, *Fantasies of Empire: The Empire Theatre of Varieties and the Licensing Controversy of 1894* (Iowa City: University of Iowa Press, 2005).

11 *The Era*, 16 May 1908, p. 22.

12 Walter Benjamin, *The Arcades Project*, trans. by Howard Eiland and Kevin McLaughlin (Cambridge, MA and London: Belknapp Press, 1999), p. 14.

13 Davis, 'The Show-Places of Paris: Night', p. 125.

14 See Anon., *John Bull's Trip to Paris* (London: Favourite Publishing, 1900); Cassell and Co., *Cassell's Guide to Paris and the Universal Exhibition of 1900* (London: Cassell, 1900); Baedeker and Co., *Paris and Environs: Handbook for Travellers* (Leipsic: Karl Baedeker, 1900); Anon., *The American Tourist in France* (New York: Tourist Publishing Company, 1900); Viscomte de Kératry, *Paris Exposition, 1900: How to See Paris Alone* (London: Simpkin, Marshall, 1900).

15 Anon., *John Bull's Trip to Paris*, pp. 35–6.

16 See Christopher Prendergast, *Paris and the Nineteenth Century* (Cambridge, MA and Oxford: Blackwell, 1992), pp. 6–13.

17 Eugen Weber, *France: Fin de Siècle* (Cambridge, MA: Harvard University Press, 1986), p. 159.

18 Adna Ferrin Weber, *The Growth of Cities in the Nineteenth Century: A Study in Cities* (Ithaca: Cornell University Press, 1968), p. 73.

19 See Jean-Marie Mayer and Madeleine Rebérioux, *The Third Republic from its Origins to the Great War, 1871–1914* (Cambridge: Cambridge University Press, 1981), pp. 120–1.

20 John Henderson, *The First Avant-Garde, 1887–1894: Sources of the Modern French Theatre* (London: Harrap, 1971), p. 22.

21  See Marvin Carlson, *The French Stage in the Nineteenth Century* (Metuchen, NJ: Scarecrow Press, 1972), pp. 9–12.

22  The arrival of the term 'avant-garde' has been attributed to an article, 'An Avant-Garde Critic', published in the Parisian review, *Art et critique*, a left-wing, Symbolist weekly publication.

23  Malcolm Bradbury, 'The Cities of Modernism', in Malcolm Bradbury and James McFarlane (eds), *Modernism: A Guide to European Literature 1890–1930* (London: Penguin, 1991), pp. 96–103 (102).

24  Weber, *France: Fin de Siècle*, p. 176.

25  Norton Atkins, 'Oui! Tray Bong! or, My Pal Jones' (London: Francis, Day and Hunter, n.d.), British Library, London, sheet music collection.

26  *Ibid.*

27  All held by the sheet music collection, British Library, London.

28  See Margot C. Finn, 'Sex and the City: Metropolitan Modernities in English Histories', *Victorian Studies* 44:1, Autumn 2001, pp. 25–32.

29  E. W. Rogers, 'When a Fellah has Turned Sixteen', British Library, London, sheet music collection.

30  Judith R. Walkowitz, 'The Vision of Salome: Cosmopolitanism and Erotic Dancing in London, 1908–1918', *American Historical Review* 108:2, 2003, pp. 337–76 (347).

31  Anon., *Tit Bits Guide to London: A Simple and Easy Way to Seeing the Metropolis in the Shortest Amount of Time* (London: Tit Bits, 1895), p. 3.

32  Cassell and Co., *Cassell's Guide to Paris and the Universal Exhibition of 1900*, p. 162.

33  *The Saturday Review*, 11 January 1896, p. 29.

34  Vivien Gardner and Susan Rutherford (eds), *The New Woman and her Sisters: Feminism and Theatre, 1850–1914* (Brighton: Harvester Wheatsheaf, 1992), p. 7.

35  E. M. Rogers (words and music), 'Three Young Ladies' (London: H. Beresford, n.d.), British Library, London, sheet music collection.

36  'The Theatrical Outlook', *The Saturday Review*, 20 August 1892, pp. 220–1 (221). This shift in the perceived social and cultural status of variety entertainment resulted in regular music-hall commentaries and listings in the two cities' mainstream dailies, notably *The Times* in London and *Le Figaro* in Paris.

37  Rhonda K. Garelick, *Rising Star: Dandyism, Gender and Performance in the Fin-de-Siècle* (Princeton: Princeton University Press, 1998), p. 4.

38  See Deborah Epstein Nord, 'The Urban Peripatetic: Spectator, Streetwalker, Woman Writer', *Nineteenth-Century Literature* 46:3, 1991, pp. 351–75 (360); Viv Gardner, 'The Invisible Spectatrice: Gender, Geography and Theatrical Space', in Maggie B. Gale and Vivien Gardner (eds), *Women, Theatre and Performance: New Histories, New Historiographies* (Manchester: Manchester University Press, 2001), pp. 25–45.

39  Schwartz, *Spectacular Realities: Early Mass Culture in Fin-de-Siècle Paris*, p. 2 onwards.

40 Phillip Dennis Cate describes *fumiste* humour as follows: 'fumisme was not a quick laugh, nor was it always obvious. A fumiste did not rely for self-satisfaction on an audience's response to his actions; rather, fumisme was a way of life, an art form that rested on scepticism and humour, of which the latter was often a black variety verging on the morbid and the macabre.' Phillip Dennis Cate and Mary Shaw (eds), *The Spirit of Montmartre: Cabaret, Humor, and the Avant Garde 1875–1905* (New Brunswick, NJ: Rutgers University Press, 1996), p. 23.

41 See Harold B. Segel, *Turn of the Century Cabaret: Paris, Barcelona, Berlin, Munich, Vienna, Cracow, Moscow, St Petersburg, Zurich* (New York: Columbia University Press, 1987); Cate and Shaw (eds), *The Spirit of Montmartre: Cabarets, Humor, and the Avant Garde, 1875–1905*; Laurence Senelick, *Cabaret Performance: Europe 1890–1920* (New York: PAJ Publications, 1989); Lisa Appiganesi, *The Cabaret* (London: Cassell and Collier Macmillan, 1975).

42 Baedeker, *Paris and Environs: Handbook for Travellers,* p. 36.

43 Segel, *Turn of the Century Cabaret: Paris, Barcelona, Berlin, Munich, Vienna, Cracow, Moscow, St Petersburg, Zurich,* p. 1.

44 Anon., *The American Tourist in France,* p. 82.

45 John Street, book review of Bernard Gendron, *Between Montmartre and the Mudd Club: Popular Music and the Avant-Garde* (Chicago: University of Chicago Press, 2002), in *Journal of the American Musicological Society* 58:2, Summer 2005, pp. 472–6 (473).

46 Lisa Tickner, 'The Popular Culture of *Kermesse*: Lewis, Painting and Performance', *Modernism/Modernity* 4:2, 1997, pp. 67–120 (78).

47 'Submerged Paris', *Saturday Review,* 19 March 1892, p. 325.

48 Dominique Lejeune, *La Belle Epoque, 1896–1914* (Paris: Armand Collin, 1991), p. 142.

49 McCormick, *Popular Theatres of Nineteenth-Century France,* p. 64.

50 Sandy Broad, 'Paris Amusements', *The Daily Northwestern,* 27 August 1895, p. 8.

51 Davis, 'The Show Places of Paris: Night', p. 125.

52 *Ibid.,* p. 129.

53 Cited in Russell Ash, *Toulouse-Lautrec: The Complete Posters* (London: BCA Publications, 1991), p. ii.

54 *The Era,* 3 September 1892, p. 13.

55 The women listed by Cate and Shaw are Rosine Bernhardt, Dominique Bonnaud, Louise France and Marie Krysinska.

56 Lynda Nead, *Victorian Babylon: People, Streets and Images in Nineteenth-Century London* (New Haven and London: Yale University Press, 2000), p. 8.

57 Jacky Bratton, *New Readings in Theatre History* (Cambridge: Cambridge University Press, 2003), pp. 10–13 and 133–70 (133).

# 2

# 'ALL THE NOBLEST ARTS . . . EXPRESSED IN THE MEASURED MOVEMENTS OF A PERFECTLY SHAPED BODY': EMBODIMENT AND SPECTACULAR PERFORMANCES OF GENDER[1]

Whilst the modern city offered new physical performance spaces and increasing financial and creative opportunities to performers, its ideological terrain factored as powerfully as its urban geography in the technologies, creation and sustention of its new celebrity culture. As Chapter one's discussions of the spectacular cultures of London and Paris have revealed, a visual language of display framed the venues, acts and audiences of the fin-de-siècle entertainment and leisure industries. London and Paris' audiences may not have been composed of numerous individual flâneurs, but as members of a metropolitan audience participating in the act of flânerie, the main function of each spectator was to look. As inhabitants of, or visitors to, the modern city this was an act in which they were well-guided, well-trained and well-practiced. The events and codes of quotidian life in fashionable metropolitan centres rotated around the dynamics of seeing and being seen, and amidst the theatre of the city the human body was positioned as the site of many gazes.

It would be unproductive to argue that problematic questions concerning gender, ideology and embodiment are not raised by any consideration of the popular female performer in a period that was preoccupied with visual spectacle. Embracing this urban environment driven by display, female stars overtly and self-consciously located themselves as the locus of the period's diverse spectatorship. Their familiar bodies, bodies that attracted and thrilled contemporary audiences, cannot be removed from the wider social context in which they appeared. The period's geographies and ideologies coalesced to shape the meanings of on-stage bodies: to some degree these physical and conceptual forces moulded the performers themselves, the performances that they offered and their audiences' responses.

Performing, both the individual act itself and the presentation of a celebrity identity on and off stage, may have offered successful individual women an opportunity to engage with and to renegotiate some dominant ideas about gender, but their acts were never isolated from the wider pattern of understandings of corporeality that were evident in the entertainment industry and society. Their performing bodies became simultaneously powerful and problematic signifiers: images that appeared both in the modern entertainment industry, and within wider ideas surrounding gender, identity and the body.

During the late nineteenth and early twentieth centuries human bodies were exhibited in many different ways: offered up to audiences in the quest for, or in the guise of, entertainment. In addition to the glamorous, comedic and contorted bodies of actors, actresses, singers, dancers, acrobats and comedians that populated city and provincial stages, the entertainment industry regularly drew upon colonised bodies to divert spectators. Audiences approved: the colonial displays and reconstructed 'native' villages staged at the regular international exhibitions proved consistently popular attractions throughout the period. Bodies labelled 'freakish' – the *phénomène* identified by Geraldine Harris – also formed common and popular sights: the physical oddities displayed in the giant, the dwarf, the beauty and the bearded woman drew spectators to circuses, café-concerts, sideshows, fairs and touring exhibitions.[2] But the body's role as a key site for the modern gaze was more than the product of commodification and its associated mass culture industries. Popular science also employed and invested in the image and materiality of the human form, fashioning contemporary spectatorial responses to corporeality.

Many of the fin de siècle's attempts to establish secure social definitions that would systematically contain ideas about gender, class and sexuality began with, and were illustrated by, the body. Current thinking, indeed cutting-edge research, about criminality, degeneration, sexuality and psychology were explored, explained and defined through visual systems of physical codes: visual systems that became familiar to the public through the popularity of science during the period. It is essential to note that the audiences of entertainment and popular science were not separate bodies of individuals. They contained many of the same members, and crossovers naturally occurred between the presentation of bodies as entertainment and the presentation of bodies as science. The glamorous body of the female performer, the eroticised, flexible body of the belly dancer, the lithe, muscular body of the acrobat and the freakish, sideshow body of the fair became objects of scientific study, whilst objects of scientific study became familiar figures, attractive to the mass audience. During the second half of the nineteenth century, as Jane R. Goodall has emphasised, 'the two cultures of science and show business became muddier, more complex, as they confused each other's principles and priorities'.[3] Bodies dominated the foreground of medical and scientific theories, exhibitions of social, scientific and technological developments, and entertainment. The methods and codes that were embedded in reading and understanding corporeality were the result of the complicated position that was occupied by the human form.

## Making a spectacle of themselves: women in public at the fin de siècle

One precept that underpinned and structured the multiplicity of bodies displayed to these mixed audiences of entertainment and science was the 'fact' of a clear and substantiated difference between female and male physical appearances, and thus female and male identities. This was not a new way of thinking, born out of recent scientific discoveries or theories, it drew on an eighteenth-century principle that had identified 'two stable, incommensurate, opposite sexes'.[4] But this old idea was spread more widely at the fin de siècle, rooted in images and ideas that were disseminated to large audiences through the growth in publicity and the popular interest in science. As the art historian Tamar Garb has noted:

> Modernity produced its own image of the body. According to the dictates of science and philosophy, modern men and women were expected to look dramatically different from one another . . . Appearance testified to the maintenance of a social order based on visible distinctions. If boundaries were transgressed, chaos could ensue.[5]

In this context, in popular print, on the stage and in everyday life, the fin-de-siècle body became an object to be 'read'. Embodiment was encoded: scientists, socialists and moralists could 'authoritatively' interpret it, but the popular audience could also understand it, to some degree. So clear and 'visible' were the established differences between female and male, that it did not require an expert eye to assess any physical case before it. It is unsurprising, therefore, that the entertainment industry – with its emphasis on visual spectacle – became, and has remained, a significant site for the expression and debate of ideas and anxieties surrounding corporeality.

Extant descriptions of anonymous female performers on the music-hall stage as 'fat-thighed [figures] with breasts like St Paul's dome and emphatic hips', who 'disclosed' themselves 'in spangles to sing slightly lewd songs in a gin-in-a-fog voice', act as a clear source of much of the justified anxiety that has been provoked by the exhibition of ornamented female bodies in a culture of spectacle.[6] But within a society that was fixated on display, no body could be exempt from its role as a visual signifier. To substantiate the established dramatic contrast between the 'modern man' and the 'modern woman', both sexes needed to be scrutinised. Each and every individual's physical attributes, dress and stature needed to be looked at closely enough that they could be mapped on to and compared with the ideological blueprint of either female or male.

At the fin de siècle, men, as well as women, were being defined according to their outward appearances, their physicality. The 'model' man of the late nineteenth and early twentieth centuries was healthy, virile and physically strong. This ideal construct, one that was to play a significant role in the early twentieth-century drive for physical culture in France and England, was founded on the contemporary preoccupation with fertility and procreation. Against the active, robust male, the model woman was passive and still: as Lynda Nead has explored, the result of this was that inactivity became an ideal feminine quality, and a corresponding social myth of frailty emerged that aligned physical weakness and femininity.

> Female dependency was reproduced and guaranteed by the belief that
> respectable women were inherently weak and delicate, and were in a
> perpetual state of sickness . . . physical frailty was a sign of respectable
> femininity and by the mid nineteenth century a morbid cult of 'female
> invalidism' had developed.[7]

Decades later this myth, and its presentation of a female body that was physically disempowered by its weakness and its characteristic predisposition to recurrent periods of extended sickness, remained powerful. Studies of visual representations of femininity at the fin de siècle have revealed that the conviction that passivity, or physical stillness, was a desirable quality in a woman continued to dominate gender ideology, and filtered through into aesthetics. Bram Dijkstra's *Idols of Perversity: Fantasies of Feminine Evil in Fin-de-Siècle Culture*, locates the extreme point of this myth in the recurring motifs in visual art that reflect what he has identified as the cults of the invalid and the collapsing woman. Images in which, as Dijkstra notes, 'the very effort of living seemed to exhaust' the women featured.[8]

As with any ideal, fixed social model, this system of visual difference between female and male contained its nemesis within itself. Promoting and normalising stable images of woman and man necessarily offered the possibility of transgression. The key role played by the visual in the process of gender classification located physical appearance as an equally powerful force for the questioning and disruption of these definitions. As Garb noted, 'appearance testified to the maintenance of a social order based on visible distinctions. If boundaries were transgressed, chaos could ensue'.[9] Deviations from the well-publicised gender 'norms' of the fin de siècle certainly provoked anxiety. Responses to the aesthetic dandy culture of the late nineteenth century in London and Paris supply one well-documented example of these concerns.[10] Another illustration of the unsettling of these defined gender roles can be discovered in contemporary female celebrity performers: women who relied upon active, physically fit and expressive bodies for their performance practices.

The clear divide between male and female embodiment both emerged out of and structured other social frameworks, including the organisation and understanding of space in modern life. In London and Paris the mid-nineteenth century's philosophy of separate spheres continued to prevail at the fin de siècle: a social structuring that separated everyday life between the public spaces of the city and the private spaces of the domestic. Man, as the virile and healthy human specimen, the source of physical, social and cultural action, occupied the public sphere. Woman, as the passive figure of restraint and physical frailty, maintained and guarded the domestic, or private, space.

The extent to which these ideas about space pervaded society in the 1860s is evinced in an account by the French social commentator Jules Michelet, where he noted that there were:

> many irritations for the single woman! She can hardly ever go out in the evening; she would be taken for a prostitute . . . For example, should she find herself delayed at the other end of Paris and hungry, she will not dare to enter into a restaurant. She would constitute an event; she would be a spectacle. All eyes would be constantly fixed on her, and she would overhear uncomplimentary and bold conjectures.[11]

During the same decade, the British writer John Ruskin's essay 'Of Queen's Gardens' appeared in *Sesame and Lilies*. In his discourse on gender, Ruskin echoed the stark differentiation between the roles of men and women and their corresponding access to space:

> The man, in his rough work in open world, must encounter all peril and trial: to him, therefore, the failure, the offense, the inevitable error: often he must be wounded, or subdued, often misled, and always hardened. But he guards the woman from all this; within his house, as ruled by her,

unless she herself has sought it, need enter no danger, no temptation, no cause of error or offense. This is the true nature of home — it is the place of Peace; the shelter, not only from all injury, but from all terror, doubt, and division.[12]

Well documented and widespread the philosophy of separate spheres may still have been at the fin de siècle. However, the ideology that it was grounded in had been under threat as early as the 1860s; a challenge that is clearly indicated in the gently mocking tone of Michelet's writing. Certainly by the end of the century the assumptions that the public/private, male/female divide were founded on were being very publicly contested. One main reason for this was the simple fact that many women – from different classes and diverse backgrounds – were necessarily on show in the modern city.[13] It was not only female performers who occupied metropolitan public spaces, new industries demanded greater workforces, including women, and the female consumer became an economic necessity of a burgeoning commodity culture. Furthermore, in the public spaces of modern cities lay access to education, professional employment and the world of politics, all areas to which a contingency of women were beginning to demand access.

As spectators, consumers and performers in the theatre of the city, women in public spaces became both active members of the urban crowd and sights within it. But what were the ramifications of making a spectacle of oneself, of constituting an event in the modern city? Griselda Pollock has noted that, at this time, '[w]omen *could* enter and represent selected locations in the public sphere – those of entertainment and display' (my emphasis). However, when they did they crossed a line that 'demarcate[d] not the end of the public/private divide but the frontier of the spaces of femininity'.[14] Whilst remaining female, these 'spectacles' contravened all established ideas of acceptable and ideal femininity by their presence in the urban public space. Two female 'figures' who self-consciously and very publicly transgressed the frontier of the spaces of the femininity, and used the forces and the institutions of the modern public space to their own ends, can be discovered in the New Woman and the Suffragette.[15] These archetypal anti-women may not feature in the foreground of postcards, lithographs, paintings and journals as frequently or as prominently as the celebrities of the day, but they were assiduously recorded by the print culture of the fin de siècle.

The press, social critics and the entertainment industry characterised the New Woman as overly intellectual and asexual. Comedic representations of this figure, adorned with her trademark accessories of 'bicycle, bangs and bloomers', countered and undermined her real demands for the right to education, employment and agency in the modern world. In the mass representation of the Suffragette, a label first used in 1906 to identify members of the Women's Social and Political Union, and their militant campaign of stone throwing and window breaking, a violent, uncontrollable and irrational female figure was offered.[16] What both of these negative representations stressed, through their focus on the comedic value and the chaotic threat contained within the figures, was their deliberate shift away from the ideals of femininity.

In the cases of the New Woman and the Suffragette, it was their extreme physical and vocal action, rather than their attacks on dominant ideas and institutions, that was framed as their greatest threat to contemporary society. The high-profile presence of these two 'anti-women' was presented to readers and to audiences as a danger to the 'natural' order of men and women. In essence, however, the public acts of the New Woman and the Suffragette occurred on the same terrain as those of the female performer, and their spectral presences haunt negative reviews and responses to women on the stage. Each of these female 'types' of the fin de siècle had unquestionably overstepped the boundaries of femininity, but what is clear is that female celebrities managed their public presence very differently. Indeed, their active, familiar bodies are rarely directly linked with the politicised icons of changes in gender roles, in spite of the similarities between the performer and New Woman, and the suffrage campaign's links with the theatre.[17] Performed against this backdrop of caricatured female figures present in the public spaces of the city and its politics, the stagings of femininity that occurred within celebrity culture complicated the late nineteenth century's ideas and assumptions about women outside the domestic sphere.

## Playing in the city's public spaces: female performers at the fin de siècle

For those women whose careers involved accessing and occupying metropolitan spaces, fulfilling their role as a passive ideal of femininity ceased to be an option. Rather than being guarded from the danger and temptation of the 'open world', they exposed themselves to it and by default they also exposed themselves to the judgements made about women that were present in the public sphere. With reference to late Victorian London, Judith Walkowitz has noted that, 'in the mental map of urban spectators [women] lacked autonomy: they were bearers of meaning, rather than makers of meaning. As symbols of conspicuous display or of lower-class and sexual disorder, they occupied a multivalent symbolic position in this imaginary landscape.'[18] Female performers – 'symbols of conspicuous display' on the popular stage – complicate Walkowitz's position further. The entertainment industry acted as a forum that continued many archaic and current myths of femininity in its output, whilst simultaneously supplying an environment where these images could be appropriated and renegotiated. The crucial difference here lies in the active and autonomous bodies of female performers: figures that made, rather than bore, meaning in the modern city.

Unusually, the absence of the body that tends to characterise performance documentation is not the case in the celebrity culture of the fin de siècle, when the bodies of female performers attracted much attention, both on and off stage.[19] Fame, for the female celebrity, brought widespread admiration in its wake, and – in the cases of many of the performers covered in this study – moral approbation in society and in the press followed. The glamorous corporeal presence of the on-stage celebrity conformed to some of the parameters set by gender ideology, whilst undeniably transgressing others. Ideas about femininity and movement were reflected, responded to and shaped by the performances of female celebrities in venues, in public and in the press. Their popularity led to the mass production of souvenirs and merchandise inspired by their styles; fans could buy accessories, clothing and memorabilia that allowed them to possess a small part of their favourite celebrity. Performances and identities were not contained in the venue. Spectators could take elements of them home with them, and emulate the appearance or the performance style of their favourite star in the domestic space: the public entered into and changed the private.

Celebrity performers became influential figures in the creation and presentation of new, alternative, images of women. This was a powerful position amidst an atmosphere of changing gender roles and current crises of masculinity and femininity. As John Stokes has identified:

> [a] central problem for feminists [in France, Italy and Britain at the end
> of the nineteenth century] was the need to present a more affirmative view
> of woman in contrast to the passive notion of the angel of the house or the
> derogatory notion of the man-hating hysteric. In such a context the image
> of woman presented on stage assumed enormous significance.[20]

However, this enormous significance, rightly attributed to the image of the individual woman on stage, needs to be considered against the

imagery of collective femininity that was used to represent the entertainment industry of the day. The makers of meaning co-existed and were in
dialogue with the bearers of meaning.

A female figure will generally feature in the majority of the visual
images that are evoked by the pleasure and leisure industries of the late
nineteenth and early twentieth centuries. From cancan dancers and
Gaiety Girls, the Moulin Rouge dance hall and the Palace Theatre
of Varieties, to the singers, dancers and actresses painted by Henri de
Toulouse-Lautrec, Edouard Manet and Edgar Degas, women are fore-
grounded in the iconography of the period's entertainment industry.
Their bodies represented the modern city, with its glamorous and spectacular reputation: as Elizabeth K. Menon has suggested, 'women were
associated with the available sex and alcohol along with the performance
aspects of song and dance that took place in the various cabarets' of
Paris.[21] Menon's statement is equally applicable to the entertainment
imagery of London, indeed many of the images of acts and performers
that appear on posters or postcards were used internationally as publicity
material. Across Europe and North America the female body became the
visual trope of the period's new mass culture industries.

The recurrent usage of the objectified female body to represent the
spectacular entertainment industry of the fin de siècle has necessarily
raised tensions and questions. The situation has been further problema-
tised by individual female celebrity performer's adherence to some of the
ideals of femininity that dominated gender constructs at the fin de siècle.
They are tensions that have proved to be influential factors in performance histories of this period, impacting on the selection of acts, performers and forms for study. Indeed, what has emerged out of this
difficult terrain is a pattern of prioritising the women involved in performance who were not positioned so overtly in the line of the gaze.[22]
Theatrical managers, or actresses who were also involved in the business
side of the entertainment industry, have received significant attention in
feminist histories of this period, whilst other popular performers have
been neglected, or only considered within very specific disciplines. In
the cases of dancers, singers and imitators, the majority of extant evidence focuses almost entirely on the body - the object of the spectators'
gazes. Visual representations and spectatorial accounts prioritise the
physical performance witnessed, on or off stage. The relative evasion
of the study of on-stage women as conspicuous objects of display in
the mass entertainment industry has inadvertently sidelined creative,
performing female bodies. On-stage corporeality – the very stuff of

performance – has been subordinated to the less gender-specific powers of the mind.

## Putting the body back in performance history

It is not only questions about gender ideology that have shaped these historiographical patterns and approaches; they have been further exacerbated by dominant intellectual assumptions about the cultural status of entertainments that centralise a performing body. This is particularly the case in the field of modernist studies. In a collection dealing with the period, James Naremore and Patrick Bratlinger have identified the relative invisibility of mass culture in academic research and scholarly histories. They suggest that one key reason for this omission can be discovered in the enduring conviction that whilst 'the supposedly cultured or civilized person responds to more than his or her physical needs and pleasures', 'the supposedly ordinary person is bound to the physical'.[23] In this equation the popular performing body is consigned to a position where it is viewed as being unworthy of study; the products and performances that it creates are rendered banal, and thus meaningless.

The problems inherent in a serious consideration of female celebrity corporeality are twofold. They are to be discovered both in ideas and anxieties concerning gender ideology and embodiment, and in pervasive hierarchical and intellectualist approaches to performance and culture. Together, these archaic, dualistic divisions between high and low culture, and the body and the mind, are powerful and questionable. Established at the birth of much Western philosophy, they have remained central to understandings and interpretations of culture and corporeality throughout history. Most interestingly, many of the ways in which feminists have dealt with questions of embodiment have also been constructed on these foundations: a tendency that, as the philosopher Elizabeth Grosz argues, has rendered the body a 'conceptual blind spot'.

In *Volatile Bodies: Towards a Corporeal Feminism*, Grosz calls for a recognition of the central role that ideological attempts to define Woman as innately connected to the body, as animalistic, irrational and primitive, have played in the continuing feminist discomfort with corporeality. These ideologies – or constructs of femininity – remain latent in performance histories: present at the core of the widespread somatophobic evasion of any way of thinking that offers corporeality as a positive force.[24] The more consideration that is given to this tendency identified by Grosz, the clearer it becomes that the avoidance and subordination of female corporeality she exposes has been the outcome of a semi-automatic response to the questions of women, embodiment and objectification. A response that has been provoked by the qualities and ideologies mapped on to the female body by discursive practices, rather than a reaction to what corporeality has actually signified to different people at a given historical moment.

When Grosz suggests that corporeality should be central to feminist thought and approaches, she offers a new direction that lends itself to performance. For if 'bodies have all the explanatory power of minds', and the 'added bonus of inevitably raising the question of sexual difference in a way that the mind does not', then individual examples of female performance practice become important sites of investigation for both histories of performance, and histories of female performance.[25] If we acknowledge the fin-de-siècle need for new images of women that more realistically reflected their roles in urban culture, alongside the somatophobic outcome of theoretical problems with corporeality and the influential presence of a stark divide between high and low culture, then female celebrities, embodied women on stage, become vital in an understanding of performance during the period.

By actively moving in and across urban public spaces and on the stage, female performers disrupted, as well as conformed to, the current imagery and ideologies that defined femininity. To return to Goodall: 'since Victorian stereotypes associated femininity with passivity and weakness, the portrayal of a purely feminine energy on stage was an aesthetic challenge of a special kind'.[26] As we shall see, the measured movements that were created and staged by the perfectly, and not so perfectly, shaped on-stage bodies of the female celebrities considered in this study demanded new vocabularies. When it came to the international star performer, the set language employed to describe women at the fin de siècle no longer sufficed.

## A Maud Allan matinee: active bodies, spaces and spectatorship

The 'perfectly shaped body' celebrated by the reviewer cited in the title of this chapter belonged to the celebrity dancer Maud Allan. Allan was one of the most famous, and arguably the most erotic, acts on the Edwardian popular stage. A Canadian-born, classically trained musician, she was raised in San Francisco until 1895, when she moved to Berlin to study classical piano at the city's acclaimed Royal Academy. After six and a half years of classical training as a musician, Allan turned to dance in 1901, claiming that she had discovered a greater capacity for creative expression in the medium. Her professional debut as a dancer occurred in Vienna two years later, in December 1903. Regular appearances followed at venues in Hamburg, Cologne, Leipzig and Berlin and, by 1908, further engagements had taken her to Budapest and to Paris, where she appeared both as a solo performer and as a member of the dancer Loïe Fuller's touring company.[27] Five years after her debut, Allan was surviving as a performer on the European variety circuit, but she had not achieved real success as an individual dancer.

Allan's transition from reasonably successful variety performer to international celebrity was the result of a private performance that she was invited to give for Edward VII at the fashionable spa resort of Marienbad. Edward's enthusiastic response to Allan's dancing led to a contract with London's Palace Theatre of Varieties, where her first British performance occurred on 8 March 1908. A flurry of publicity and sensationalism surrounded her premiere; hype that had been engineered by the Palace's entrepreneurial manager Alfred Butt who, as Judith Walkowitz has noted, had recently been forced to remove the popular tableaux vivants from his nightly programme and was seeking an alternative main attraction.[28] Four days before her first public appearance, Butt had arranged for Allan to dance before a carefully selected, invited audience. By gaining the approval of this representative body of influential London society – including Members of Parliament, artists, writers and figures from the national and provincial presses – Butt aimed not only to publicise the new dancer in town, but also to give a moral and aesthetic stamp of approval to his latest act. His plan worked: Allan's celebrity status was rapidly secured in the British capital, and it endured.

Audiences in London and across Britain, as well as international followers of performance, quickly became familiar with Maud Allan's name, and with images of her body. In April 1908, *The Era* recorded that her 'poetical dance interpretations of music' had become a 'society craze'.[29] Dance schools and private dance teachers offered pupils lessons in the Allan style, and racehorses were named after the fin de siècle's new star.[30] A year later her fame showed no sign of abating: in April 1909 the Empire Theatre of Varieties, Leicester Square (one of the Palace's main competitors) staged the burlesque *Come Inside*. The humour of the show, *The Times* noted, 'depend[ed] almost entirely, as is the way of . . . modern humour, on personalities'. At this time these figures were supplied by 'two [of the] most prominent ladies of the day', the 'rather well-worn personalities' Maud

Allan and Christabel Pankhurst, performer and Suffragette.[31] Two years on, and Allan was still a popular figure in the British capital: in 1911, a burlesque of a Maud Allan matinee was advertised as a new scene in H. G. Pelissier and the Follies' programme.[32] In the meantime, as well as performing at the Palace regularly, Allan had taken extended engagements in Paris and in Boston; her celebrity status was international.

It is important to acknowledge that Maud Allan was a variety performer throughout her entire career. At the Palace Theatre of Varieties her dancing featured as one of the acts in wider matinee and evening programmes of entertainment. Audiences attending an Allan performance did not only see her dancing, it was presented amidst a diverse range of other acts. In July 1909, at the height of her fame in London, Allan appeared on a bill alongside a short drama, A Woman's Revolt by W. L. Courtney. Mixing drama, dance, music, acrobatics and comedy was standard practice for variety programmers. However, the contrast between responses to this short play and to Allan's familiar dancing style clearly illustrates the power of the female celebrity's corporeality to raise and engage with ideas about gender.

The Times reviewer sent to cover this summer matinee at the Palace appears to have been both confused and amused by the themes and characters presented in A Woman's Revolt. The paper recorded that the drama focused on the marriage of a successful actress, Gabrielle (unsurprisingly a woman with 'a not immaculate "past" ') to Launcelot Wrayne, 'the hero – no! no! – the leading villain'. A villain, surmises this professional spectator, because he 'had actually dared to ask [Gabrielle] to share his name and his large income as his wedded wife'. As the reviewer noted, 'we did not realize at first how wrong this was of Launcelot. In fact, we thought it moderately decent behaviour on his part, since Gabrielle admitted that she was hardly strong enough for her work, and rather liked the idea of settling down and being looked after. But we were to learn.'[33] A succession of amorous encounters and domestic conflicts entangling Gabrielle, Launcelot and Launcelot's guardian, Colonel Routledge, followed. The drama concluded with Gabrielle's rejection of the financial support and affection of both men: with ironic echoes of Henrik Ibsen's Nora Helmer, she left, 'thanking her Creator that she could "live her own life" '.[34]

A Woman's Revolt was interpreted and presented by The Times as a poor pastiche of contemporary gender politics and developments in sexual equality. Certainly it seems to have drawn upon caricatural representations of the New Woman that would have been familiar to early twentieth-century audiences. Courtney's troublesome anti-heroine Gabrielle is a rather clichéd compound of images of the New Woman and the actress: images that predate the play's production by at least two decades. In her treatment of the two men who admire and court her, Gabrielle engages with questions about marriage and emancipation that are reminiscent not only of the female characters created by Henrik Ibsen, but also those from successful mainstream plays by Arthur Wing Pinero and Sydney Grundy that appeared on the London stage in the 1890s. Yet, in spite of these precedents, and the critic's dismissal of this short production, there is a genuine and intriguing sense of confusion underlying the review's concluding statement, which records: '[b]ut for [the play] we might have gone on believing marriage to be an honourable state for both sexes, and to help those in trouble a plain duty. But "feminism" is very enlightening.'[35]

Having attempted – albeit unsuccessfully – to dismiss the baffling gender politics of Courtney's play, the *Times* reviewer turned next to Maud Allan's performance at this matinee. A distinct contrast to the scathing reduction of the character and behaviour of Gabrielle, and by extension to new ideas about feminism, is evident here: 'Miss Maud Allan, in several new dances, gave a display of feminism of a more agreeable order. One has to be very careful these days. We may be offering Miss Allan a gross insult in saying that we liked her new dances very much.'[36] Allan's performance attracted the reviewer's full attention. In this seemingly flippant dismissal of current ideas about feminism, and the need 'to be very careful' about what one said to women, the celebrity dancer becomes the locus of questions surrounding ideas about 'acceptability', and – more specifically – about acceptable behaviour towards women. In her programme of short dances, a non-narrative physical performance, Allan's moving body speaks and questions in a way that Courtney's Gabrielle does not. During this 1909 afternoon of entertainment, it was the corporeality of the dancer that engaged with and raised questions about gender. Bearing in mind the sensationalism and furore that was caused by Allan's dancing in other contexts, this becomes even more striking and significant.

For anyone with an interest in fin-de-siècle European culture, it is difficult to separate the name Maud Allan from the figure of Salome. Images of key poses from her popular and controversial work *The Vision of Salome* were mass produced as postcards during the period (Figure 3). These images have become widely accepted as representations of her performance style. Historically, Allan has been understood as a dancer

3  Maud Allan as Salome, postcard (1908)

whose performances were largely affiliated with this one role. There are numerous reasons for this connection, and they are discussed further in Chapter eight. These photographs – freeze-frames extracted from a whole performance – and descriptions of Allan's dancing body in this piece have been variously identified with cultures of eroticism, exoticism, objectification and imperialism.[37] The transparent skirt, small beaded bodice and strings of pearls that Allan wore to perform this piece, and her use of a papier-mâché head to stage the decapitation of John the Baptist, provoked debate and scandal. In June 1908, the Manchester Watch Committee ruled that *The Vision of Salome* was unsuitable entertainment for the city's audiences, and they banned Allan from performing there. Engagements were cancelled, but, most significantly, the edict incited a flurry of comments in the press. Critics, reviewers, journalists and letter writers commented on Allan, her performances, the reason for the ban and its appropriateness.

The sheer column space devoted to supportive and critical views and opinions on the nature of Allan's dancing made her a household name. The *Clarion*'s 'Stageland' column published on Friday 12 June 1908 used the Manchester ban as a means to mock the establishment, and to lambaste contemporary ideas about morality. Pointing out the ludicrous nature of the situation, they concluded that the whole situation could only be viewed as 'funny', 'very funny'.[38] In spite of, or encouraged by, the debate incited by the Manchester ban, Allan's London performances continued to sell out. This was publicity that even the entrepreneurial Alfred Butt would have struggled to engineer.

### 'New ideas of the power of the human body to act emotions and moods'[39]

Returning to contemporary responses to Maud Allan's performances, particularly those appearances that occurred after the Manchester debate had died down, reveals that critics and spectators discovered more in Allan's performances and her celebrity than the furore and the ideas that were provoked by *The Vision of Salome*. As *The Penny Illustrated* noted, 'she can well afford to leave sensationalism to the others . . . She is the High Priestess of a purer art, and breathes the voiceless music of our dreams.'[40] Reviewing her first London performance, the *Daily News* identified Allan as an 'extraordinary artiste': a dancer whose performance offered 'new ideas of the power of the human body to act emotions and moods'. 'The dancing itself is a poem', the reviewer continued, 'and none but the most prurient could see the slightest appeal to any sense but that of beauty of motion and of pose.'[41] Amidst the controversy provoked by her appearances, it was clear to these commentators that Maud Allan was using her on-stage body in a new way: her dancing offered London audiences a different form of corporeal expression.

Whilst Allan may have resigned her role as a classical musician in 1901, music was to remain central to the performance style that she developed, and her fusion of movement and music, the two mediums that she had experience within, led to much serious discussion and admiration of her work. The *Daily News*' summary of her performance as a 'poem' echoes other responses that interpreted her dance as a staging of aesthetic synthesis. In strikingly similar language the *Standard* recorded that Allan's dancing demonstrated, '[a] new Art form. They are not dances in the ordinary sense. They are really the translation of poetry and music to movement.'[42] In order to achieve this synthesis, Allan rejected the familiar airs and songs that were selected by many popular performers of her day. Instead she worked with compositions by contemporary composers, choreographing pieces to works by Frédéric Chopin, Claude Debussy, Marcel Remy, Jean Sibelius, Edvard Grieg and Léo Delibes, amongst others. For some works – such as the ballet *Khamma*, choreographed in 1910 – she commissioned new musical scores: for this piece, one publication noted, 'Debussy is at the moment engaged in completing the music for a new and curiously subtle departure in the way of a composition specially adapted to her fascinating form of art.'[43]

Allan choreographed over forty dances during her stage career, many of which engaged with very different material and ideas to the erotic dance of the seven veils connected with the biblical myth of Salome. Nonetheless, they proved popular with audiences. In *Marche Funèbre*, a work choreographed to a recent work by Chopin, Allan portrayed a grieving woman, desperately searching for the body of her dead lover amongst the corpses strewn on a battlefield. *Valse Triste*, created to visualise the music of Jean Sibelius, was the tale of a dying, old woman who entered a fit of delirium: Allan danced her vision, in which she re-encountered the ghostly friends and lovers of her youth. In *Anitra's Dance*, from the score for *Peer Gynt* composed by Grieg, Allan again used popular dance performance as a means of experimenting with, and achieving, a new level of expression. As *The Times* reported in February 1909:

> It is a joyful experience to see Miss Allan dance a phrase that appears first in the major and then in the minor, for she makes the one phrase of her

dance repeat the other, yet with the fitting change of aspect that must have been in the musician's mind. This was particularly beautiful in more than one movement of Grieg's first *Peer Gynt* suite, in which 'Anitra's Dance' was the most charming of the sections.[44]

Professionally and creatively, Maud Allan claimed that there was only 'one woman in the world' that she desired to 'rival' in her performances. That woman was the 'great and glorious' Sarah Bernhardt,[45] the Victorian actress that Sos Eltis has described as embracing 'celebrity with the greatest enthusiasm'.[46] Watching the performances of 'The Divine Sarah', Allan was particularly struck by the star actress' 'wonderful talent', and her expressiveness. For the dancer, it was the 'beautiful movements of [Bernhardt's] body' that enabled her characteristic performances. The power of her corporeality and physical performance exceeded that of her vocal technique; as Allan noted in her autobiography, she seemed 'to express more with [her body] than with her lips'.[47] A desire to achieve a similar level of physical expression through dance was at the core of Allan's performance practice and, as the *Daily News* affirms, early in her celebrity career her diverse works were being recognised as both expressive and experimental.

Certainly as the twentieth century entered its second decade, the original excitement and controversy that had been raised by Allan's Salome costume and her use of that prop head subsided. In 1911 she returned to the stage of the Palace Theatre of Varieties after a long American tour; the articles and reviews that covered this new set of London appearances scarcely mention *The Vision of Salome*. Although the dance still featured in her repertoire, this press coverage focused almost entirely on new works including *Danse Sacrée et Profane* (Debussy) and *Moment Musical* (Schubert), as well as reflecting a continuing interest in some of her earlier dances that she still regularly performed, including *Marche Funèbre*.[48]

Maud Allan did not disappear from public view, or from celebrity culture, when *The Vision of Salome* ceased to provide one of the city's main talking points. Instead, at this point, her other works began to attract serious critical attention and artistic appreciation: attention and appreciation that were also there at the beginning of her celebrity career, but that were subsumed under the controversy that reactions to her performances provoked. As a performer and a hugely influential celebrity figure, Maud Allan represented more than the sensationalism of Salome to Edwardian audiences.

## 'These matinees are like no other matinees'[49]

At a sold-out performance – and Allan sold out the majority of her London appearances – around 1,700 spectators filled the Palace Theatre of Varieties. Even if one takes into account the number of spectators who may have been late on that afternoon in July, as well as those audience members who may have chosen not to attend the first half of the evening's entertainment, opting instead only going to watch Allan dance, a large number of people would still have seen *A Woman's Revolt*. Because of Allan's fame, Courtney's short play, with its theatrical presentation of ideas about marriage, economic dependence and gender stereotypes, would have been presented to a near-maximum capacity house. In the *Times* reviewer's response there is an assumption that all of those individuals that attended the matinee shared his reactions to the piece: '*we* were to learn' he informed the reader, and '*we* did not realise' (my emphasis).[50]

Existing accounts of the audiences who regularly attended Maud Allan matinees make it clear that this unified response was unlikely. Reflecting the diversification of spectatorship that characterised the fin-de-siècle entertainment industry, a large proportion of the dancer's spectators and followers were women; a fact that did not escape the press, and social critics and caricaturists. In one press pastiche, 'The Maud Allan Matinées', the writer noted:

> These matinees are like no other matinees. The atmosphere is smokeless and fragrant with the fumes of afternoon tea. The audience looks suburban and is almost entirely feminine . . . The majority of the women look like as if they had 'serious interest' in life, so have nothing much to show you in the way of clothes. 'Suitable' is the modistic ideal after which they seem to strive, though some of them – the 'nutty ones' I'm sure – wear weird sat-upon kind of hats and waistless bodices.[51]

In this writer's mind, this is not just an audience dominated by women; it is an audience dominated by a certain 'type' of woman. As in Courtney's *A Woman's Revolt*, the figures pastiched here mirror the traits identified and emphasised in earlier caricatures of the asexual New Woman. For the writer the 'serious interest in life' displayed by these women reduces their femininity: as a collective body they show no interest in their individual appearances, they have 'nothing much to show you in the way of clothes', they are united by their misled 'modistic ideal'. Furthermore their behaviour reveals them to be ignorant of contemporary mores: they are loud and appear socially uneducated; they chatter throughout Allan's performance and remain entirely oblivious to its aesthetic qualities:

> 'Don't you think it must be very easy?' [asked] the flapper. 'I'll try when I get home'. 'It must be very fatiguing, I should think', her mother suggests. 'Did you see how she lay down at the end of the last dance: Tired out, I suppose'. 'Silly! That was part of the dance,' shouts the serious-minded cousin [from another box], 'She does that every time'.[52]

Although this contingency of educated, 'unappealing' women seemed to dominate the auditorium in the eyes of this particular satirist, it is clear that they did not make up the whole of the audience. Allan's performances attracted a mixture of her fans, regular Palace-goers and members of London's fashionable set. In spite of this, in the same way as the *Times'* reviewer, what this journalist offers is one response from within the Palace's spectatorship presented as a generalised audience response. Taken as evidence, without interrogation, these accounts have direct implications for interpretations of Allan's work, and compromise an understanding of the mass popularity of her performances.

## Feminism of a more agreeable order?

Maud Allan the star, and Maud Allan the performer, had a significant influence on ideas about fin-de-siècle women. Her corporeal presence, on stage and in postcard and photographic images, formed crucial elements of her fame, and played a key role in responses to her high-profile identity. Any performance is an embodied act, but in the case of dance, discussions of the body cannot be evaded. Unlike the singer or the actress, the dancer's body is the sole vehicle of the form and many anxieties about female bodies have been mapped on to fin-de-siècle dance, notably those concerning voyeurism and how performers consciously or unconsciously colluded with gender ideology. More than any other celebrity covered in this study, and arguably more than all female performers on stage at the fin de siècle, in Maud Allan's dance those seeds of feminism are unapologetically embodied. The result of this is that it raised questions about femininity, movement, aesthetics and gender.

As Maud Allan's high-profile celebrity, and the initial scandal that was caused by her interpretation of Salome, suggest, female performers' bodies were subject to objectification on the fin-de-siècle popular stage. In an article on the dancer that focuses on her performances of *The Vision of Salome*, Judith Walkowitz has emphasised that 'despite their respectful praise, reviewers subjected [Allan's] body to an obsessive scrutiny'.[53] Indeed they did, but this occurred within a culture of scrutiny: Allan's performing body was simultaneously active and controlled, and a reflection of current debates about gender and aesthetics. The ideological terrain on which Maud Allan performed is problematic, but it was this context that shaped her performances, provoked concern and secured their popularity.

In Edwardian London, and internationally, Maud Allan's body was a powerful and familiar sight and signifier. Moving and stationary her corporeality was interpreted in multiple ways; it meant different things and offered different things to different spectators. Allan may have been banned from Manchester, and her performances associated with the erotic, but her female fan base and her followers performing versions of her style in their own drawing rooms complicate a simple reading of what Allan's body represented. What is clear is that the 'perfectly shaped' body of this dancer did not have one fixed meaning. Amidst the sights, and as the sites, of the multiple gazes of the modern entertainment industry, the meanings expressed by and interpreted from the bodies of female performers oscillated. Roles included erotic object, positive and expressive force and figure of emulation: and all of these roles could co-exist. To return to Grosz, Allan's performing body becomes a model for a body that was not 'inert, passive, noncultural and ahistorical'. Instead it was 'the crucial term, the site of contestation, in a series of economic, political, sexual and intellectual struggles'.[54] In the 'feminism of a more agreeable order' on display at a Maud Allan Palace matinee, an example of popular stage performance that is truly enlightening can be discovered.

The geographical and ideological spaces created and developed in the modern city were complex and contradictory territories. Their meanings shifted. Against this urban backdrop, the popular stage offered a space where female and male bodies did possess the potential to harbour the explanatory powers of minds. The following two chapters explore this in more detail in relation to two specific and very different metropolitan sites: the Gaiety Theatre in London and the Salpêtrière hospital in Paris. In their representation and performances these spaces harnessed and enmeshed the forces of the popular stage, spectatorship and corporeality.

## Notes

1 *Daily Mail*, 7 March 1908, Maud Allan clippings file, Mander and Mitchenson Collection, London.

2  Gery Harris, 'But is it Art? Female Performers in the Café-Concert', *New Theatre Quarterly*, 1989, pp. 334–47. See also Harris, 'Regarding History: Some Narratives Concerning the Café-Concert, Le Music Hall and the Feminist Academic', *The Drama Review* 40:4, 1996, pp. 70–84.

3  Jane R. Goodall, *Performance and Evolution in the Age of Darwin* (London: Routledge, 2002), p. 185. See also Elizabeth Coffman, 'Women in Motion: Loïe Fuller and the "Interpenetration" of Art and Science', *Camera Obscura* 17:1, 2002, pp. 73–105.

4  Thomas Laquer, *Making Sex: Body and Gender from the Greeks to Freud* (Cambridge, MA: Harvard University, 1994), p. 5.

5  Tamar Garb, *Bodies of Modernity: Figure and Flesh in Fin-de-Siècle France* (London: Thames and Hudson, 1988), p. 11.

6  Ursula Bloom, *Curtain Call for the Guv'nor* (London: Hutchinson, 1954), p. 23.

7  Lynda Nead, *Myths of Sexuality: Representations of Women in Victorian Britain* (Oxford: Blackwells, 1988), p. 29.

8  Bram Dijkstra, *Idols of Perversity: Fantasies of Feminine Evil in Fin-de-Siècle Culture* (Oxford: Oxford University Press, 1986), p. 70.

9  Garb, *Bodies of Modernity: Figure and Flesh in Fin-de-Siècle France*, p. 11.

10  See C. E. Forth, 'Moral Contagion and Will: The Crisis of Masculinity in Fin-de-Siècle France', in Alison Bashford and Claire Hooker (eds), *Contagion: Historical and Cultural Studies* (London: Routledge, 2001), pp. 61–75.

11  Jules Michelet, cited in Griselda Pollock, 'Modernity and the Spaces of Femininity', in Norma Broude and Mary D. Garrard (eds), *The Expanding Discourse: Feminism and Art History* (Boulder: Westview Press, 1992), pp. 244–67 (254).

12  John Ruskin, *Sesame and Lilies: Three Lectures* (Orpington: G. Allen, 1894).

13  For discussions of women in the city see Deborah Epstein Nord, *Walking the Victorian Streets: Women, Representation and the City* (Ithaca: Cornell University Press, 1995); Elizabeth Wilson, *The Sphinx in the City: Urban Life, the Control of Disorder and Women* (London: Virago, 1991); Judith R. Walkowitz, *City of Dreadful Delight: Narratives of Sexual Danger in Late Victorian London* (London: Virago, 1992).

14  Pollock, 'Modernity and the Spaces of Femininity', p. 259.

15  See Angelique Richardson and Chris Willis (eds), *The New Woman in Fiction and in Fact: Fin-de-Siècle Feminisms* (Basingstoke: Palgrave, 2000) and Mary Louise Roberts, *Disruptive Acts: The New Woman in Fin-de-Siècle France* (Chicago and London: The University of Chicago Press, 2002) for discussions of the figure of the New Woman in England and in France.

16  P. Marks, *Bicycles, Bangs and Bloomers: The New Woman in the Popular Press* (Lexington: University Press of Kentucky, 1990); Lisa Tickner, *The Spectacle of Women: Imagery of the Suffrage Campaign* (Chicago: University of Chicago, 1988).

17  As revealed in Vivien Gardner and Susan Rutherford (eds), *The New Woman and her Sisters: Feminism and Theatre, 1850–1914* (Brighton: Harvester Wheatsheaf, 1992).

18  Walkowitz, *City of Dreadful Delight: Narratives of Sexual Danger in Late Victorian London*, p. 21.

19  Anna Cutler, 'Abstract Body Language: Documenting Women's Bodies in Theatre', *New Theatre Quarterly* 54:2, 1998, pp. 111–18 (111).

20  John Stokes, in John Stokes, Michael Booth and Susan Bassnet, *Bernhardt, Terry and Duse: The Actress in her Time* (Cambridge: Cambridge University Press, 1988), p. 2.

21  Elizabeth K. Menon, 'Images of Pleasure and Vice: Women of the Fringe', in Gabriel P. Weisberg (ed.), *Montmartre and the Making of Mass Culture* (London: Rutgers University Press, 2001), pp. 37–71 (67).

22  Although exceptions to this can be discovered in the work of Tracy C. Davis and Jacky Bratton, see Tracy C. Davis, *Actresses as Working Women: Their Social Identity in Victorian Culture* (London: Routledge, 1991) and J. S. Bratton (ed.), *Music Hall: Performance and Style* (Milton Keynes: Open University Press, 1986).

23  James Naremore and Patrick Bratlinger (eds), *Modernity and Mass Culture* (Bloomington, IN: Indiana University Press, 1991), p. 3.

24  Elizabeth Grosz, *Volatile Bodies: Towards a Corporeal Feminism* (Bloomington; IN: Indiana University Press, 1994), p. 3.

25  *Ibid.*, p. 20.

26  Goodall, *Performance and Evolution in the Age of Darwin*, p. 190.

27  See Felix Cherniavsky, *The Salome Dancer: The Life and Times of Maud Allan* (Toronto: McClelland and Stewart Inc., 1991), pp. 146–8.

28  Judith R. Walkowitz, 'The Vision of Salome: Cosmopolitanism and Erotic Dancing in London, 1908–1918', *American Historical Review* 108:2, 2003, pp. 337–76.

29  *The Era*, 4 April 1908, p. 18.

30  *The Times*, 1 April 1909, p. 18 notes that 'Maud Allan' ran in the Royal Artillery Point to Point in Kent.

31  *The Times*, 12 April 1909, p. 9.

32  *The Times*, 14 March 1911, p. 8.

33  'Palace Theatre', *The Times*, 8 July 1909, p. 7.

34  *The Times*, 8 July 1909, p. 7.

35  *Ibid.*, p. 7.

36  *Ibid.*

37  See Amy Koritz, 'Dancing the Orient for England: Maud Allan's "The Vision of Salome"', *Theatre Journal* 46:1, 1994, pp. 63–78; Walkowitz, 'The Vision of Salome: Cosmopolitanism and Erotic Dancing in London, 1908–1918'; Michael Kettle, *Salome's Last Veil: The Libel Case of the Century* (London: Hart-Davis, 1977).

38 Hilda Thompson, 'Stageland', *The Clarion*, 12 June 1908, p. 5.
39 *Daily News*, 7 March 1908, Maud Allan clippings file, Mander and Mitchenson Collection, London.
40 *The Penny Illustrated*, 25 February 1911, p. 25.
41 *Daily News*, 7 March 1908.
42 Cited in 'A Few Press Tributes to Miss Maud Allan', *The Revival of Classical Dancing*, undated pamphlet, published by Gale and Polden, London, Mander and Mitchenson Collection, London, p. 6.
43 Unidentified press clipping, Maud Allan clippings file, Mander and Mitchenson Collection, London.
44 *The Times*, 13 February 1909, p. 13.
45 Maud Allan, *My Life and Dancing* (London: Everett and Co., 1908), p. 36.
46 Sos Eltis, 'Private Lives and Public Spaces: Reputation, Celebrity and the Late Victorian Actress', in Mary Luckhurst and Jane Moody (eds), *Theatre and Celebrity in Britain, 1660–2000* (Basingstoke: Palgrave Macmillan, 2005), pp. 169–90 (169).
47 Allan, *My Life and Dancing*, p. 36.
48 'Maudelightful than Ever', Maud Allan clippings file, Mander and Mitchenson Collection, London; *The Sphere*, 22 February 1911, Maud Allan clippings file, Mander and Mitchenson Collection, London.
49 'The Maud Allan Matinées', Maud Allan clippings file, Mander and Mitchenson Collection, London. Although this clipping is undated, the writer refers in the piece to the trend for imitating Allan, taking classes in her dance style and practising at home. The popularity of these activities was concurrent with Allan's height of fame at the Palace in 1908–9.
50 'Palace Theatre', *The Times*, 8 July 1909, p. 7.
51 'The Maud Allan Matinées'.
52 *Ibid.*
53 Walkowitz, 'The Vision of Salome: Cosmopolitanism and Erotic Dancing in London, 1908–1918', p. 351.
54 Grosz, *Volatile Bodies: Towards a Corporeal Feminism*, p. 19.

# Part II
## SPACES

'An eden [the Salpêtrière hospital] was for me, so much in this world being relative.' (Jane Avril)

# 3

# Epidemics of enchanting creatures: Loïe Fuller and the Gaiety Theatre, London

At the fin de siècle, London's Gaiety Theatre and its famous resident company of glamorous female performers – the Gaiety Girls – formed a familiar feature of the British capital's spectacular culture. As Norton Atkins recorded in 1898, when he penned the lyrics to his comic music-hall song 'Happiest Chappie', it was 'the best dressed' men in London – those chaps who are 'well-known everywhere' – that spent their evenings going 'off to the Gaiety'.[1] Constructed in 1868, the venue was a quintessential and self-consciously modern entertainment space, a product of the theatre-building boom of the second half of the nineteenth century. Occupying a prime site on the Strand, at the heart of London's fashionable social centre, the Gaiety was a landmark of the capital's new commodity culture. Eating at its restaurant, mingling in its foyer and seeing each new show became fashionable acts for both citizens and visitors to the city. The Gaiety was the place to be seen, as one contemporary recalled: 'Nobody said "what's on at the Gaiety?" They said "Let's go to the Gaiety." '[2]

In 1886, the well-known London entertainment entrepreneur George Edwardes took over the management of the Gaiety, retaining the venue until 1903 amidst his changing portfolio of London leisure attractions. Edwardes had inherited a viable financial concern from the theatre's first manager John Hollingshead. Under his regime the Gaiety's popularity increased further, as the theatre became renowned for its musical comedies and long-running burlesques: forms that offered audiences attractive stage spectacles that staged the codes and trends of fashionable metropolitan life 'against a colourful backdrop'.[3]

Between 1886 and 1903, the careers of numerous celebrity actresses, singers and dancers began on the Gaiety Theatre's stage, whilst many well-established stars also chose to perform at the high-profile venue. Amongst these individual performers was a relatively unknown American actress and singer, trying her luck in the British capital. Edwardes contracted Loïe Fuller in the early 1890s, and the period of time that she spent at the venue reveals that she used the space, style and reputation of the Gaiety to establish and develop her own performance form, celebrity identity and career management. It is no coincidence that eighteen months after leaving the Gaiety, Loïe Fuller was an international star.

The European premiere of Fuller's *Serpentine Dance* at the Folies-Bergère music hall in Paris in October 1892 marks the beginning of her international celebrity status. This debut performance comprised a forty-five-minute programme featuring four dances: *The Serpentine Dance, The Violet Dance, The Butterfly Dance* and *The White Dance*. Combined with carefully timed publicity in the daily newspaper, *Le Figaro*, this first Parisian performance rocketed Fuller to fame overnight.[4] Across the city she rapidly became known as 'La Loïe Fuller' – *the* Loïe Fuller – recognition not only of her acceptance into French culture, but also of her status as the creator of a new performance style.[5] Fuller claimed that previous, less successful performances of her new dance in London, New York and Boston had convinced her that cities where she was consistently billed as a divertissement were unlikely to offer her the fame and the creative respect that she desired. In this context, her decision to relocate to Paris – 'a city where, as I had been told, educated people would like my dancing and would accord it a place in the realm of art' – appears to have been an unmitigated success.[6]

However, in spite of the emphasis on the artistic appeal of Paris as a performance environment contained in Fuller's retrospective celebration of the city, it is also evident that she was acutely aware that the French capital's love of spectacle, and its reputation as the worldwide centre of the entertainment industry, would offer her greater financial stability and more performance opportunities than were available in other key metropolitan centres. Fin-de-siècle Paris' unique urban environment supplied Fuller with a career in the entertainment industry and the opening to be recognised as a creative innovator. Moving to the city was a tactical manoeuvre in Fuller's creation of herself as a star performer and celebrity artist, but her success when she arrived was the outcome of her experience of the American and British entertainment industries.

After Fuller's hugely successful debut at the Folies-Bergère, additional matinee performances were added to her schedule. These still did not satisfy audience demand, and ten days' advance booking was needed to secure tickets for any of her appearances.[7] The dancer's followers did not only watch her perform on stage, they read – and demanded – countless interviews and articles with their favourite celebrity; they witnessed posters and images of her cover cities; and they provided the market for a Loïe Fuller merchandise industry. 'Paris has gone mad over Miss Loïe Fuller,' reported *The Sketch* in 1893, 'not only is there the Loïe Fuller skirt, but the Bon Marché and Louvre are selling Loïe Fuller hats, Loïe Fuller ribbons, Loïe Fuller shoes and even Loïe Fuller petticoats.'[8]

Fuller accessories and merchandise were not only available in France; similar products were also on sale in department stores and by mail order in the metropolitan centres of Britain, Spain and America. International tours followed her Parisian success, and for the next three and a half decades La Loïe remained a popular act at metropolitan music halls, dance halls, café-concerts and theatres in Europe and North and South America. What was this popular dancer, untrained in the form, doing on stage to achieve such a universal level of acclaim?

Fuller identified her work as dance, whilst simultaneously commenting on the inadequacy of the definition, and stating that 'there ought to be a word better adapted to the thing'.[9] Her celebrated performances choreographed movement, music, light and fabric; their effects created by the play of 'colored lights on swirling draperies and floating veils'.[10] In a completely darkened auditorium La Loïe would appear before her audience, framed within a black, silk-draped stage space and clothed in loose fabric gowns and veils that were made to her own designs. As the orchestra began its accompaniment, she moved swiftly across and around the performance space, animating the cloth: throwing large swathes of fabric into the air and manipulating them with the movement of her arms, or with the aid of long canes that were stitched into the loose sleeves of her costumes. James McNeill Whistler's sketch of Fuller performing at the Folies-Bergère captures the movement of her dance (Figure 4).

## 'Her creations became a law in the theatres of the world'[11]

What mesmerised and thrilled Fuller's audiences were the sequences of amorphous moving images created by this technique: series of shapes that changed through spectrums of colour, and faded in and out of light and darkness. As one spectator recorded: 'the theatre being pitch dark, the dancer can be brought slowly into view and can be made to slowly disappear', 'she can appear in any colour, or combination of colours'.[12] The effects of these illusive on-stage visions are captured in a review of a touring programme of dances that were performed by Fuller

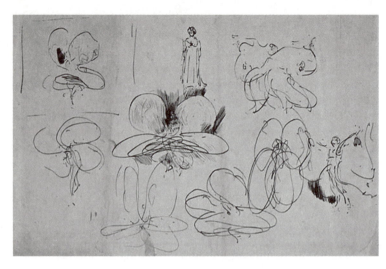

4  Whistler, 'Loïe Fuller Dancing' (1892)

at the Folies-Bergère, the Palace Theatre of Varieties in London, and at
venues in New York and Boston in the mid-1890s:

> In the third [dance, *The Firmament*] a most entrancing effect is produced
> when the dancer's gauzy garments, irradiated by multi-coloured lights,
> have the appearance of fleecy clouds. In 'La Nuit' [*The Night*] we see black
> robes become incandescent with tiny stars and in 'Le lys' [*The Lily*] the
> dancer looks like a winged spirit ready to fly to the realms of blue ether.
> The spectacle is dreamy, poetic, fascinating and admirable music
> enhances its very remarkable and novel effects. It was watched with the
> deepest interest and with universal approval.[13]

This was an 'elusive and transitional' visual performance;[14] a fusion of
physical movement, choreography and technological experimentation
that led spectators to describe it as 'dreamy, poetic', 'fascinating',[15] 'aston-
ishing',[16] 'terrifying'[17] and 'phantasmagorical'.[18]

Nonetheless, extended periods of meticulous planning and choreography lay behind the effects and the success of each of her performances:
some of her dances took up to three years to develop and to stage.[19] In
her own words, each movement of Fuller's body in performance was
'expressed in the folds of the silk, in a play of colours and draperies that
could be mathematically and systematically calculated'.[20] In performance, she claimed, 'I leave nothing to chance.'[21] By employing established

stage machinery and technology, including magic lantern projections, and combining it with the carefully designed use of controllable electric-lighting effects and chemical dyes, Loïe Fuller's popular performances pushed at the boundaries of stage spectacle at the fin de siècle.[22]

It is clear that Fuller herself was convinced of her important practical and aesthetic achievements as a performer and an innovator, as well as a mass celebrity. In an unapologetic piece of self-promotion that she drafted for a second volume of her memoirs (which never appeared in print), she recorded that:

> Her creations became a law in the theatres of the world. She was the creator of colored lights on swirling draperies and floating veils. She was the creator of the dark draperies to replace scenery. She was the creator of obscurity in the theatre. She was the creator of shading the lights in the orchestra, and she began it by using black paper with the music written on it in white.[23]

In the 1990s, Fuller's words were reiterated and updated by a critic writing for the French newspaper *Libération* who stated: 'cinematic art, multimedia, abstract, performance, interactivity, contemporary dance: at the end of the nineteenth century, Loïe Fuller had already invented everything'.[24] The connections and the similarities between this dance, for the want of a better word, and the experiments and innovations of individual practitioners including Edward Gordon Craig, Adolphe Appia, Isadora Duncan and Ruth St Denis are striking. La Loïe may have been an international star, but her performance practice was avant-garde.

On the stages of music halls and variety theatres, the performances of this celebrity fused ideas, practices and innovations that would now be considered tropes of modern and post-modern performance. An aesthetic experiment and statement in its own right, its synthesis of forms attracted the interest of contemporary avant-garde artists and writers, but it was a synthesis that fundamentally depended on the spaces and the technologies of the popular entertainment industry. Without the material conditions of mass entertainment and the modern city environments of London and Paris, Loïe Fuller's style, developments and inventions would simply not have occurred.

Fuller was thirty on the night of her 1892 Parisian debut, and had already amassed fifteen years of popular stage experience. Previous engagements had included contracts as an actress and as a singer in musical comedies and operettas, at theatres across America and in London. Shortly before her rapid ascent to fame in Paris, she had spent eighteen months performing in the British capital, arriving in late October 1889 to take up the lease of the Royal Globe Theatre on Newcastle Street. She had hired the venue to stage *Caprice*, a production of a comedy by Howard P. Taylor that she had already mounted and managed in Jamaica. In spite of reasonable reviews in the London press, *Caprice* was not a success, and it closed after a short run.

Rather than returning to America immediately, Fuller opted to stay in London and seek alternative opportunities. After an initial struggle to find employment, she managed to secure a succession of small roles at many of the capital's well-known playhouses, working at the Royal Avenue Theatre, Terry's Theatre, the Opéra-Comique, the Theatre Royal, Drury Lane and the Shaftesbury Theatre. In addition to these engagements at some of London's choicest venues, between 13 October 1890 and 4 July 1891 Fuller spent nine and a half months appearing with the Gaiety Theatre company, by far the longest of her British contracts. On stage at the Gaiety during this 1890–91 season was the long-running burlesque *Carmen up to Data*. A parody of Bizet's *Carmen* penned by the celebrated burlesquers George R. Sims and Henry Pettit and choreographed by John D'Auban, the show had proved a hit with London's audiences, going through two versions during its extended run.

Burlesques were characteristic Gaiety entertainment: they offered the manager, the designers and the cast the opportunity to indulge in the opulent costumes and the spectacle that had become central to the reputation and success of the venue. One critic, writing for *The Saturday Review*, encapsulated the nature of these productions, affectionately remarking that:

> A Gaiety burlesque is almost as composite a piece of work as a Chinese puzzle; a beginning and an ending it must necessarily have, but the construction of the middle seems to depend entirely on chance . . . So far as what, by a figure of speech, is still termed the 'burlesque' is concerned, it is, as of yore, deemed necessary to make believe that a 'story' runs through it, and that a plot is also to be discovered by those who will devote themselves to a strenuous search for it.

With reference to the current production the reviewer noted that, 'the plain fact is that the production (*it happens to be called Carmen up to Data this time*) is nothing more than a piece of patchwork; . . . there are beautiful women, and beautiful stage-pictures, and beautiful dresses' (my emphasis).[25]

*Carmen up to Data* starred two of the Gaiety's most popular performers, Letty Lind and Sylvia Grey. Lind and Grey were familiar to

London's audiences as actresses, singers and dancers, but predominantly they were known as Gaiety Girls, representatives of the venue's female company. Fuller was not hired as a cast member for *Carmen up to Data*: instead she played the lead, Alice Montrose, in the season's curtain-raiser, a one-act operetta entitled *His Last Chance*. However, following the standard practice of the Gaiety company, she would also have been cast as an understudy for one of the actresses in the main burlesque. The *Daily Express'* obituary for the dancer noted that, 'she followed Letty Lind' during the run,[26] a statement further endorsed by William Davenport Adams in his 1904 *Dictionary of the Drama*, where he notes that Fuller did actually play Lind's role for a period of time during the run of *Carmen up to Data*.[27] Appearing in the Gaiety's curtain-raiser, acting as understudy to one of the venue's most popular female performers, and the exposure to the celebrity construct of the Gaiety Girl that this extended engagement involved, were to have a significant influence on Loïe Fuller's performance style and on her celebrity personality.

## 'The Gaiety Girl was, above all, feminine. She was womanhood incarnate'[28]

Under John Hollingshead's management the figure of the Gaiety Girl had emerged as one of the theatre's main attractions and talking points; under George Edwardes she became the venue's internationally recognisable image. The iconography of the Gaiety Girl that was created and sold by the venue in the late 1880s and 1890s embraced current ideals of femininity. As Edwardes' contemporary Walter Macqueen Pope explained:

> no longer was there the lavish display of feminine limbs and charms . . . Skirts replaced tights, and mystery, deep, alluring and irresistible, surrounded the female form. Above all else, Edwardes exalted femininity . . . Edwardes put the 'Girl' into the Gaiety.[29]

Attractive images of these popular, 'irresistible' female performers blanketed the posters, programmes and merchandise that were commissioned by the theatre (Figure 5). Initially, this use of a commodified 'exalted femininity' to sell entertainment to large audiences suggests that this fashionable metropolitan venue acts as a model of Elizabeth Menon's conviction that women were used as motifs to represent both the performers and the pleasures of the contemporary entertainment industry (discussed in Chapter two).[30] To some extent this is the case, but considering some of the individual performers that fulfilled the role of the

5  Souvenir programme for *A Gaiety Girl* (1894)

Gaiety Girl reveals that this was a far more complex construct than this position suggests.

The vocabulary and imagery repeatedly utilised by the press, performers and management to describe the Gaiety's female company members were grounded in ideals of femininity, not of sexuality or sexual availability. In part, this reflected a widely held belief in the moral and cultural improvement of the female performer at the fin de siècle. Just after the turn of the twentieth century Stanley Naylor remarked that:

> [i]t is a pleasing sign of the improved condition of the stage that the 'chorus girl' of the old school is so quickly passing away . . . [The Gaiety Girls] are undoubtedly more beautiful, more ladylike, and dressed in better taste than were their predecessors of a generation ago.[31]

London's Gaiety Girls were public personalities, celebrity figures that attracted international interest; their lives regularly made the British, European and American presses. A triumph of fin-de-siècle marketing and branding, in this familiar and popular figure, examples of professional women in the public sphere, who were widely considered to be respectable and wholesome representatives of their sex, can be discovered. The construct of the Gaiety Girl was inherently dualistic; it served as both 'a criterion for all that was enchanting', and as a model that gave successful and creative performers access to a performance space and to celebrity culture.[32]

The repeated representation and wide acceptance of the Gaiety Girl as a positive representation of women is particularly striking because the performers she represented were occupants and active members of the metropolis' modern urban terrain. As a direct result of the sexual ideology that the ideal nature of the figure was grounded in, this appealing construct of femininity simultaneously adhered to and challenged contemporary ideas about gender. The figure of the Gaiety Girl, and the female company members that were associated with her mysterious 'allure', occupied a fundamentally ambiguous position amidst social and cultural ideas: a position that reflected that of many other female celebrity performers who were not connected to Edwardes' venue.

Much of the appeal of the Gaiety Girl was connected to the theatre's successful marketing campaigns, and the imagery and ideas about identity that these depended on. As Peter Bailey has commented, George Edwardes was responsible for designing his company's image, and maintaining control over their appearance and behaviour on and off stage. In addition to producing a successful and popular body of performers, Edwardes presented society with an ensemble of respectable and ladylike women. His success is evinced by the public's interest in the real-life 'Cinderella narratives' that involved Gaiety Girls. Numerous press articles and interviews told of members of Edwardes' company who had attracted the attention of high-class admirers and made society marriages, relinquishing their stage careers for the lifestyle of the minor aristocracy.

In 1884, Constance (or Connie) Gilchrist, an actress and dancer who had been one of the Gaiety's top-billing stars in the 1870s and early 1880s, retired from the company to live with the Duke of Beaufort. This period of non-marital cohabitation did nothing to damage Gilchrist's reputation, nor her eligibility; she went on to marry Edmond, Earl of Orkney in 1892. Gilchrist's married life was conservative; she appears to have spent much of her retirement engaged in philanthropic acts for the benefit of the community. Having left the stage, Connie Gilchrist remained, on one level, a performer: as the charitable society wife she was 'appearing' in a different context, performing the vision of ideal and respectable femininity that had been shaped and promoted by Edwardes at the Gaiety.

Gilchrist was not alone in her move from theatrical circles to those of high society. In his 1911 work *Love Romances of the Aristocracy*, Thornton Hall devoted a whole chapter – 'Footlights and Coronets' – to the 'epidemic' of 'romantic alliances between the peerage and the stage' that had dominated the gossip columns of recent years.[33] Hall's accounts are romantic; they contain no sense of disapproval of the increasing number of these marriages in society. The sentimental nature of these well-known tales, and the public's fondness for them, both endorsed and furthered the aura of respectability that surrounded the Gaiety Girl.

Attitudes, it seems, were changing, and amidst this wider improvement in the image and the status of the female performer, the Gaiety Girl was an influential figure. The extent of this shift was recorded by the music-hall gossip column of *The Era* in 1892, where, after reporting on another liaison between a stage star and a social figure, the journalist noted that '[t]his is an age of rapid evolution – revolution, we might say. Dancers become countesses, and countesses dancers.'[34] Women were moving between spaces previously understood to be diametrically opposed: not only were dancers marrying into aristocracy, but the aristocracy were taking to the stage. Ideas were in flux, and previously solid conceptions of social roles and femininity were blurred.

The Gaiety Girl's dual role – as a performer and as a public representative of ideal womanhood – meant that the individual actresses, singers and dancers that she represented were placed, and understood, within multiple categories at the fin de siècle. Bailey has identified the theatre's distinctive image as simultaneously standing for a 'working woman, stage persona, public image, and private person'. These different identities were, in this case, inseparable: they 'constantly intersect[ed] and elide[d]', but what is unusual – in this celebrity construct – is that they do not appear to have conflicted.[35] During the 1880s and 1890s the Gaiety Girl became a nexus of ideas about femininity, the changing nature of women in public and in performance. Undeniably, the display of beautiful women was interwoven into the fabric of the spectacular Gaiety show, but individual stars that worked at the venue also created and embodied new ideas about female celebrities and performance.

In the modern city, the entertainment industry supplied a space that embraced and fostered the period's changing social constructs and ideas. Theatres and music halls offered female performers the opportunity to establish celebrity identities within popular stage forms. Amongst the women performing and shaping their careers at the Gaiety Theatre in its age of deep, alluring and mysterious femininity were practical, creative and talented performers: women who appropriated the ultra-feminine role that was associated with Edwardes' venue to gain a performance space. In this context *The Era*'s 1892 use of the words 'rapid evolution' and 'revolution' to refer to current shifts in ideas about the female performer may not be as misplaced as it initially appears. Certainly an evolution was occurring in what popular entertainment spaces could offer to performers. In the figure of the Skirt Dancer, one of the representative images of the Gaiety Girl, and a construct that was to play a crucial role in the successful careers of Letty Lind, Sylvia Grey and Loïe Fuller, these ideas can be further traced.

## 'One of the most lucrative of modern properties – a new dance'[36]

The definition 'Skirt Dance' has been called upon by its contemporaries and by historians to classify and describe many variations and developments of a basic style that emerged in London in the 1870s. Its creation was attributed to Kate Vaughan (1852–1903), an actress, trained ballet dancer and Gaiety Girl. In its earliest form the dance was characterised by a series of swaying movements, softened and emphasised by the light fabric of the long, pleated petticoats and skirts worn by the performers. Its pleasing visual effects were described by Reginald St Johnston in his 1906 publication *A History of Dancing*, where he drew attention to the Skirt Dance's 'swift rush of floating draperies through the air'. A skilled performer, he noted further, would manipulate these draperies with 'a certainty and precision whose very apparent absence declares its art'.[37] The talented Skirt Dancer would, it seems, make her performance appear an entirely natural act, a pleasing sight for the spectator that required minimal physical exertion on the part of the female performer.

Visually pleasing, inherently graceful and based on the impression that it did not require any physical exertion, it is no surprise that the Skirt Dance became a popular form of the day, for it reflected important mainstays of gender ideology. For those who were not attracted to a career on the stage, gentle skirt dancing was recommended as a beneficial leisure activity. Indeed it became widely viewed as a good way for young women to improve their postures, and to take gentle exercise. Dance instructors quickly realised the financial potential of teaching the Skirt Dance: with its long dresses and gentle movements it was the ideal style to be taught to young ladies, who could practise and perform it in the home. As Elizabeth Garratt, a successful dance teacher, explained in an interview with the *Pall Mall Budget* following an 'at-home' at which many of her pupils performed: 'girls dance after a dinner-party as, formerly, they gave a song. You see, the style of dress that is required for these dances is almost identical with the ordinary dinner dress . . . the umbrella-shaped skirt of this season is just the right thing for skirt dancing.'[38]

If lessons were not a financial or practical option, then paper-guides also offered basic instruction in the popular style. Routledge's 1893 publication *How to Dance* was designed as 'a new guide to the latest fashionable dances', with the Skirt Dance's steps explained simply enough to be followed at home by the novice.[39] Mrs Foreman's *Illustrated Portfolio of Artistic Dancing* included several photographs of a child – a girl of around six or seven – to demonstrate the main poses from the 'Society Skirt Dance'. The accompanying notes strongly recommend 'early instruction' in the form as a means to encourage the 'natural grace of childhood'.[40] As part of a visual sign system that encompassed the stage and the drawing room, the semiotics of the Skirt Dance were grounded in positive ideologies of graceful and gentle femininity. It was interpreted and marketed as a feminine form, a connection that supplies the key reason for its association with the Gaiety Theatre and the Gaiety Girl. As St Johnston commented, for 'most people the word 'skirt-dancing' will call at once to mind the Gaiety Theatre, and not without reason; for with the Gaiety Theatre . . . skirt-dancing has ever had its closest ties'.[41]

The Gaiety's first manager, John Hollingshead, had spotted Kate Vaughan on the music-hall stage. Hollingshead was a theatrical entrepreneur who recognised the talent and skill of popular performers on the variety stage. He frequented London's music halls on a regular basis to seek out new stars for his own company, and also travelled to Paris to search for fresh talent and ideas. In his memoirs he aligned this scouting with commercial forces, comparing it to that of 'a silk-buyer selecting silk by the touch, or a tea-taster, selecting tea by the palate'.[42] The variety star was the commercial product, and for the Gaiety that product had to be of the highest standard. But, as with Edwardes' later use of the Gaiety Girl as the representative image of the venue, for individual performers the relationship could be mutually beneficial. Vaughan accepted Hollingshead's offer of a Gaiety contract, and at the theatre she further developed her trademark performance: a dancing style that used gentle, balletic movements far removed from any association with the Skirt Dance's frenetic, wider-skirted cousin, the Paris cancan. In this first incarnation of the Gaiety Skirt Dance, and the theatre's first Skirt Dancer, we can discover a model for many of the celebrity performers that were to follow.

Kate Vaughan quickly established herself as one of the most popular first-generation Gaiety Girls, and her performances became one of 'the leading attractions in the [theatre's] burlesques'.[43] The immense popularity of her dancing style with audiences, and its approbation by critics, resulted in imitations and appropriations of the Skirt Dance appearing across European theatre and music-hall programmes. By the early 1890s, the craze for the Skirt Dance – likened in the press to an 'epidemic' – had swept from London, through Europe and to America.[44] Venues including the Palace Theatre of Varieties, the Royal Music Hall, the Folies-Bergère, the Empire Theatre of Varieties and the Tivoli music hall all hired and promoted their own Skirt Dancers.

Lucrative opportunities for female performers and dancers were also offered by the dance form: May Palfrey, Topsy Sinden, Clara Wieland, Jennie Joyce, Mabel Love, Estrella Sylvia and Ida Heath all offered versions of the style in their acts in the period between 1892 and 1896. The dance that accompanied Lottie Collins' equally loved and hated 'Ta-ra-ra-boom-de-ay' was based on a combination of the basic moves of the Skirt Dance, coupled with her trademark high kicking during the song's chorus. Whilst Vaughan had imbued the Skirt Dance with 'an air of refinement', making it 'a distinct and graceful style of dancing' that was 'far removed from the acrobatic and the gymnastic', many of these later adaptations eroticised the balletic movement that was initially associated with the form.[45] As Collins' high-kicking routine suggests, away from the Gaiety stage the Skirt Dance became increasingly energetic.[46] But, in spite of these appropriations, the form remained connected with ideas of femininity and grace. Like many of the popular cultural trends and entertainments of the fin de siècle, including the Maud Allan and Loïe Fuller styles, the popularity of the Skirt Dance bridged mass cultural and domestic spaces, and femininity and celebrity.

Skirt dancing, and the figure of the Skirt Dancer, became extensions and endorsements of the image of the Gaiety Girl. Like the Gaiety Girl, they also were inherently dualistic. Seemingly based on and supporting current ideas about femininity, for individual performers the dance simultaneously realised the potential for female creativity and relative economic independence. The Skirt Dance's wide appeal and multiple meanings secured its financial viability, its moral approbation and its enduring popularity. A significant part of its stature, success and cultural prominence was owed to its connection with the Gaiety Girl.

### 'A stage personality which was like no one else's': Letty Lind[47]

As St Johnston's 1906 note has indicated, after Vaughan's retirement from the venue, the Skirt Dance continued to be a core part of the Gaiety Theatre's image. One of the first performers to fill her position as the Gaiety's first dancer was the actress and singer Letty Lind. Raised in a theatrical family, Lind began her professional career as a child performer, singing, acting and dancing at provincial theatres around the country. Shortly after moving to London in her mid-twenties she was spotted on the variety stage by George Edwardes who was impressed by her dancing, her singing and – no doubt – her attractive appearance. He offered her a contract as a burlesque actress and dancer with the Gaiety company, which she accepted, and – according to Macqueen Pope – she was an immediate success from her first appearance at the theatre in 1887:

> Kate Vaughan herself said that she considered her the best [Skirt Dancer] she had ever seen – with a reservation in favour of herself. Indeed, she became a Letty Lind 'fan', and those 'fans' . . . ran into tens of thousands.[48]

Lind's dancing style was celebrated for its femininity, its gentleness and its grace; responses to her performances echo the praise offered to her predecessor Kate Vaughan. These were still popular and marketable qualities in the late 1880s and 1890s, and Lind was to locate them at the core of the celebrity identity she constructed.

As an actress she quickly became identified with the 'bright and graceful . . . heroine', associated with pantomime princesses, the Harlequinade's heroine Columbine, Greek goddesses and geishas. Off stage, celebrations of her femininity were printed by journals and reviews, and were familiar to contemporary readers. In the postcard image of Lind 'Going, Going, Gone'

6  Letty Lind, postcard showing the Skirt Dance

(Figure 6) the two are combined. A sense of light-hearted fun and femininity characterises the image.

In *Carmen up to Data* Lind was cast in a relatively small role, the character of Mercedes. Yet in spite of this small part, the musical synopsis for the burlesque reveals that she performed two solo songs and that she danced alone. What is more interesting is that she was the only female cast member, aside from Florence St John who played Carmen, to perform alone: an indication both of her status within the Gaiety company, the popularity of the Skirt Dance and the public's affection for her as a performer. Unlikely as it seems, one of Lind's solo songs – 'The Farmyard' – incorporated her trademark animal impressions; the most celebrated being those of pigs and horses. The piece featured between 'a chorus of smugglers' and a hornpipe,[49] but no attention was given in any published responses to the burlesque of the potential or actual incongruity of the song's presence in this narrative. Contemporary responses instead note the presence of Lind's trademark act without surprise, commenting on the characteristic 'sweetness' of her performance in the song.[50] The *Illustrated Sporting and Dramatic News* was the only voice of dissent, and then it was slight: their reviewer noted that 'Miss Letty Lind . . . sings her well-known song with farmyard imitations. It is, like her dancing, well received, but of the two I think her dancing much the better.'[51]

Gaiety audiences wanted to see Lind perform the pieces and the styles that she was famous for, and 'The Farmyard' and her dance were simply pieces of the accepted patchwork construction of burlesque identified earlier in *The Saturday Review*. In spite of the representative image of the Gaiety Girl that was projected by the venue and the press, it is clear that a number of female performers in the company managed to establish individual celebrity identities and performance styles alongside their role as a Gaiety Girl. Members of the audience and critics appear to have expected and welcomed performers offering their own set pieces as part of a Gaiety musical comedy.

The choreography of Lind's solo dance fitted a little more neatly with the Spanish theme that loosely framed the burlesque than her pig and horse impressions. The piece was based on Skirt Dance moves, and choreographed to incorporate the sweeping and evasive manoeuvres of the toreador in the bull-ring. Amongst the souvenir merchandise that was produced for *Carmen up to Data* was an ornate cardboard, ribbon-tied folio, containing ten individual colour prints of the main characters in the play.[52] Percy Anderson – the costume designer for the production – created these images, and they can thus be judged as offering a reasonably accurate account of the burlesque's design and the performers' visual appearances. Anderson's sketch of Lind shows her in motion; one leg is raised, and the full skirts of her costume billow around her: the appeal of Lind's performance was in its movement.

Anderson's image of Lind emphasises the way in which the Skirt Dance had been appropriated to incorporate both the expected undulation of petticoats and the movements of the cloth used to taunt the bull. The dance fed and fuelled the public's fondness for national dance styles as exhibition pieces at the time. It also reflected the popularity of Spanish dance performers on the variety stage, including the internationally successful Caroline Otero, known as 'La Belle Otero'. A strikingly similar representation of Lind appears on Augusta Boecher's poster for the production, in the line illustration that was included in the *Theatre*'s review of the burlesque and in other press and publicity images.[53] Lind's dancing forms the most popular visual motif from *Carmen up to Data*; the individual performer, with her signature performances programmed into the show, becomes the representative Gaiety Girl for this production.

Lind's success as an actress, singer and dancer continued, in spite of the fact that she was forced to take a three-year break from her performance career between 1891 and 1894 as a result of extended illness. She became a regular performer at the fashionable Daly's Theatre, and toured internationally, taking engagements in America and Australia. Celebrated performances in *An Artist's Model* (1895), *Go-Bang!* (1894), *The Geisha* (1896) and *A Greek Slave* (1898) ensured Lind remained a high-profile figure in the entertainment headlines. In 1895, a year after her return to the stage, a column devoted to the London favourites – 'Are Liked in London' – was published in the American periodical *The Gazette*. The writer indicated the difference between Lind's performance and that of other actresses in musical comedies:

> [Lind's] face is piquant – an honest, little face – but of absolute beauty she has scarcely any . . . Her charm, however, does not depend on the beauty of face or voice. She seems a sprite, her every glance an unreserved expression of the part she plays . . . She is a born comedienne. Seldom does a dancing member of a comic-opera company give any semblance of reality to the lines of the libretto.[54]

The most significant element of Lind's fame and her popularity with critics was that she was neither a technically skilled or trained singer nor dancer, although she was clearly a skilled actress and performer. As responses to Allan and Fuller drew attention to their unconventional footwork and technique, commentators were not afraid to draw attention to the fact that Lind had 'so little of the artistic equipment of the prima donna of the ballet' or little beauty of voice. What made her performances successful was their seeming simplicity: 'her steps and poses were easy and graceful – that was all'.[55] Lind's fin-de-siècle success as a celebrity performer was not connected to admirable technical expertise. It was grounded in her personality, the appeal of the roles that she played to metropolitan mass audiences and her careful selection and individual presentation of popular styles.

It is clear that by the time Loïe Fuller arrived in London in 1889, Lind was well established as a Gaiety favourite and a celebrity of the London entertainment scene. Her reputation had also spread internationally: one American journal's warm praise of a new dancer described her performance as 'grace personified', one that 'can well compete with even Letty Lind'.[56] Understudying this popular performer during the run of *Carmen up to Data* offered Fuller adequate opportunity to study both her dancing style and the way that she managed her personality, and the public's enthusiastic response to both of these elements of her celebrity. The works that Fuller was to become famous for, and her self-promotion and image creation, were to bear more than a passing resemblance to the Gaiety Skirt Dance's characteristic 'swift rush of floating draperies through the air', and the graceful and ladylike celebrity figure of the Gaiety Girl embraced and epitomised by Lind.

## She 'is not expressive, not descriptive, and certainly not rhythmic'[57]

The Skirt Dance craze formed the subject of extended debate in the 1890s' press. Journalists, critics and performers published extensively on the question of the artistic value of the form. Many framed their argument by comparing and contrasting the new trend to other familiar dance styles, in particular the rigidity of ballet and the physical demands it placed on the ballerina's body. In February 1891, Lind entered into this ongoing discussion: during an interview with the *Daily Graphic* she was asked: 'What do you say to XX's assertion that the "voluminous petticoats" worn by skirt dancers cover a multitude of steps?' She responded that,

> it is quite true in many instances, and . . . many girls acquire a knowledge of singing and skirt manipulation to be merely pleasing and graceful, but in no sense can they be called dancers in the highest and most thorough meaning . . . I will only repeat that the steps suited to short skirts and tights are of a perfectly different order to those that we of this Gaiety school want, and which our imitators think are so easily acquired that they can do them without a complete dancing education.[58]

In this interview Lind is turned to as an authoritative figure, a performer with an authorised creative voice speaking for the recognised 'Gaiety school'. Arguing articulately against critiques of the Skirt Dance as an unskilled performance style, the dancer offers the form as a different kind of skill, one that demands to be recognised. After all, her own 'complete dancing education' was not that of conventional ballet training.

In addition to the contributions to the Skirt Dance debate that were offered by popular dailies and journals, specialist entertainment publications also entered the arena, with *The Theatre* publishing an extended series of articles and letters concerning the form. One of these – a gently satirical article written by Philip Hayman and entitled 'The Magic of Dancing is Sorcery Sweet' – argued for the recognition of the Skirt Dance as true Terpsichore: the creative superior of the ballet. Published in London in May 1891, Hayman's account appeared in print during Fuller's run at the Gaiety, and offered the 'Gaietina' as a strong contemporary challenge to the figure of the ballerina.[59]

As the title suggests, Hayman's approaches to the questions of dance and the female performer are scarcely revolutionary. In relation to both forms, he is primarily concerned with an aesthetics that centres on beautiful female bodies on stage. However, some modern ideas are pre-empted in his identification and discussion of the physical demands that were made of the ballet dancer. Rather than projecting an idealised image of female corporeality, Hayman sees ballet as staging a deformed vision of the dancer's body. The ballerina, he argues, is imprisoned by the techniques of her form; a captivity that denies her the potential of expression. Whilst, 'in all [her] postures and motions she may be active, agile, athletic, gymnastic, acrobatic', she is, 'not expressive, not descriptive, and certainly not rhythmic'. Furthermore, Hayman notes that in every ballet the female dancer's part is 'virtually the same': the ballerina is never placed in a position from which she can 'aid the motif of the piece, she portrays no emotion, heightens no effect'.[60]

In contrast to the repetitious displays of rigid technique that nineteenth-century choreography offered to the romantic ballerina, Hayman presented the more rhythmic and creative Skirt Dance. His only caveat being that the 'Gaietina' needed to develop and explore her form more, in order to avoid becoming, 'the slave of the petticoat'.[61] Three months after Lind's interview appeared in the *Daily Graphic*, this article echoes her argument that those dancers who were concerned merely with being graceful and pleasing were entirely different to 'dancers of the highest order'. In the popular press and in publications dedicated to the theatre, serious and productive discussions of dance, female celebrities and musical comedy appeared: an indication of their new power and role in the entertainment industry and of the influence of the Gaiety Theatre in ideas about performance.

## 'In dancing, as in most other things, it is ideas that carry the day'[62]

Seven years later the Skirt Dance was still attracting a significant amount of critical and popular attention. In 1898, another of the Gaiety favourites, the dancer and actress Sylvia Grey, used the press to add her contribution to the seemingly endless debate about dance and aesthetics. Lind and Grey were the two performers regularly singled out by critics as the most talented of the Gaiety company's dancers and – like Lind – Grey continued to manage a successful career in the entertainment industry after her time at Edwardes' theatre.

St Johnston describes Grey's dancing as 'graceful in the extreme', noting that she was a performer who 'wisely understood that to dance with the feet alone does not constitute the whole of the Terpsichorean art'.[63] In the article she wrote for *The Theatre*, entitled simply 'Dancing', this idea is apparent. Grey was committed to dance as an artistic, as well as an entertainment, form and insisted that experience and study were essential if one was to perform well. Grey's style in this article is intriguing. She begins the piece with a modest account of the 'perplexing' struggle she encountered when attempting to write about dance, recording that: 'first of all, I am in doubt where to begin; secondly, I am at a loss how to go on; and lastly, I have not an idea how, or where, to end'. But she then continues confidently, asserting that good dance and a strong performance can only be the result of training, research and new ideas. To achieve a level of skill, Grey argues, a dancer should experience and perform in every dance form that they can. Only when they have studied and understood a diversity of styles can they begin creating their own approach. And it is new approaches that are crucial for the continuing success of the form, for, 'in dancing, as in most other things', Grey concludes, 'it is ideas that carry the day'.[64]

Grey begins this article by adopting a role; in a similar way to Lind's use of the feminine image of the Gaiety Girl as the basis of her celebrity, Grey offers a modest and retiring female voice. Throughout the piece, from underneath this faux modesty the authoritative voice of a practitioner emerges. What is clear in this press coverage of the Skirt Dance craze, and from contemporary responses to Loïe Fuller and Maud Allan, is that dance was a form associated with women. Whilst this construct of the dancer did cause problems in relation to female corporeality on stage, as we have seen in the cases of Allan, Fuller, Lind and Grey it could also offer female performers both a performance space and a creative voice.

There are elements of Hayman's and Grey's arguments for the aesthetic recognition of the Skirt Dance in late nineteenth-century culture that would have appealed to Fuller. Hayman's interpretation of true Terpsichore as a, 'bodily expression of feeling' that, 'originating as an expression of emotion . . . becomes dramatic', echoes Fuller's own conception of dance as the expression of, 'all the sensations and emotions that [the human body] experiences'.[65] Indeed Fuller's Skirt Dance can be interpreted as a response to Hayman's direct challenge to the 'Gaietina' to move away from being the slave of the petticoat. Grey and Fuller knew each other; not only did they perform together on Edwardes' stage, they also both featured in a four-act comedy, *Zephyr*, at the Avenue Theatre in March 1891, and the Opéra Comique in May 1891. Their shared belief in the importance of new ideas and research in dance link the professional aims and aesthetic agendas of this successful variety performer and the international star. Illustrating, staging and extending the current debate surrounding the Skirt Dance, Fuller's dances were more than just grace- ful and pleasing performances, and they certainly involved the study and knowledge of other popular forms on the mass stage. The *Serpentine Dance* took the Skirt Dance as its raw material and pushed the creative potential of the form to its limits.

Many of the autobiographical narratives that Fuller published during her stage career are misleading; some simply fallacious. However, whilst multiple romanticised and mythologised versions of the tale behind the creation of her *Serpentine Dance* appeared in print, Fuller remained consistent about when and where the first public appearance her 'new' form took place. She dated its debut to the autumn of 1891, during the American run of a play called *Quack MD*, just months after her return from London and her experiences at the Gaiety Theatre. Taking into account the international fame of the Gaiety Skirt Dancer it is perhaps unsurprising that there is no direct reference to Edwardes' theatre in Fuller's memoirs, but in her account of the advice that she was offered by the theatre managers who saw early versions of the *Serpentine Dance*, London's influence is made very clear.

Overall, the entertainment industry's initial responses to Fuller's new dance were not encouraging. The general opinion expressed by the theatre managers and programmers she approached was that 'there is nothing new to be done in dancing'. To guarantee a large and satisfied audience, they explained, all that it was necessary to do was engage, ' "dancers like – " then they would mention half-a-dozen English skirt- dancers'. The public had their favourites, and offering them any other performer or performance style was simply an unnecessary risk.[66] Amidst the list of popular dancers that followed, Fuller recalled only two names – Lind and Grey. She noted that one manager's rejection was based on the opinion that '[w]hen I engage a dancer she will have to be a star. The only ones I know are Sylvia Gray [sic] and Lettie [sic] Lind in London.'[67] It is unlikely that it is mere coincidence that the only two dancers whose names Fuller recalled in this context also happened to be members of the Gaiety company during her recent period of time at the venue. Both were known for their skirt dancing; she had understudied one of them, and performed with the other at the theatre and other venues. The influence of these two English stars – and the construct of celebrity they embod- ied – should not be underestimated.

In performance Loïe Fuller's appearance was frequently likened to that of a fairy: 'the fairy of electricity'. It was a metaphor for her work that she actively encouraged, for in her public accounts she favoured the impression that her dances were the spontaneous fulfilment of creative energy. Like the ideal Skirt Dancer, Fuller realised the importance and advantage of giving the impression of a natural performance, a work that appeared in spite of a seeming lack of effort. As we know, however, Fuller's performances were actually the outcome of extended and laborious periods of experimentation with lighting, chemicals and fabrics, as well as the awareness and appropriation of other popular contemporary styles. If – as Fuller herself stated – 'new things are made out of parts of old ones' – the Gaiety Skirt Dance certainly played a significant role in the debut of the *Serpentine Dance*.[68]

## 'Loïe Fuller is not merely a Skirt Dancer – she is *the* Skirt Dancer'[69]

Fuller's *Serpentine Dance* increased press interest in skirt dancing: to what extent her celebrated performances were an appropriation of the popular form connected with the Gaiety Theatre and the British music hall formed the subject of extended debate during the early period of her dancing career. It was widely agreed that the origins of the two forms were the same: Crawford Flitch, who wrote an authoritative history of modern dance in 1912, confidently stated that although the discovery of Loïe Fuller's *Serpentine Dance* was, 'accidental', her characteristic style never-theless remained 'a derivation of the Skirt Dance'.[70] Although some writers denigrated the enthusiastic response to La Loïe, accusing her of imitation and a lack of originality, it was also widely agreed that, in spite of their roots, the performances she offered were entirely individual. In 1898 *The Times* argued that '[w]hether Miss Fuller was the originator or not of this very elegant dance, she is undoubtedly its ablest exponent, and deserved to the full the enthusiastic reception she met with'.[71] A senti-ment echoed two years later in the journal *Black and White*'s statement that, 'Loïe Fuller is not merely a Skirt Dancer – she is *the* Skirt Dancer'.[72]

A unique blend and management of the intelligent appropriation and development of other popular contemporary styles is evident in Fuller's performances, and in her celebrity identity. Her interest in the develop-ing technologies of modernity, in art, music and literature, and the ways in which she marketed herself as an individual performer made her a celebrity in her own right, a cultural icon of interest to the popular and the avant-garde. The London period offered Fuller both her form – the Skirt Dance – and a strong, workable construct of femininity and respectability – the Gaiety Girl. Pushing the Skirt Dance to its limits, she also moulded and presented herself as a respectable woman. Her success at this is evinced in an article written by Mrs M. Griffith for *The Strand Magazine* in May 1894, which concluded that:

> Miss Fuller has done wonders in improving the public taste, and proving that dancing is not an art that degrades . . . It may truly be said that there is not a discordant note in her whole performance, or a gesture or a movement which would wound the susceptibilities of the most modest-minded of British matrons or maidens.[73]

Building on the foundations of form and reputation that had been largely offered by the Gaiety Theatre, Fuller discovered a space from where she could actively shift contemporary understandings of dance and the female performer. La Loïe reshaped current thinking about dance from being a diversion within a longer play, to its acknowledgement as a performance medium in its own right.

Fuller's 255-night run on the Gaiety stage during the 1890–91 season contextualises the 'creation' of her characteristic *Serpentine Dance*. It locates the Gaiety Girl and the Gaiety Skirt Dancer as popular cultural constructions that enabled and affected ideas about female celebrity and performance. The modern metropolitan entertainment space occupied by Edwardes' venue offered a unique environment for female performers. For Loïe Fuller it provided an urban entertainment space in which her *Serpentine Dance*, her celebrity identity and her management of the technologies of fame could be initiated. It is clear that she drew on her experience at the venue and on its international reputation. Appearing as a dancer in between the acts of a French musical comedy, *Uncle Celestin* (at the Casino Theatre in New York), Fuller was billed as follows: 'Incidental to the third act the serpentine dance by Miss Loïe Fuller (specially engaged), as performed by her 100 nights at the Gaiety Theatre, London'.[74] This was deliberate use of an international entertainment site.

Alongside the posters, programmes and diverse merchandise produced by London's Gaiety Theatre, contemporary press responses and reviews reveal that the display of female bodies was at the core of its output. In this context, the Skirt Dance may seem to have been used largely as a way to fill gaps in performances: to offer beautiful visions of femininity as a popular part of the Chinese puzzle of the burlesque. The successful careers of performers contracted by Edwardes at the fin de siècle, including Letty Lind, Sylvia Grey and Loïe Fuller, relay a second and separate narrative. In their acts and their celebrity identities, the performance space and cultural construct of the Gaiety Theatre, coupled with the iconography of the Gaiety Girl, were harnessed by active female performers. One of London's chicest mass cultural spaces – a venue that mirrored and reflected the theatre of the modern city – simultaneously acted as a site that could be used by individual female performers to construct and to enhance their identities and performances.

## Notes

1  Norton Atkins, (words and music), 'The Happiest Chappie: A Comic Song' (London: Jeffreys Ltd, n.d.), British Library, London, sheet music collection.

2  W. Macqueen Pope, *Gaiety: Theatre of Enchantment* (London: W. H. Allen, 1949), p. 13. See also Jim Davis and Victor Emeljanow, '"Wistful Remembrancer": The Historiographical Problem of Macqueen-Popery', *New Theatre Quarterly* 17:4, November 2001, pp. 299–309.

3  Ursula Bloom, *Curtain Call for the Gov'nor* (London: Hutchinson, 1954), p. 14. For more on the musical comedy see Len Platt, *Musical Comedy on the West End Stage, 1890–1939* (Basingstoke: Palgrave Macmillan, 2004).

4  Loïe Fuller, *Fifteen Years of a Dancer's Life, with Some Account of her Distinguished Friends* (London: Herbert Jenkins, 1913), p. 57; 'Loïe Fuller, an American girl, came to Paris', MS dated 1924, The Loïe Fuller Collection, New York Public Library, Performing Arts Division, Jerome Robbins Dance Collection.

5  At the Folies-Bergère Fuller was billed as La Créatrice de la danse serpentine (The creator of the *Serpentine Dance*). See Folies-Bergère programme for 24 March 1893, held by the Theatre Museum, London.

6  Fuller, *Fifteen Years of a Dancer's Life, with Some Account of her Distinguished Friends*, p. 46.

7  *Le Figaro*, 9 November 1892, p. 6.

8  'A Chat with Miss Loïe Fuller', *The Sketch*, 12 April 1893, pp. 641–3.

9  Fuller, *Fifteen Years of a Dancer's Life, with Some Account of her Distinguished Friends*, p. 70.

10  Unidentified press clipping, Maud Madison Scrapbooks, New York Public Library, Performing Arts Division, Jerome Robbins Dance Collection.

11  'Loïe Fuller, an American girl, came to Paris'.

12  Albert A. Hopkins, *Magic: Stage Illusions and Scientific Diversions (Including Trick Photography)* (London: Sampson Low, Marston and Co., 1897), p. 344.

13  *The Era*, 14 December 1895, p. 16.

14  Sally R. Sommer, 'Loïe Fuller's Art of Music and Light', *Dance Chronicle* 4, 1981, pp. 389–401 (392).

15  *The Era*, 14 December 1895, p. 16.

16  *The Times*, 11 December 1895, p. 5.

17  See the programme for Fuller's performances at the Hippodrome in January 1907, held by New York Public Library, Performing Arts Department, Jerome Robbins Dance Division.

18  *Reynold's Newspaper*, 29 December 1895, p. 8.

19  Fuller recorded that *The Lily Dance* took her three years to design and perfect, 'La Loïe Talks of her Art', *The New York Times*, 1 March 1896, p. 10.

20  Fuller, *Fifteen Years of a Dancer's Life, with Some Account of her Distinguished Friends*, pp. 33–4.

21  *Ibid.*, p. 10.

22  Two important nineteenth-century studies of stage illusion and machinery, Hopkins, *Magic: Stage Illusions and Scientific Diversions (Including Trick Photography)* and Georges Moynet, *Trucs et décors: la machinerie théâtrale* (Paris: Librarie Illustrée, 1900), use images of Fuller dancing as their frontispieces.

23  'Loïe Fuller, an American girl, came to Paris'.

24  Cited in Dee Reynolds, 'The Dancer as Woman: Loïe Fuller and Stéphane Mallarmé', in Richard Hobbs (ed.), *Impressions of French Modernity* (Manchester: Manchester University Press, 1998), pp. 155–72 (161).

25  *The Saturday Review*, 11 October 1890, p. 424.

26  *Daily Express*, 2 January 1928, Loïe Fuller clippings file, Theatre Museum, London.

27  William Davenport Adams, *A Dictionary of the Drama* (London: Chatto and Windus, 1904), p. 555.

28  Pope, *Gaiety: Theatre of Enchantment*, p. 395.

29  *Ibid.*, p. 11.

30  For more information on the relationship between the popular female performer and advertising see Veronica Kelly, 'Beauty and the Market: Actress Postcards and their Senders in Early Twentieth-Century Australia', *New Theatre Quarterly* 78, May 2004, pp. 99–116 and Vivien Gardner, 'Gertie Millar: Celebrity and Musical Comedy', in Jane Milling and Martin Banham (eds), *Extraordinary Actors: Essays on Popular Performers* (Exeter: University of Exeter Press, 2004).

31  Stanley Naylor (ed.), *Gaiety and George Grossmith: Random Reflections on the Serious Business of Enjoyment* (London: Stanley Paul, 1913), p. 122.

32  Walter Macqueen Pope, 'Gaiety Girls in Town Again', *The Sphere*, 28 January 28 1950, p. 130.

33  Thornton Hall, *Love Romances of the Aristocracy* (London: T. Werner Laurie, 1911), p. 255.

34  'Music Hall Gossip', *The Era*, 23 July 1892, p. 15.

35  Peter Bailey, *Popular Culture and Performance in the Victorian City* (Cambridge: Cambridge University Press, 1998), p. 177.

36 'Evolution of La Loïe's Dance', *New York Herald*, Sunday 27 August 1893, press clipping, Maud Madison Scrapbooks, New York Public Library, Performing Arts Division, Jerome Robbins Dance Collection.

37 Reginald St Johnston, *A History of Dancing* (London: Simpkin, Marshall, Hamilton, Kent, 1906), p. 117.

38 'The Dancing of the Day: An 'At Home' at Miss E. Garratt's', *Pall Mall Budget*, 14 April 1892, p. 535. In the interview Garratt also comments on the influence of the theatre on popular entertainment forms: 'You know there was some step-dancing in the Guards' theatricals. Well, it pleased so much that last year after the performances people began to do a little step dancing in private. And now it is all the rage.'

39 *The Saturday Review*, 14 January 1893, p. 55.

40 See Mrs H. A. Foreman, *Illustrated Portfolio of Artistic Dancing* (New Portland, OR: Peaslee, 1894).

41 St Johnston, *A History of Dancing*, p. 117.

42 John Hollingshead, *Gaiety Chronicles* (London: Archibald Constable, 1898), pp. 346–7.

43 Charles E. Pascoe (ed.), *Our Actors and Actresses: The Dramatic List* (London: Benjamin Blom, 1880), p. 52.

44 Unidentified press clipping, Maud Madison Scrapbooks, New York Public Library, Performing Arts Division, Jerome Robbins Dance Collection.

45 Hollingshead, *Gaiety Chronicles*, pp. 336–9.

46 See David Price, *Cancan!* (London: Cygnus Arts, 1998).

47 Obituary for Letty Lind, 28 August 1923, Letty Lind clippings file, Theatre Museum, London.

48 Pope, *Gaiety: Theatre of Enchantment*, p. 254.

49 Synopsis of music in *Carmen up to Data*, held by the Theatre Museum, London.

50 'Our Play Box', *The Theatre*, 1 November 1890, pp. 237–9 (239); see also *The Saturday Review*, 11 October 1890, p. 424.

51 *The Illustrated Sporting and Dramatic News*, 1 November 1890, p. 246.

52 The merchandise and the programmes from the Gaiety production of *Carmen up to Data* can be found in the collections of the Theatre Museum, London.

53 See the *Illustrated London News*, 25 October 1890, p. 524, for an example of this.

54 'Are Liked in London', *The Gazette*, 20 November 1895, p. 9.

55 'The Drama', *New York Times Illustrated Review*, 25 September 1898, p. 8.

56 Press clipping, Maud Madison Scrapbooks, New York Public Library, Performing Arts Division, Jerome Robbins Dance Collection.

57 Philip Hayman, 'The Magic of Dancing is Sorcery Sweet', *The Theatre*, 1 May 1891, pp. 237–9 (238).

58 *Daily Graphic*, 13 February 1891, press clipping, Theatre Museum, London.

59  Hayman, 'The Magic of Dancing is Sorcery Sweet', p. 237.

60  *Ibid.*, p. 238.

61  *Ibid.*, p. 239.

62  Sylvia Grey, 'Dancing', *The Theatre*, 1 January 1898, pp. 34–7 (34).

63  St Johnston, *A History of Dancing*, p. 176.

64  Grey, 'Dancing', p. 34.

65  Hayman, 'The Magic of Dancing is Sorcery Sweet', p. 238; Fuller, *Fifteen Years of a Dancer's Life, with Some Account of her Distinguished Friends*, p. 70.

66  'A Chat with Miss Loïe Fuller', p. 642.

67  Fuller, *Fifteen Years of a Dancer's Life, with Some Account of her Distinguished Friends*, p. 35.

68  'How did Loïe Fuller happen to make a ballet and a film from a fairy story of Her Majesty the Queen of Romania?', Autobiographical fragment, The Loïe Fuller Collection, New York Public Library, Performing Arts Division, Jerome Robbins Dance Division.

69  *Black and White*, 8 September 1900, p. 392.

70  J. E. Crawford Flitch, *Modern Dancing and Dancers* (London: Grant Richards Ltd, 1912), p. 81.

71  *The Times*, 12 July 1898, p. 4.

72  *Black and White*, 8 September 1900, p. 392.

73  Mrs M. Griffith, 'Loïe Fuller – The Inventor of the Serpentine Dance', *Strand Magazine*, May 1894, pp. 540–5 (545).

74  Unidentified press clipping, Maud Madison Scrapbooks, New York Public Library, Performing Arts Division, Jerome Robbins Dance Collection.

# 4

## MADNESS, DANCING AND THE DANCER: JANE AVRIL AND THE SALPÊTRIÈRE HOSPITAL, PARIS

To call such movements [the Serpentine and the Ta-ra-ra] dancing is ridiculous. Regarded as an expression of the modern spirit the serpentine dance has a kind of interest of its own. It is that phthisis of the soul, that moral anaemia which is the malady of our time, translated into woven paces and waving hands. It is not the poetry of motion, but the poison of rhythm, having no closer connexion with the dance than skating or walking.[1]

It may seem an incongruous journey to cross the Channel at this point: leaving an opulent, fashionable theatre in London's West End to arrive at Paris', and arguably the nineteenth-century world's, most famous research and teaching hospital. Its path is guided by questions of corpo-reality. Embodiment's function as a representative of both popular science and entertainment resulted in connections between the female performer and physical and mental health factoring significantly in con-temporary imagery and ideology. In the new international culture of the period, these ideas were to become as pervasive and commonplace as the widely acknowledged, intrinsic affiliations between the female performer, beauty and eroticism. Whilst the Gaiety Theatre fused corporeality and performance space in the figure and complicated spectacle of the Gaiety Girl, the Salpêtrière hospital constructed and disseminated ideas about female embodiment and psychology in the world of performance through the image of the madwoman.

In January 1896, amidst the mid-1890s' run of publications on modern dance forms and the Skirt Dance, *The Saturday Review* published a long article concerned with the art of dancing and the figure of the dancer. As the citation above reveals, its author was preoccupied with the ways that current forms of popular stage dancing intersected with social concerns. This account offers a strikingly different reading of the aesthet-ics of the new dance styles of the 1890s to those published by Hayman and Grey in the same decade. Dance is understood as a form that incorporated the 'poison of rhythm', rather than the 'poetry of motion' associated with the Gaiety Skirt Dancers, amongst others. For this writer, the dancer is a compound of the performer and the madwoman. Her on-stage movements simultaneously exposed and expressed the characteristic 'malady' of the time: a malady that was identified as psychological, but expressed and decoded through the physical.

In the press, modern dancing bodies were not only offered as examples of art, entertainment, performance or aesthetics, they were also offered as powerful cultural and social signifiers. Gender ideology is embedded in the resonant imagery employed by this journalist. The styles of dance and the movements described in the *Saturday Review*'s article clearly classify the performing bodies in question as female. Furthermore, the writer's assumptions and tone evince that the dancer's physical forms, movement and fashionable performance styles, such as the Serpentine and the Ta-ra-ra (a shortened reference to the dance style popularised by Lottie Collins), were a familiar site for the interrogation of wider social and cultural ideas and anxieties. No context or explanation is offered for the metaphorical use of the dancing body and its associations with psychological illness. As Felicia McCarren has identified, remarkable similarities can be drawn between the histories of dance and medicine at the fin de siècle; similarities that must have been widely documented and discussed at the time, for this article is directed at a set of readers that will be au fait with and follow its references.[2] The women that performed these woven paces are not timeless, female, graceful images. These dancers are iconographic figures of the fin de siècle, inherently linked to its social and cultural climates.

Thematically and stylistically, the *Saturday Review* article is grounded in well-established discursive relationships between women's bodies, irrationality and acts of madness: links that had a significant influence on contemporary constructions of femininity.[3] These connections had ramifications for the dancer and, by extension, for all women who performed on stage, but for the Parisian dancer Jane Avril they were peculiarly significant. In December 1882 Avril was admitted to Paris' Salpêtrière hospital, where she spent eighteen months as a patient.[4] She had been diagnosed with 'St Vitus' Dance': a psychological condition classified as one of the 'dancing manias' that became central to the study of women and madness at the fin de siècle. Avril's medical history and her treatment at Paris' renowned 'lunatic asylum' were to shape her performance style, help crystallise her celebrity identity and impact on responses to her work during her successful stage career.[5]

## Jane Avril's stage apprenticeship: belly dancing and horseback acrobatics

In the period between being discharged from the Salpêtrière hospital in 1884 and her success as a popular performer in the early 1890s, Avril gained some experience of the day-to-day running of Paris' entertainment industry. In May of 1889, against the backdrop of the recently completed Eiffel Tower, Paris' universal exhibition opened. Avril took a job as a cashier at a venue on the rue de Caire (the Cairo Road), a recreated 'Egyptian' street located close to the foot of the tower. Regular international exhibitions became important forces in the creation and promotion of national identities and mythologies in the late nineteenth and early twentieth centuries. They were committed and contributed to the network of international connections that created a transatlantic celebrity culture, uniting the 'modern' European and American countries that they were located in, against a savage, 'un-modern' other. Regardless of their geographical setting, these events shared a 'great organizing principle . . . the idea of a universal culture, a complex notion defined, in part, by European (often with a French accent) opposition between civilisation and savagery'.[6]

It was no coincidence that the 1889 French exhibition coincided with the centenary of the 1789 revolution. To mark this 100-year anniversary, Paris self-consciously put itself on display to the world, exhibiting a modern, republican and metropolitan identity that distanced the city from the chaos and violence associated with the revolution. To achieve this gargantuan public relations exercise and national advertisement, the event's organising committee depended upon the same forces of promotion and publicity that were employed by the city's burgeoning entertainment industry.[7] Paris' 1889 exhibition reveals the theatricality of the modern city in action. Displays of industrial and technological prowess, colonial power and cultural sophistication were presented as pleasurable diversions, framed in a language of entertainment.

Consequently, the exhibition site's main attractions responded to the mass audience's demand, whilst reflecting current politics and ideology. It proved a popular mix; before the event closed in early November more than 32 million people had visited.[8] Special editions of tourist guides that included plans, revised transport timetables, and detailed accounts of the site and its displays were available in Britain and in America. Publishers clearly anticipated that overseas visitors would plan special trips to the city for the event.[9] The success of Paris 1889 was largely due to its reliance on the trends and technologies of the popular stage: on the Cairo Road Jane Avril spent her days working amidst these forces.[10]

The Cairo Road's staging of colonised bodies, ostensibly displayed for the pleasure of the fin-de-siècle spectator's gaze and concurrently emphasising France's colonial power, made the area one of the event's most popular attractions. Four pages of one 1889 edition of the *Magasin pittoresque* were dedicated to an extensive account of this one small section of the exhibition site. In this 'perfect' reconstruction of Egypt, the journalist Jean Guérin noted, visitors could wander slowly down the winding street, taking in its twenty-five different shops and its restaurants, all staffed by Egyptians. They could also watch potters at work, peruse and purchase unusual spices and perfumes from the bazaar, sit in cafés and listen to Egyptian music, or attend traditional entertainments including belly dancing, sabre dancing or snake charming.[11] On the Cairo Road, Paris presented a sanitised, colonial representation of Egypt for its international mass audience. The street formed one big stage set.

After the exhibition closed, Avril took her first engagement as a professional performer at Charles Zidler's Hippodrome circus, where she was employed as a bareback rider. Extravagant and exciting circus displays were hugely popular entertainment forms in fin-de-siècle Paris, and horseback acrobatics featured as one of the most popular and daring of the regular acts on offer.[12] Working as an equestrienne was physically demanding; it required extreme agility, physical fitness and a good dose of fearlessness. Alongside her circus contract, Avril was also dancing regularly as an amateur: since leaving the Salpêtrière hospital she had been a frequent visitor to Paris' public dancing gardens. On the dance floors of these venues she was not a performer, but a member of the public seeking leisure, entertainment and a space in which to dance. The idiosyncratic style that was soon to secure her position as one of Paris' most familiar dancers had already made Avril a familiar figure amongst the regular student and artisan clientele that attended the Bal Bullier dancing garden, at the place de l'Observatoire, on Thursday nights.

The Bullier, as the venue was known across the city, was comprised of a small dance hall (about 100 feet square) and large pleasure gardens that contained small tables, grottoes, fountains, waterfalls and rocking horses, all illuminated by coloured lights. The overall effect was fairytale-like, as one visitor noted in 1895, 'the scene resembled what one sees on the stage more than an actual occurrence'. Anyone admitted to the venue could dance in this space, and interestingly it was the dancing of the women who attended that attracted this visitor's specific attention. He noted that the 'freedom of action' demonstrated by 'these females was quite shocking'. 'They seemed to dance because they liked it, and danced with a vim and abandon which convinced one that they did like it.'[13] In this leisure space women were associated with activity, not passivity, and they celebrated it. In this context, on the dance floor of the Bullier, Avril's regular dancing with her partner Marcel Lenoir drew much interest:

> Jane and Marcel then stepped down onto the floor, of which thenceforth they were the only occupants. Everyone looked on and the customers out in the garden . . . left their tables to swell the throng of admiring onlookers. And indeed the performance was well worth the trouble. The two partners turned and glided with an incomparable airy grace; interweaving their movements with incredible skill and harmony, they improvised figures as dainty as they were daring.[14]

Long before she began dancing professionally, Avril had accrued experience in the entertainment industry. As an employee and a performer, she was not only familiar with its themes and sights, she had also started to develop her own distinctive performance practice.

## The Moulin Rouge: 'things of beauty, but not a joy forever'[15]

It was towards the end of 1889 that Jane Avril began to perform at the venue that her image has remained inseparable from: the Moulin Rouge. The Montmartre dance hall was a new entertainment site in Paris, opened earlier in the same year by two of the city's most experienced entertainment entrepreneurs, Zidler (the manager of the Hippodrome circus) and Joseph Oller. Zidler and Oller shared a conviction that the Parisian public were in need of a new form of entertainment: a form they believed that they could supply at their new venue by combining a programme of skilled variety performers with a dance floor that was open to the public, the formula that had proved so successful for many of the city's dancing gardens, including the Bullier. Choosing to locate the Moulin Rouge on the place Blanche in Montmartre – the city's eighteenth arrondissement located to the north of central Paris – further ensured its popularity. Associated with the Parisian underworld and the romanticised bohemian lifestyles of artists and performers, the area was known to attract those eager for a frisson of alcohol and sex. For many, Montmartre offered an authorised and temporary experience of the darker side of modern metropolitan life.

Zidler and Oller established the Moulin Rouge as a space in which they could experiment with their extensive knowledge of the desires of the mass audience. It was a huge success. During the early 1890s, the dance hall appears as frequently and as prominently on tourist maps of the city as either the Louvre museum or the Eiffel Tower. In 1895, one American journalist noted that ever since he had arrived in Paris all that he had been asked was, 'have you been to the Moulin Rouge'.[16] By 1900, *Le Guide de l'étranger à Montmartre* ( *The Visitor's Guide to Montmartre*) could claim that the whole world knew of the Moulin Rouge.[17] In the venue's original design, many of the popular aesthetics that shaped the 1889 exhibition site in the city centre were mirrored. Entering the dance hall, Avril would have been familiar with the themes that had guided its interior décor from the time that she had spent working on the Cairo Road: in the words of one observer the Moulin Rouge was a Temple of Dance, discovered within the world of *One Thousand and One Nights.*[18]

Moorish in style, the Moulin Rouge was comprised of a cabaret theatre, a large polished-oak dance floor and low galleries that swept around two sides of the building and offered multiple spectatorial positions from which its audiences 'could drink wine and look at the dancing'.[19] Exoticism and opulence were at the root of its design scheme: large mirrors, careful lighting and spicy, earthy colours inside the building were complemented by large, landscaped pleasure gardens outside. Both served as multifunctional entertainment areas. The gardens could hold up to 600 spectators, and housed a covered stage, surrounded by seats and small tables. Here programmes of entertainment that featured song, music, low comedy and farce were offered between eight thirty and ten fifteen in the evening.[20] To one side of the stage stood a 30-foot-high elephant sculpture, the interior of which acted as an intimate performance space, accessed by a spiral staircase concealed in one of the pachyderm's legs. After the performances in the garden finished, the five or six hundred spectators would move into the dance hall to join later arrivals, and to watch and participate in the numbers on the dance floor, including the waltz, the polka and the infamous quadrille. On an average evening around 1,500 spectators would fill the dance hall for this part of the evening's entertainment.

The Moulin Rouge's exotic nature, its location in Montmartre and its associations with eroticised performance placed the dance hall in an ambiguous location amidst the international culture of the fin de siècle. Descriptions of the venue repeatedly oscillate between the dance hall as desirable, and the dance hall as threatening. In 1895 the American correspondent Richard Harding Davis presented a vignette of the Moulin

Rouge for readers of the American journal *Harper's New Monthly Magazine*, he recorded that the building:

> glows like a furnace, and the glare from its lamps reddens the sky and lights up the surrounding streets and cafés and the faces of the people passing like a conflagration. The mill is red, the thatched roof is red, the arms are picked out in electric lights in red globes, and arches of red lamp-shades rise on every side against the blackness of the night. Young men and women are fed into the blazing doors of the mill nightly, and the great arms, as they turn unceasingly and noisily in a fiery circle through the air, seem to tell of the wheels within that are grinding out the life and the health and souls of these young people of Montmartre.[21]

Harding Davis' infernal vision of the dance hall places it at the heart of the physical and moral degeneration of Montmartre, of the city of Paris as a whole and – by implication – of the new international entertainment industry.

Concurrently, the Moulin Rouge was a fashionable venue: one that was attended by both Parisians and visitors; an entertainment site that was regularly listed and recommended in the press and in guide books and that was immensely popular with English and American tourists. By 1900 one guide to the city reported that although the dance hall required the spectator to, 'leave [their] scruples behind', the 'night festivals' staged there 'are rather festive; they are things of beauty, but not a joy forever – very gay, but terribly mixed'.[22] Indeed, Harding Davis' account also hints at the seductive nature of this modern space; there is something undeniably alluring about his language and imagery. Evidently it was not only the female celebrity performer that was placed in a dualistic position by the entertainment industry: its terrain was inherently dichotomous and complex. Jane Avril's lasting association with the Moulin Rouge locates her at the core of this network of ideas.

## Cancan!

Today, the name of the Moulin Rouge automatically conjures up images of the representative nineteenth-century Parisian popular entertainment form, the cancan: an association that bears witness to the power that marketing, nostalgia and the cultural imagination have had in historicisations of the fin de siècle. In Paris at this time cancan (or quadrille) was not only on offer at the Moulin Rouge, performances could also be seen elsewhere in Montmartre and in central Paris. At the Moulin Rouge itself the dance formed only a small part of the nightly entertainment on offer. As has already been suggested, the programme was diverse, it also featured singers, other dancers and novelty acts – including Le Pétomane, who delighted audiences with his tuneful farting of popular chansons and musical works. Nonetheless, it was through its associations with the quadrille, and with beautiful dancing women, that the Moulin Rouge forged and maintained its national and international reputation as the epitome of Paris' spectacular entertainment industry.

Shortly after the venue opened Zidler had offered Avril a Moulin Rouge contract. In the first instance she refused this regular salary, preferring to be paid on a nightly basis when she appeared at the venue in an attempt to maintain a greater degree of creative freedom over her performance. At the same time she continued to dance for her own pleasure as a member of the public at dance halls and dancing gardens across Paris. This remained the case until Zidler left the venue in September 1892, and Oller succeeded in persuading Avril to take a permanent contract and to dance regularly in the venue's quadrille. It is from these Moulin Rouge performances that the mass marketed, twenty-first-century manifestation of Jane Avril emerges.

Familiar representations of Avril by Henri de Toulouse-Lautrec have become part of Montmartre's modern-day tourist industry.[23] The dancer's image appears on a range of souvenir items that can be bought from street vendors, in cheap gift shops, in department stores, at the Eurostar terminal and Charles de Gaulle airport, and at museum boutiques. China figurines, mouse mats, fridge magnets, Christmas tree baubles, tee-shirts, tote bags and costume jewellery adorned with Avril's dancing figure are widely available. However, this retrospective commodification of Avril has distanced ideas about her from her fin-de-siècle celebrity status, and from her actual performances. She has become compounded with – and a representative of – the collective image of the cancan dancers of the Moulin Rouge and of a romanticised vision of the late nineteenth-century city of Paris.

In direct contrast to her factually questionable legacy, Charles Zidler had quickly recognised that Avril possessed a unique talent. Whilst her dancing may have lacked the explicit eroticism that characterised the performances of many of the Moulin Rouge's other stars, having 'none of that carnal frenzy which gave La Goulue [Louise Weber, 1866–1929] her lubricious fame', it nonetheless attracted a large number of followers, who were taken with the way that her movement formed 'a language' of its own.[24] Generally Avril opted to dance alone, performing to slow music and watching herself in the mirrored walls that surrounded the dance floor. Describing her movement as the 'dance of shadows', shadows that reminded him of figures from a dream, the English Symbolist poet Arthur Symons captured the dancer's solipsism. Against the frenzied, lubricious performances of the other dancers, Avril's movement could be identified by its uncharacteristic lack of engagement with the crowds who surrounded her.[25]

Realising the allure of the unusual, Zidler was eager to retain this emerging star, and he allowed Avril a level of creative freedom over and above that offered to the other dancers at the Moulin Rouge. In addition to choosing when she performed, the effects of Avril's dancing were developed and enhanced by Zidler's concession that she could have greater freedom with her costume. Instead of the plain, white underwear that the venue's dancers were obliged to perform in, Avril could choose to wear any combination of colours on the dance floor. Rather than wearing clothes loaned by the fashion houses or the department stores that regularly dressed the stars of the metropolis' vaudeville stages, the dancer optimised the freedom Zidler offered her, and designed her own costumes.

As Loïe Fuller's costume designs were central to her stage effects, Avril's dresses became important expressive elements of her performance. Fabrics, colours and shapes were brought together to complement and develop the effects of the dance style, rather than acting as ornaments that adorned and drew attention to Avril's moving body. Thanks to a controlled use of contrasting and tonal shades and diverse fabrics, Moulin Rouge spectators saw Avril perform in layered costumes that revealed spectrums of colour as she moved. As her first biographer José Shercliff recalled:

> her first gown was scarlet and underneath it tiers of skirts shaded down the whole gamut of reds to the palest shell pink. Another was cherry-coloured silk, the petticoats fading through tones of heliotrope and lavender. Under a flame-coloured gown that made her hair look almost platinum blonde, she wore tulip green, ice-blue under cyclamen, primrose under green.[26]

Costume became an essential tool in Avril's attempts to open up the dance hall as a performance space by creating new forms of expression on its dance floor. It was a tool that was accessible, reasonably affordable and conformed to the conventions of the popular stage, but its role was to maximise the innovative effects that the female celebrity could achieve through active, physical, individual performance.

The strikingly different nature of Avril's performances rapidly established her reputation as one of the Moulin Rouge's star dancers and she continued to perform at the dance hall for the majority of her early stage career. During her occasional short breaks from the venue, engagements were forthcoming from other fashionable establishments. In Paris, Avril danced at the Divan Japonais, the Casino de Paris, the Folies-Bergère and the Jardin de Paris. In the mid-1890s, she visited London, touring with Mlle Eglantine's troupe to appear at the Palace Theatre of Varieties. Later tours followed to Madrid, and to other cities in France. In the 1890s Avril was also familiar to Parisian audiences as a singer and an actress: she appeared in the stage version of Colette's novel *Claudine à Paris* (staged at the Bouffes-Parisien), and in *La Belle de New York*.

## Exhibiting madness: the Salpêtrière hospital

In spite of Jane Avril's diverse and successful career in the entertainment industry, responses to the dancer from the fin de siècle, and later interpretations of her performances, have been contained and defined by cultural constructs of femininity. It is not only the pervasive image of the Moulin Rouge cancan dancer that has impacted on understandings of Avril, the figure of the madwoman has had a powerful effect on interpretations of her dance style. Avril's professional performance career did not begin until seven years after her admission to the Salpêtrière hospital. But her medical history and her connection to the hospital were widely known across the city, and frequently turned to as a means of explaining the performances of a dancer whose movements were reminiscent of 'whirlwinds', 'phantoms',[27] 'feverishness'[28] and 'melancholia'.[29]

In the nicknames attributed to Avril by her friends and her fans, the established connections between the dancer and madness are emphasised. From L'Etrange, or the Strange One, to La Mélinite, the term used for a relatively new and very powerful form of explosive, and Jane la Folle, or Crazy Jane, these affectionate aliases are grounded in understandings of her movement as unpredictable and irrational. Oscillating between the unthreatening and gentle figure of Crazy Jane and the inherent danger of violent explosives, these names reflect the sense of the unknown, and the indefinable, that was perceived to be at the core of Avril's dancing. Avril rejected all of these names in her professional life: she used none of them to refer to herself, or to promote or describe her performances. Regardless of what terms Paris' gossip columns, or the crowds at the city's dance halls, were using to identify her performance, she was always billed as Jane

Avril. But she did not avoid a connection with madness as a result of this. As the names and descriptions suggest, the legacy of the time she spent at the Salpêtrière hospital, coupled with her unusual, solipsistic performance style, positioned the dancer as a site and a representation of a wider cultural pattern of ideas that interconnected femininity, entertainment and madness.

It was not only the readers of London's *The Saturday Review* that were interested in and concerned about madness. In a social environment preoccupied with questions of degeneration, much time, money, professional research and popular speculation were devoted to why large numbers of women were displaying symptoms that were ascribed to psychological disorders by fin-de-siècle medicine. On occasions, these areas of interest merged in popular accounts of science: in the same year as *The Saturday Review*'s discussion of dance appeared, an account of Parisian research into nervous disorders was published by *Reynold's Newspaper*. Under the headline 'Piano on the Nerves', it detailed that no less than 12 per cent of a case study group of 6,000 girls were being treated for nervous disorders: notably chlorosis, neurosis and neurasthenia. The results of the study attributed the cause of this high number of patients to the constant repetition of exercises involved in piano lessons. Interestingly the *Reynold's Newspaper* report is framed scientifically; it places great emphasis on the authorised nature of the research it is documenting, and the 'carefully drawn statistics' it was based on.[30] The fin-de-siècle public was fascinated by the new sciences of the mind, and their patterns, ideas and languages. It was a natural progression for these popular scientific approaches and theories to filter through into the period's leisure and entertainment industries and, as stressed in Chapter two, into understandings of corporeality.

As director of Paris' Salpêtrière hospital, Jean-Martin Charcot led the late nineteenth-century world's largest and most renowned centre for psychological treatment and research. Amongst the scientific community he was widely recognised as an exceptional practitioner and scholar, respected for his pioneering new psychological approaches and acknowledged as the figurehead of this new medicinal discipline. As Christopher G. Goetz has noted, Charcot, the Salpêtrière and the emergence of clinical neurology in the nineteenth century 'are so closely linked in their reputations that when one is mentioned, the other two are immediately recalled'.[31] Alongside the professional status and reputation he had achieved, Charcot the clinician was also a talented showman. This was a doctor that was adept at employing and manipulating the metropolitan spectacle that shaped the theatre of the city in the interests of science and research.[32]

The theatricality of Paris, the popular showman and public interest in science collided at the Salpêtrière hospital, creating a unique, modern, metropolitan site that had direct ramifications for ideas surrounding women and performance. Charcot cannot be identified as being single-handedly responsible for the popular interest in madness that can be easily traced in the late 1880s and 1890s. However, he did play a key role in advertising the birth and the rapid growth of clinical neurology as a discipline and in generating public enthusiasm for its subjects, practices and discoveries. During 1887 and 1888 a regular open, weekly lecture programme was launched at the hospital at which Charcot offered research presentations based on the psychological conditions that he was currently investigating and treating: groundbreaking neurological research that was largely driven by his fascination with the interrelationship between the physical and the psychological. In order to illustrate and emphasise the processes and hypotheses guiding his work, he would often rely on displaying one of the patients that he was treating at the time to his audience. At the front of an institutional lecture theatre in the hospital, against a backdrop of 'statues of contorted patients [and] plaster casts of their deformities . . . spotlighted as altar icons', Charcot exhibited a real, embodied example of the condition he discussed.[33]

By all accounts, Charcot was a very capable performer. He held his audience, pronouncing 'his sentences distinctly and slowly, with a seemingly conscious effort to communicate ideas to the entire audience, French and foreign, medical and non-medical'.[34] The combination of his skilled and enigmatic presentation style, the contemporary interest in madness and the display of physical 'models' of madness drew wide audiences to the Salpêtrière hospital, and the Tuesday lessons became popular cultural and social events.[35] Audiences assembled in the medium-sized lecture theatre described above, which had a capacity of around 400. Spectatorial bodies that were composed of 'tout Paris, authors, journalists, leading actors and actresses, fashionable demimondaines' came together to watch Charcot's demonstrations and presentations, seated alongside and amidst the more intimate and specialised gazes of the hospital's alienists.[36]

The diverse spectatorship attracted by the lectures shared much with that of the modern metropolitan entertainment venue, and the connections between the two sites did not end with their audiences. Regular attendees at Charcot's sessions included the actress Sarah Bernhardt, the writer Guy de Maupassant and the philosopher Henri Bergson.[37] At the Salpêtrière hospital these influential figures watched and studied Charcot's exhibitions of psychological disorders: madness made visual. These movements and physicalisations of insanity were then incorporated into their own interpretations and presentations of madness, and offered to other audiences in theatrical, literary and philosophical outputs. Charcot's research – presented using similar techniques and styles to those of the entertainment industry – fed back into the period's widely disseminated, popular images and representations of madness.

### Dancing with the madwomen

The Tuesday lessons were not the only popular social events that occurred at the Salpêtrière hospital. Throughout the year the hospital authorities also organised a series of balls and parties, a programme that reflects a wider project of bringing entertainment funding into French nineteenth-century institutions. As its location as a fashionable site increased, events at the Salpêtrière became more than occasions designed for the entertainment of staff and their partners, or philanthropic opportunities to raise funds for the hospital. Instead the balls and parties quickly developed into appealing and popular occasions that became part of the Parisian social calendar, and invitations were sent out to, and sought by, famous artists, scholars, sculptors, actors and scientists.[38]

The 'madwomen's balls', as they were known throughout Paris, and across Europe and America, occupied a space between contemporary constructions of fantasy and reality: they occurred at the transgressive, liminal point where the two intersected. As Yannick Ripa has noted, at these balls and parties, 'sane people would adopt imaginary personalities, play with fantasy, mingle with the insane disguised as countesses, bakers, caucasian princes'.[39] Liberating and carnivalesque for the spectators and, as we shall see, for some of the individual patients, these occasions were very different events to the Tuesday lectures. At the balls and parties, visitors to the hospital did not 'watch' displays of madness whilst remaining distant from them because of their physical role as a spectator. In the ballroom and on the dance floor attendees actively participated in the ideas and the forces that were associated with the hospital. Like the Cairo Road, here was a 'modern' experience, temporarily offered to the spectator within a reassuringly familiar framework.

The public events hosted by the Salpêtrière hospital changed the meaning of the modern medico-research space. On these occasions a scientific and institutional site welcomed in large numbers of visitors and spectators as a public, metropolitan space. During the late nineteenth century, the institution's reputation was so strong that it would have been nearly impossible for the individuals who attended the Tuesday lectures, and constituted the crowds at the parties and balls, to be unaware of the scientific discourses and research connected with the establishment. Whilst its status as a cutting-edge research institution was one of the main appeals of the hospital for its visitors, it was not its only drawing factor.

The familiarity of the hospital as a site on the city's social circuit erased any possibility of the space only signifying science and research. Geographically removed from the urban spaces and areas that were explicitly connected with Paris' spectacle and leisure, in the public mind the hospital space was nonetheless coupled with ideas about display and entertainment. At its lectures, balls and parties, medicine, research and psychiatry entered into the arena of fin-de-siècle mass culture: doctors and patients were positioned as performers, and they interacted with visitors living out fantasy roles. At the Salpêtrière a disparate set of forces were in action; forces that are directly comparable with those that sustained the modern entertainment industry. Madness and the entertainment industry were not only linked through the body of the female performer; the connections between them were extensive, pervasive and influential in the formation of ideas concerning gender, corporeality and rationality.

Avril's memoirs devote several pages to the period of time that she spent at the Salpêtrière hospital, as a patient under the care of Charcot.[40] They form an intriguing response to treatment for a psychological condition, for the language selected by Avril seems incongruous with our retrospective perceptions of the actual experience of neurological treatments in the nineteenth century: the hospital was, Avril recalled, 'an eden . . . for me, so much in this world being relative'.[41] As the daughter of a famous, but jaded, Second Empire courtesan Elise Richepin (La Belle Elise), Avril had endured a difficult and penurious childhood. Her mother's poverty and fading beauty led to her repeatedly trying to force her daughter into prostitution; when Avril refused she was beaten. Although the retrospective – and slightly romanticised – nature of Avril's autobiographical narrative demands to be acknowledged, what her descriptions suggest is that the hospital acted as a refuge from the instability and violence of her home environment.[42] After being discharged from the Salpêtrière's care, she willingly returned on several occasions, both to perform at charity events and to attend some of Charcot's Tuesday lectures.[43]

More interesting than Avril's affectionate remembrances of the sanctuary offered by the hospital are the sections of her memoirs that reveal her identification and acknowledgement of the performance and performances that constructed its unique environment. This awareness is most notable in her focus on the hospital's most famous female patients at the time: the 'stars of hysteria'. Here Avril takes on the 'ailment' that was creating a 'sensation' at the time, exposing what she considered to be the questionable acting skills and the deliberate role-playing adopted by her co-patients, or the 'crazies' as she more frequently refers to them.[44] Although on her admission Avril had been diagnosed with St Vitus' Dance, not hysteria, she was placed on the same ward as the hospital's most famous patients. The reasons behind this decision are unclear, but Avril's extended residency on the ward positioned her as a spectator, offered an unusually high level of access to the fashionable condition.

Watching the hysterics' behaviour 'on and off stage', in the presence of the hospital's medical staff, in the lecture theatre and in each other's company, enabled Avril to recognise the myths about madwomen that were engendered by the hospital and to observe the behaviour that those myths provoked. Whilst a significant amount of productive research has been undertaken on the question of the fin de siècle's interest in hysteria and the hysterics, it is not in the interest of Avril's performance practice to enter into that debate here. Rather it is the particular constructions of display and spectacle that were propagated by the Salpêtrière hospital, and the public acts of its famous hysterics, that are fundamental to an analysis of Avril's ideas about performance, and the ways in which she would later negotiate celebrity culture. This scientific, metropolitan site, with its investment in the codes and forces of the entertainment industry, provided Avril with a clear example of how personality could be constructed in the modern city.

## The 'stars of hysteria'[45]

Hysteria was amongst the most renowned of the psychological conditions investigated by Charcot during the culmination of his career at the Salpêtrière hospital. Although his research revealed that its seizures and symptoms affected members of both sexes, it was the female patients diagnosed with the condition that became – and have continued to be – its representation. Since identified by Georges Didi-Huberman as both an invention and an iconography, fin-de-siècle hysteria was not just a medicinal construct; the condition also formed a reflection and a distortion of social images of femininity and madness.[46] Furthermore, its iconography was significantly influenced by the celebrity culture of the day: created by the cultural moment and the performance environment of the Salpêtrière hospital, the hysteric became a star, a familiar figure across Paris and Europe, a celebrity presented by Charcot, the doctor, scientist, showman and mesmerist.[47]

During the mid-1880s Charcot had further developed his interest in the therapeutic potential of hypnotism: a technique that he believed could be employed to control, to study and to treat some psychological conditions.[48] In terms of his lectures hypnosis also supplied a very practical tool. Staging demonstrations of individual conditions made it desirable to be able to offer visual examples of their symptoms and seizures on demand. The provocation of an attack by the means of hypnotic control over the subject became a key way for Charcot to stage hysteria. One contemporary spectator's account of these presentations records that, under hypnosis, female patients:

> smelt with delight a bottle of ammonia when told it was rose water, others would eat a piece of charcoal when presented to them as chocolate. Another would crawl on all fours on the floor, barking furiously when told she was a dog, flap her arms as if trying to fly when turned into a pigeon, lift her skirts with a shriek of terror with a suggestion of a snake.[49]

The ways that the hysterical attack was displayed indicates that the exhibition was designed to be – at least in part – entertaining. The acts directed by the hypnotiser clearly reflect the popularity of mesmerism and mesmerists as popular stage attractions throughout the nineteenth century.[50] They also signal a further link between spectacle, the madwoman, the performer and the entertainment industry: the smelling of 'perfume', the love of chocolate and a terror of snakes expressed through shrieking and the lifting of skirts are intrinsically 'feminine' actions. Individually, and out of this context, they would not represent actions that were either 'mad' or irrational: they are recognisable ideas affiliated with women and the gentleness of femininity, framed by the hysterical seizure. Aligning the condition with a love of perfume and of chocolate reinforced its identification with the female in the popular and scientific mind: as Roy Porter has noted, '[h]ysteria came to be seen as the open sesame to impenetrable riddles of existence: religious ecstasy, sexual deviation and above all, that mystery of mysteries, woman'.[51]

The fashionable position of the stage mesmerist and the hysteric drew psychology and entertainment more deeply into the same physical and conceptual spaces. Moreover, it advertised an inherent connection between performance – or simulation – and hysteria present at the core of many contemporary understandings of the condition. Charcot himself came to the conclusion that a 'degree of simulation was at work in hysteric self-presentation',[52] whilst in the notes of Robert Carter, another contemporary scientist, the claim is made that 'nature knew no such being as a solitary hysteric: Hysteria was a public complaint presupposing an audience – mass Hysteria definitionally so'.[53] Someone needed to be positioned as the spectator of the hysterical act, to be present to observe its sequence of shapes and contortions, or its irrational activities. 'Hysteria was a condition chiefly rendered visible by the medical presence', but it was also displayed to and advertised by the public's presence and interest.[54]

## Rejecting the hysteric: Jane Avril

Contemporary understandings and scientific explanations of hysteria as a performative act reinforce the conclusions that Jane Avril came to during her time at the Salpêtrière hospital. However, whilst later readings see the condition as offering a limited source of expression to its sufferers, suggesting that 'in hysteria, the afflicted subject has recourse to her or his body as a medium of expression precisely because symbolic language for some reason no longer suffices', Avril's clear and uncompassionate dismissal of the behaviour of her co-patients carries within it an explicit rejection of their performances.[55] Her repeated return to the complete absence of rationality in the 'crazies'' behaviour negates any agency that could be read in their 'acts': she noted that 'there were those deranged girls whose ailment named Hysteria consisted, above all, in simulation of it . . . how much trouble they used to go to in order to capture attention and gain stardom'.[56] Avril may have recognised a designed and premeditated performance here, but in her reading of it, it was not performance that was linked to expression or to creation.

Avril's accounts simultaneously identify and dismiss the meretriciousness of the hysterics: the central deceit that she located at the core of the 'hysterical act'. Its result was a predictable and directed performance that she neither approved of, nor respected. 'For me it was a comic show to see these crazies come away so proud and delighted to have been chosen and pointed to by the "master"' she recalled.[57] Charcot – the 'master' – pointed, and the performance commenced: a reading that contains an implicit rejection of a performance act where the primary aim was to please the eye, and to satisfy a pre-established set of demands. On stage at, and in the wards of, the Salpêtrière hospital were examples not of performance agency, but of comedy: in many ways Avril was pre-empting the same questions raised by later scholars of the condition and its public representatives. Her position can be aligned with identifications of the central tensions in hysterical performance when, as Martha Noel Evans has commented, '[d]esirous of attention, it seems at almost any price, hysterics appeared to be playing their audience, almost enjoying their symptoms'.[58]

The sections of *Més mémoires* that are dedicated to hysteria form the most notable section of Avril's account of her time at the Salpêtrière hospital.[59] They have been singled out for comment by both of her biographers, José Shercliff and François Caradec, and also raised in an article on the dancer and neurological history by Michel Bonduelle and Toby Gelfand. In spite of their different stylistic approaches and aims, all three of these studies reveal an interesting alignment in the ways that they document and discuss Avril's honest – and sometimes barbed – reactions to the hysterics. It appears that all four of these writers share a sense of surprise at the stark absence of female community amongst the women treated by Charcot that is revealed in the accounts. They are linked by the assumption (directly on the part of the authors, but also a reflection of a much wider cultural assumption) that the wards of the Salpêtrière hospital induced a female solidarity: a notional 'sisterhood' that Avril's forthright rejection of the hysterics transgressed. Caradec, for example, notes that Avril observed, and later documented, the new and curious world of the Salpêtrière with a degree of unkind mischief.[60]

Pervasive and appealing this mythologised vision of the Salpêtrière hospital and 'medicine's hysteria romance' may be, but it appears to be the combined product of romanticised images and retrospective reclamations of the hysteric as a figure of resistance, rather than the outcome of any historically based understanding of the hospital environment.[61] Avril's self-conscious distancing of herself from any association with the hysterics' celebrity and performances unsettles the mythical status of this historicised site, and the divisions and tensions it reveals offer access to a productive debate about women and performance at the fin de siècle.

### 'Alas! I was cured'

In addition to offering Avril physical protection from her difficult and violent home environment, the Salpêtrière hospital also offered her space to mould her performance practice and her creative identity. Deliberately aligning itself with the growing recognition of a connection between mental and physical health, the hospital had introduced a relatively comprehensive educational programme for its younger patients. Academic lessons were devoted to the major subjects, and strong emphasis was also placed on improving the physical health and fitness of the patients. As part of this programme Avril attended gymnastic classes three times weekly: her first experience of taught rhythmic movement, and one at which – she notes – she excelled.[62] Later descriptions of her dancing style, with its incorporation of movements such as *The Fan*, where the dancer stood on one leg with the other extended straight up and clasped in front of her face, while her coloured skirts cascaded around her, reveal how she had incorporated the flexibility and physical control that had formed the basis of these classes into the agility of her dance. During her time at the hospital, she was also taught the basic rudiments of balletic dance by a patient who had been a professional performer prior to her time in the hospital.

It was at the Salpêtrière hospital that Avril's first experience of public performance occurred, during a ball arranged to celebrate the eve of *mi-carême* in 1884.[63] In the following account of this evening, Avril's words are recalled by her first biographer, José Shercliff:

> The greatest moment of the evening came when the orchestra struck up a valse for which [Avril] had no partner. She was standing alone . . . At the first notes of the rhythm something seemed to wake in her. She felt a tingling feeling run through her limbs and a strange, excited happiness surged into her heart to make her pulse beat quicker and her breathing lighter. Almost unconsciously she began to dance alone . . . One by one the dancers began to notice her, to draw aside, then to fall out of the dance. Enchanted and amazed they watched her rapt face, the perfect movements of her feet and hands. Then suddenly she was aware of what had happened.[64]

In her memoirs, Avril's recollection of the impact that this first dance performance had on her is almost identical to that cited here.[65] Both focus on the idea that the dancer was somehow taken over by the music and the movement, highlighting her experience of being momentarily, but completely, unaware of the other people in the room. The entire event is framed in a vocabulary of apotheosis: 'Alas!' Avril noted, after this evening, 'I was cured.'[66] And it seems she was; less than a week later Avril was discharged from the hospital, but its ideas and dynamics were to remain with her.

Contemporary press fascination with the celebrities of the fin de siècle meant that Avril's period of treatment at the Salpêtrière hospital was common knowledge. In spite of her immediate response to and later published condemnations of the hysterics, the iconography of the madwoman was to follow the dancer throughout her performance career. As her descriptions of that first performance, with their identification of it as a moment that crystallised the therapeutic treatment process she had undergone, suggest, the dancer did not actively discourage these connections. Arguably she fostered them. However, where much of the iconography of the hysteric and the madwoman focused on their corporeality – the systematic physicalisations of the condition – in relation to Avril associations with madness were linked to stagings of the mind. Descriptions of her dancing convey the sense of a 'disembodied performance'; she becomes an almost haunting figure disassociated from her own corporeality.

If hysterical behaviour occurred in a medically initiated trance, Avril, it seems, went into her own, self-induced trance when dancing. Claiming to be unaware of her surroundings whilst she performed, it was a distance in which she discovered a creative space. It was a trance that intrigued and threatened her audience because of the 'otherness' it suggested. Attempts to explain the effects and attraction of Avril's dancing – from Shercliff's identification of her 'very strangeness', a quality that 'roused strange desires and drew men and women of all kinds round her like moths',[67] to descriptions of her as a whirlwind – reinforce these ideas. Avril's action was unpredictable, but it was neither irrational nor chaotic in its physical movement; it was wholly removed from the extreme freneticism of the cancan. In Paul-Jean Toulet's view the uniqueness of her dance was to be discovered in her use of a rapid succession of unpredictable new rhythms. His language suggests that her dance conveyed multiple performance personalities and styles: '[s]uddenly, she departs from her own rhythm, breaks it, and creates a new one; she seems never tired, always reinventing herself'.[68]

These descriptions are connected by the sense that the effects of Jane Avril's performances were indefinable. They rely on a psychological vocabulary – an evocation of mental and emotional states – rather than a description of the physical act of performance. There is a sense in the images, descriptions and nicknames contemporary with Avril's performances that her dance was founded on a sense of the unexpected: a disruption of conventional systems of movement and rhythm. This has been affiliated with madness. However, involuntary and purposeless movement of the limbs and general muscular weakness are the main symptoms of St Vitus' Dance – the condition Avril was diagnosed with. These are simply not consistent with the ideas and images associated with Avril's dancing, which demanded high levels of physical strength, co-ordination and agility. Trademark movements such as the 'fan' demanded exceptional balance, flexibility and control: gained through gymnastics training and her time as a horseback rider.

Metaphors of the unconscious frame descriptions of Avril's performances, and they are reinforced by her own discussions of dance as a therapeutic art form. But the affiliation of her dance with madness and femininity is strikingly different to the iconography of the hysteric. What Avril's records of her actual experience of psychological illness and of her treatment at the Salpêtrière offer are an illustration of the sheer complexity of the relationship between spaces, women, embodiment and madness. Her comments complicate the key questions surrounding femininity and insanity that are raised by responses to her work. Elizabeth Dempster has questioned what stories are told and which are silenced through the process of inscribing and reading performing bodies with the ideas and myths of the discursive practices of their historical moment.[69] It is all too easy to align Avril with the hysteric, the representative madwoman of the fin de siècle, but this alignment removes the history of a whole experimental performer.

Immersion in the environment of the Salpêtrière hospital undoubtedly shaped Jane Avril's performance practice but, as her reaction to the hysterics suggests, she did not mirror or replicate its ideas or constructs of celebrity in her performances. Indeed the creation of her work can be seen as a response to, a comment on, the space, in spite of the ways that she was described. Whilst McCarren's alignment of dance and medicine had powerful effects, there is also agency here: for Avril dance offered a medium that could be consciously used, developed and created. It was not only created at the Salpêtrière, it was also built on and incorporated the Cairo Road, the Hippodrome circus and the Moulin Rouge. In this context Avril's dance cannot be read as unthinking and lacking in autonomy – a 'symptomatic act' – rather it represents a conception of performance that constituted a deliberate and considered creative process, one in which the dancer simultaneously adopted, rejected and expressed the ideological forces that she was subjected to. Jane Avril's performance formed a historical performative product that both adopted and commented on contemporary ideas about women and madness, and transformed the popular stage into a site of innovation and development in theatrical dance. As a 'cultural production dynamically interacting with the sociocultural matrix of which it is a part', Avril's performing body staged ideas about femininity and insanity.[70]

The two strikingly different urban spaces represented by the Gaiety Theatre, one of the iconic sites of London's Victorian and Edwardian theatre industries, and Paris' Salpêtrière hospital created constructs of femininity that dominated the fin-de-siècle entertainment industry. At the Gaiety, the fashionable skirt-dancing Gaiety Girls offered Loïe Fuller a means of transforming vaudeville dance into an autonomous and culturally respected art form. In Paris, Jane Avril learnt and appropriated the model of the hysteric she discovered in the complicated space occupied by the Salpêtrière hospital. In the reputations and ideas of these two modern, metropolitan spaces lies a reflection of the presence of corporeality at the core of contemporary ideas about science and entertainment.

The problematic nature of examples of how we recover and define historical performance spaces is illustrated by the Salpêtrière hospital. As a space it formed part of the theatromania of the fin de siècle, responding to and shaping ideas about entertainment and performance. Along with the streets of London and Paris, the Gaiety Theatre and the Moulin Rouge, the hospital demands attention, both as a physical performance space, and as a construct shaped and reshaped by its output. Existing spaces and constructs of femininity could be used and reworked by performers, manipulated to achieve celebrity and a space for creative practice. But this was not just about the performance space; the female performer needed to disseminate their new model more widely, using the technologies of fame. The popular press, the mass advertising industry and the environment of competition and imitation helped to secure a performance space for many women.

## Notes

1  'Dancing', *The Saturday Review*, 18 January 1896, p. 52.
2  See Felicia McCarren, 'The "Symptomatic Act" Circa 1900: Hysteria, Hypnosis, Electricity, Dance', *Critical Inquiry* 21:4, Summer 1995, pp. 748–74 (748).
3  Elaine Showalter has revealed the ways in which the female body has been adopted throughout history as a cultural symbol of irrationality in *The Female Malady: Women, Madness and English Culture, 1830–1980* (London: Virago, 1987), p. 5 and following.
4  St Vitus' Dance is now identified as 'Huntingdon's Chorea', or 'Sydenham's Chorea'. Its most obvious symptom is involuntary muscular twitches of the face and body. The onset of St Vitus' Dance was understood to be related to either a pre-existing neurological condition or to the repeated experience of

extreme levels of stress. In the late nineteenth century treatment focused on calming the patient with sedatives, and protecting them from any further nervous excitement. Sydenham's choice of terminology for the illness is revealing: chorea is the ancient Greek word for dance.

5 'Submerged Paris', *The Saturday Review*, 26 March 1892, p. 353.

6 James Gilbert, 'World's Fairs as Historical Events', in Robert W. Rydell and Nancy Gwinn (eds), *Fair Representations: World's Fairs and the Modern World* (Amsterdam: VU University Press, 1994), p. 17.

7 See Caroline Mathieu, 'Exposition Universelle 1889', in Marc Bascou, Ted Gott *et al.* (eds), *Paris in the Late Nineteenth Century* (Canberra: National Gallery of Australia Press, 1996), pp. 58–65.

8 Paul Greenhalgh, *Ephemeral Vistas: The Expositions Universelles, Great Exhibitions and World's Fairs, 1851–1939* (Manchester: Manchester University Press, 1988), p. 37.

9 See Cassell and Co., *Cassell's Guide to Paris and the Universal Exhibition of 1900* (London: Cassell, 1900); Viscomte de Kératry, *Paris Exposition, 1900: How to See Paris Alone* (London: Simpkin, Marshall, 1900).

10 Avril records her fond memories of working on the Cairo Road in the series of autobiographical articles that she gave to *Paris-midi* in 1933. See note 40.

11 Jean Guérin, 'Rue (la) Caire à l'Exposition', *Magasin pittoresque*, 1889, pp. 215–19.

12 See Henry Thétard, *La Merveilleuse Histoire du cirque* (Paris: Prisma, 1947); Julia Frey, *Toulouse-Lautrec: A Life* (London: Weidenfeld and Nicolson, 1994).

13 Sandy Broad, 'Paris Amusements', *The Daily Northwestern*, 27 August 27 1895, p. 8.

14 James Laver (intro.) and Henry Davray (ed.), *XIXth Century French Posters* (London: Nicholson and Watson, 1944), p. 13.

15 Kératry, *Paris Exposition, 1900: How to See Paris Alone*, p. 162.

16 Broad, 'Paris Amusements'.

17 Victor Meusy and Edmond Depas (eds), *Guide de l'étranger à Montmartre* (Paris: J. Strauss, 1900), p. 45.

18 *Ibid.*

19 Broad, 'Paris Amusements'.

20 *Ibid.*

21 Richard Harding Davis, *About Paris* (New York: Harper Bros., 1895), p. 95.

22 Kératry, *Paris Exposition, 1900: How to See Paris Alone*, pp. 161–2.

23 See Gabriel P. Weisberg (ed.), *Montmartre and the Making of Mass Culture* (London: Rutgers University Press, 2001) for a discussion of the relationship between Montmartre and commercial entertainment.

24 Henri Perruchot, *Toulouse-Lautrec* (London: Constable, 1994), p. 154.

25 Arthur Symons, 'La Mélinite: Moulin Rouge', in *Arthur Symons: Poetry and Prose*, ed. R. V. Holdsworth (Cheadle: Carcanet Press, 1974), pp. 41–2.

26 José Shercliff, *Jane Avril of the Moulin Rouge* (London: Jarrolds, 1952), p. 38.

27 Raymond Escholier, 'La Mélinite chez Toulouse-Lautrec', *Journal*, 2 March 1938, Jane Avril clippings file, Site Richelieu, Bibliothèque Nationale de France.

28 'Le Sourire de Jane Avril', *Comedia*, 24 April 1924, Jane Avril clippings file, Site Richelieu, Bibliothèque Nationale de France.

29 'Jane Avril est morte', *Petit Parisien*, 3 February 1943, Jane Avril clippings file, Site Richelieu, Bibliothèque Nationale de France.

30 *Reynold's Newspaper*, 23 February 1896, p. 2.

31 Christopher G. Goetz (trans. and comm.), *Charcot the Clinician: The Tuesday Lessons* (New York: Raven Press, 1987), p. xix.

32 *Ibid.*

33 Christopher G. Goetz, Michel Bonduelle and Toby Gelfand, *Charcot: Constructing Neurology* (Oxford: Oxford University Press, 1995), p. xviii.

34 *Ibid.*

35 See Goetz (trans. and comm.), *Charcot the Clinician: The Tuesday Lessons*; and Julia Borossa, *Ideas in Psychoanalysis: Hysteria* (Cambridge: Icon Books, 2001).

36 Axel Munthe was a Swedish physician who visited Paris in the late nineteenth century and was struck by the 'multicoloured' nature of the audiences that regularly attended Charcot's lectures. Cited in Elaine Showalter, 'Hysteria, Feminism and Gender', in Sander Gilman, Helen King, Roy Porter, G. S. Rousseau and Elaine Showalter (eds), *Hysteria Beyond Freud* (Berkeley: University of California Press, 1993), pp. 309–32 (311).

37 See Rae Beth Gordon, 'From Charcot to Charlot: Unconscious Imitation and Spectatorship in French Cabaret and Early Cinema', *Critical Inquiry* 27:3, 2001, pp. 515–49.

38 Shercliff, *Jane Avril of the Moulin Rouge*, p. 49.

39 Yannick Ripa, *Women and Madness: The Incarceration of Women in Nineteenth-Century France*, trans. by Catherine du Pelous Menagé (Cambridge: Polity, 1990), p. 111.

40 Avril published her memoirs in *Paris-midi* between 9 and 26 August 1933. They have since been reissued in Claudine Brécourt-Villars and Jean-Paul Morel (eds), *Jane Avril: mes mémoires* (Paris: Phébus, 2005).

41 Avril, *Mes mémoires*, pp. 25–9.

42 See Thomas Postlewait, 'Theatre Autobiographies: Some Preliminary Concerns for the Historian', *Assaph C* 16, 2000, pp. 157–72.

43 Martha Noel Evans' study of hysteria, *Fits and Starts: A Genealogy of Hysteria in Modern France* (Ithaca: Cornell University Press, 1991), comments that 'even Jane Avril, Toulouse-Lautrec's famous poster subject, [was a visitor] at these demonstrations', p. 65.

44 Avril, *Mes mémoires*, pp. 25–9.

45 *Ibid.*

46 See Georges Didi-Huberman, *Invention of Hysteria: Charcot and the Photographic Iconography of the Salpêtrière*, trans. by Alisa Hartz (Cambridge, MA: MIT Press, 2003).

47 Michel Bonduelle and Toby Gelfand, 'Hysteria Behind the Scenes: Jane Avril at the Salpêtrière', *Journal of the History of the Neurosciences* 7:1, 1998, pp. 35–42 (37).

48 See McCarren, 'The "Symptomatic Act" Circa 1900: Hysteria, Hypnosis, Electricity, Dance'.

49 Gilman, King, Porter, Rousseau and Showalter (eds), *Hysteria Beyond Freud*, p. 311.

50 See Alison Winter, *Mesmerized: Powers of Mind in Victorian Britain* (Chicago: University of Chicago Press, 2003).

51 Roy Porter, 'The Body and the Mind, the Doctor and the Patient', in Gilman, King, Porter, Rousseau and Showalter (eds), *Hysteria Beyond Freud*, p. 227.

52 Elisabeth Bronfen, 'The Language of Hysteria: A Misappropriation of the Master Narratives', *Women: A Cultural Review* 11:1/2, 2000, pp. 8–18.

53 Porter, 'The Body and the Mind, the Doctor and the Patient', p. 242.

54 *Ibid.*

55 Bronfen, 'The Language of Hysteria: A Misappropriation of the Master Narratives', p. 8.

56 Avril, *Mes mémoires*, pp. 25–9.

57 *Ibid.*

58 Evans, *Fits and Starts: A Genealogy of Hysteria in Modern France*, p. 32.

59 Avril, *Mes mémoires*, pp. 25–9.

60 François Caradec, *Jane Avril au Moulin-Rouge avec Toulouse-Lautrec* (Paris: Fayard, 2001), p. 21.

61 Elisabeth Bronfen, *The Knotted Subject: Hysteria and its Discontents* (Princeton: Princeton University Press, 1998), p. 101.

62 Avril *Mes mémoires*, p. 29.

63 *Mi-carême* was a traditional festival marking the middle of Lent, customarily celebrated with a series of revels.

64 Shercliff, *Jane Avril of the Moulin Rouge*, p. 50. Shercliff's biography was written in conjunction with Avril, with the final text being constructed from a set of interviews and more informal conversations between the two women.

65 Avril, *Mes mémoires*, pp. 25–9.

66 *Ibid.*, p. 30.

67 Shercliff, *Jane Avril of the Moulin Rouge*, p. 101.

68 Paul-Jean Toulet, cited in *Ibid.*, p. 87.

69 Elizabeth Dempster, 'Women Writing the Body: Let's Watch a Little How She Dances', in Ellen W. Goellner and Jacqueline Shea Murphy (eds.), *Bodies of the Text: Dance as Theory, Literature as Dance* (New Brunswick, NJ: Rutgers University, 1995), pp. 21–38 (22).

70 *Ibid.*

# Part III
## IMAGE

'A living death-like poster, that was just what I intended.' (Yvette Guilbert)

# 5

# 'THEY ARE WISE WHO ADVERTISE, IN EVERY GENERATION': IMAGE AND THE FEMALE CELEBRITY[1]

Go forth in haste,
With bills and paste,
Proclaim to all the nation:
That they are wise
Who advertise
In every generation.[2]

In 1895 the Irish-American novelist and short-story writer Walter Lecky published an article on the downfall of the Naturalist writer and critic Emile Zola's fame and popularity. He opened the piece with the lines that are cited above: lines that he claimed to have seen a few years earlier 'ornamenting a dead-wall' in a London suburb. Lines that 'may or may not be poetry – that is a matter of taste in these days', but were 'sense, and sanity rules the roost in the long run'.[3]

In Lecky's view, advertising was a crucial factor of fame and success at the fin de siècle. To effectively create and manage a clear public identity, an understanding of marketing techniques had become a basic necessity. This was not only the case in the world of fiction and writers for, as the familiar figure and strong cultural identity of the Gaiety Girl have illustrated, the contemporary entertainment industry was dominated by the power of image and the cult of celebrity. Indeed, the stage offers a model of fin-de-siècle image culture that is simultaneously clearer and more complicated than any other: the successful performer did not only need to establish a strong, on-stage performance identity, they also needed to ensure that their off-stage personality was recognisable and appealing. Powerful promotional tools were on offer to the celebrity to help them achieve this cultural prominence, including the poster, the interview and the autobiography.

## 'Postermania!'[4]

The objects that promoted and familiarised female celebrity images were themselves outputs of the modern city and its leisure industries. New technologies opened up a new level of mass production, whilst current trends and public investment in the spectacular culture of the metropolitan environment created receptive audiences for the visual stimuli and the gossip offered by posters, press interviews, photographs, postcards and autobiographies. At this historical moment the female performer had access to an unprecedented level of identity creation and self-promotion techniques. Located at their core was the most culturally ubiquitous of the fin de siècle's advertising forms: the entertainment poster.

Recent advances in mechanised chromolithography led to the production of reams of brightly coloured poster images that engulfed the modern city. Advertising the products and experiences available to the metropolitan consumer, they covered the walls, hoardings, *colonnes Morris*, omnibuses, handcarts and sandwich boards of London and Paris. In this context the entertainment lithograph demands to be understood as a cultural product embedded in, and inseparable from, the urban and technological cultures of its time. Aside from its functional role as a means of promoting the cities' leisure industries, the poster also formed a familiar and popular part of the period's urban spectacle. It is unsurprising therefore that the powerful visual impact of poster images became the subject of extended commentaries and debate on both sides of the Channel.

In Paris, the collector and art critic Ernest Maindron, a self-professed fan of the poster and author of the 1896 collection, *Les Affiches illustrées, 1886–1895*, satirically noted that the French capital's 'poster hangers use every unoccupied space, without restraint and without respect', to the 'point of robbing us, poor Parisians, of the sight of our monuments'.[5] A similar situation was documented in London where, as part of a more extensive and ongoing debate concerning the poster, a writer to *The Saturday Review* complained that, 'every vacant wall or hoarding which is accessible to the billsticker blazes with pictures which do not precisely educate the public taste, and are rather a serious addition to the minor evils of life'.[6] Peculiarly, ideas about this advertising and art form were subject to a similar set of concerns and judgements as the female celebrity performer, for the combination of its popularity and prominence resulted in the poster quickly becoming a locus of wider cultural anxieties provoked by the modern, international world of metropolitan commodity culture.

The wide availability of reproductions of these late nineteenth-century images today, and their popular presence in permanent art collections and touring exhibitions, makes it easy to forget just how modern the poster was at the fin de siècle. As early as 1944 the art critic James Laver noted that because the poster had so quickly become 'part of the normal décor' of life, its 'modern' nature had already been forgotten.[7] Nonetheless, it was the medium's striking newness and its function as advertisement that were directly responsible for the significant impact that posters had on the quotidian visual urban experience. Contemporaries celebrated the lithograph's 'riots of colour . . . triumphant in their certainty of fascinating and bewildering the passer by',[8] whilst the language chosen by the reviewer of an early New York poster exhibition in 1896 further reinforces the sense of novelty and excitement that the form evoked:

> the newspapers, the great publishers, magazines and the patent medicine people were represented in brilliant reds, blues, greens, yellows and purples; some wildly chaotic, others more sane, few uninteresting, all more or less startling.[9]

The poster was simultaneously a modern advertising form and an exciting new visual medium: its 'bewildering' and 'startling' images demanded – and won – the attention of the modern city's large body of spectators leading to an outburst of postermania, or *l'affichomanie*.

In spite of the concerns that were raised about the number of posters on display in the modern city and the potential detrimental effect that these images could have on 'public taste', many artists discovered a creatively liberating and challenging new medium in the flat blocks of colour and strong lines characteristic of the modern lithographic form, as well as an opportunity for financially lucrative commissions from the commercial sector. Poster images by Henri de Toulouse-Lautrec, Adolphe Willette, Jules Chéret and Alphonse Mucha (amongst others) reflect some of the main visual tropes associated with modernist art, and locate the medium as the site of important artistic innovations, and images. In lithographs commissioned and designed to promote venues, or advertise cosmetics, performers, newspapers, novels and medicinal products, it is possible to trace the current popularity of Japonisme, the interest in the wood-cut print, and the stark use of strong colour favoured by Paul Gauguin and the Pont-Aven School, and adopted by later groups of artists including the Nabis and the Symbolists.

Encouraged by their attractive nature and their association with emerging young radical artists, a large body of poster collectors quickly emerged across Europe and America, and these new and quintessentially modern cultural products became fashionable, sought-after items. Such was the desire to own new works by popular artists, that the 'postermania' craze frequently witnessed the surreptitious removal of newly hung images from city walls and hoardings. Amongst the many bill-posters – 'all-powerful personage[s]' for the fan of the lithograph – were a contingency who could be tempted with cash to 'liberate' new and desirable posters to order. As Arsène Alexandre noted, amongst this trade existed a number of individuals who 'came to serve the name of the un-paster of posters', rather than bill-poster.[10] Court cases and convictions for theft did little to assuage the problem, so artists and printers attacked it from a different angle, arranging for specialist stores to sell limited editions of posters that were held back from major commercial print runs.

## 'A day of little things': the poster as an art form[11]

As this level of poster connoisseurship suggests, the form became the subject of aesthetic discussion and theory, as well as a desirable possession and decorative object. In response, specialist journals including the London-based publication *The Poster* and Paris' *Maitres de l'affiche* (*Masters of the Poster*) were established, offering image reproductions, collectible series of prints and serious discussions of the medium. Moreover, in Europe and America large exhibitions of posters proved to be popular entertainments for diverse spectatorships that included critics and artists amongst a wider body of enthusiasts and the intrigued. Endorsing their position in gallery spaces, the French critic Jules Claretie stated that the poster had given Paris 'a museum of pictures', 'an open-air exhibition of art' that distinguished the city from other modern capitals.[12] A view that was supported by Maindron in his claim that every day Paris' inhabitants and visitors awoke amidst the presence of original artworks, offered to them by the poster images that covered the city.[13] For Claretie, Maindron and many others, the poster was an art form.

The London-based collector and self-appointed poster expert Charles Hiatt adopted an alternative position. Whilst he remained a committed fan of the poster, Hiatt believed that its primary function as advertisement meant that it was simple foolishness to argue that examples of the form could be considered as art. The 'aesthetic qualities' of the poster, he argued, must, without exception, 'be subordinated to its commercial qualities': in this popular, new medium the artist will always remain primarily 'the servant of the tradesman'.[14] It may have been the case that art is 'supposed to be inimical to commerce and commerce inimical to art', but in the case of the poster, 'we have the two combining in the advantage of both, and succeeding in making the beautiful an incident of the necessary'.[15] To claim that the poster was pure art was – in Hiatt's view – to rather miss the very point of its existence.

Their disagreements aside, one thing that the poster's supporters and critics did concur on was that the popularity of this cultural phenomenon was not going to be short-lived. As one journalist sent to cover the first British exhibition of posters, held at Westminster's Royal Aquarium in December 1895, conceded, 'these posters, and the questions, artistic or other, which they give rise to, are things which have to be considered seriously'.[16] In many ways the time was right for this serious engagement with the medium, and for its cultural acceptance as art. As an object the poster was aligned with the wider appreciation of the small arts and everyday objects that had driven the Arts and Crafts movement, and was to be an important factor in the brief popularity of Art Nouveau design. In 1892, the American journalist Brander Matthews adopted a popular approach when he suggested that the immense popularity of the poster across Europe and America could be explained within this wider aesthetic movement, a movement that favoured 'little things'. It would, he argued, not be,

> wholly unfair to suggest that this nineteenth century of ours is a day of little things, and that our silverware, our pottery, our tiles, our wallpaper, our wood-cuts, our book covers, each in its kind, and when at its best, are better than our historic painting, our heroic sculpture, our grandiose architecture. The minor arts have their place in the hierarchy of the beautiful.[17]

Clearly Matthews is not employing 'little' to refer to the scale of the object in the case of the lithograph: late nineteenth-century posters were, after all, large in size and often printed on several individual sheets that were then pasted together to construct the entire image. Rather 'small' refers to the cultural hierarchy that classified and defined objects at the fin de siècle: a cultural hierarchy in question.

The high cultural status accorded to the poster – a 'minor art' assigned a place in the 'hierarchy of the beautiful' – located the form in an ambiguous cultural position. Reflecting a more generalised blurring of the boundaries between high and low, or minor and major, art forms, the lithograph's striking shapes and colours simultaneously embodied a work of art and a cultural product realised by the forces of commodification. In lithography a mass-produced object became an accepted form of art that existed in a liminal space that opened out between the popular entertainment industry and the world of high art.[18]

The economic forces that drove this successful and competitive area of the fin de siècle's print-culture industry are strikingly similar to those of the popular stage. Both were the products of new technologies and commodity culture, with their success dependent on their reflection and creation of current trends, and a strategic use of image. Furthermore, both became representatives of anxieties about progress and degeneration, and ideas about art, entertainment and audiences.

## The entertainment poster and the female celebrity

Poster images did not only mould cities' vistas in the eyes of their citizens and tourists, they also shaped perceptions of the people, places or products that they advertised. Within an international metropolitan culture that was preoccupied with visual spectacle, these advertising products became powerful objects and forces. In 1900, the Australian correspondent for the London-based journal *The Sphere* reported on two successful charity events that had recently taken place in Melbourne: a poster ball and a poster pageant. Organised to raise funds for the city's children's hospital, *The Sphere* recorded that the pageant alone had attracted over 20,000 spectators. The account of this occasion, at which the organising principles drew heavily upon the current fad for the poster, reveals a microcosmic illustration of the forces at play in the lithograph.

As the large number of spectators suggests, many had been attracted by the idea of watching members of society and familiar industry and entertainment figures dressed up to represent poster images for Pears' Soap, John Bull Oats, Quaker Oats, Dewar's whiskey and Yankee Doodle tobacco. Other popular brands of champagne, ale, tea, soap, tyres and jam also featured, as did Australian journals and newspapers, and famous entertainment sites, including the city's Geisha tearooms. Funds were not only raised by charging admission to the event, each advertiser also had to make a substantial donation in order to have a character represent their product. In the context of fin-de-siècle marketing this pageant was viewed as a chic, unusual and important event: the tone of the *Sphere* article makes it clear that the journal was not only proud to have been involved, but that they considered it a coup to be the only London journal represented.[19]

*The Sphere*'s account was accompanied by a significant number of visual images, even for a journal that characteristically offered its readers numerous illustrations. What these photographs reveal is that poster pageant was an accurate definition: this was a theatrical event. As the title of the journal's report – 'Posters as Living Pictures' – suggests, the show fused recognisable practices from poster advertisements and from popular entertainment. The designs of the costumes displayed were not loosely based on the familiar figures that featured on current posters; they were created from, and decorated with, imagery and typography that were copied directly from popular lithographs. Moreover, the poses that were adopted by the famous figures modelling the creations echoed the poses of the figures represented on poster images. The pageant's success depended entirely on an audience that was familiar with, and embraced, these tropes and conventions: an audience trained in reading the new iconography of commodification. That audience existed, for as the *Sphere*'s reporter concluded, 'nothing so colossal in the way of either function [the pageant and the ball] had been previously seen in this part of the world'.[20]

The poster, the entertainment industry and leisure time were insepa-rably linked at the fin de siècle, and many of the commercial lithographs produced during the period were commissioned as advertisements for venues and performers. These images were particularly well received by the wider public, for, as Maindron recorded, they reminded their viewers of noisy and pleasurable evenings, and offered the recognisable profiles of figures that they liked to watch on stage.[21] However, amongst the numer-ous sites and diverse figures connected with the popular stage, it was the female celebrity that became most clearly affiliated with the iconography of the entertainment poster and marketing. As we have already seen in the case of the Gaiety Girl, representative images of female performers were frequently used as motifs of the entertainment industry, and its promises of spectacle and diversion. Figure 7, an 1895 poster for the Palace Theatre of Varieties advertising the Minstrels Parisiens, further illustrates this trend. The name of this act reveals that the entertainers were a group, but the main image of the lithograph is still of one prominent female figure, an attractive and curvaceous dancing woman.

Fin-de-siècle advertising images necessarily raise the problematic question of woman as object, but it is important to locate these concerns within their contemporary context. In nineteenth-century Europe, the use of an alluring woman to sell a product was completely revolutionary. As John Hewitt has revealed in an essay on the poster debate in London, there was no pre-existing debate surrounding the subject of its represen-tation.[22] Instead these debates were being carved out in journals and newspapers. The numerous and unprecedented images of women that covered cities, appeared in art galleries, and entered into the drawing

7  Poster for The Palace Theatre of Varieties advertising the Minstrels
Parisiens (1895)

rooms of collectors and journal readers demanded new languages and a new set of responses. In addition to this, alongside the representative female iconography employed to represent leisure and pleasure, individual stars commissioned striking lithographs. Celebrities relied on, and managed, this fashionable advertising form and cultural trend to ensure that the public were aware of their identities and performances. Artist and celebrity, poster and act, were products of their cultural moment, created by and dependent upon the technological developments of modernity. Neither group would have enjoyed such levels of success and public attention without the dynamic and powerful relationship that existed between them.

## Celebrity culture: harnessing the fin de siècle's 'sweet uses of advertisement'[23]

As cultural objects, entertainment lithographs provide an important visual record of the themes, acts and performers of the popular stage, as well as supplying information about the leisure industry as a whole. Thanks to the avid poster collectors of the late nineteenth century, many examples of advertising imagery still exist, as well as comprehensive catalogues and journals that document the number, nature and iconography of these lithographs. Their subjects, tropes and colours document what was popular, offering a clear insight into the ways in which fame was established and represented at the fin de siècle. Because the creation and advertisement of a familiar visual image formed a requisite element of the female celebrity's public identity, the lithographs that they commissioned reveal ideas about the cultural environment in which their fame emerged, and how that fame could be controlled and manipulated through a strategic use of image.

For some individual performers, the technologies of this new advertising industry offered more than an opportunity to crystallise a public identity. The new environment also enabled them to draw attention to their capability as modern entrepreneurs and businesswomen. In 1899, a celebratory interview in *The Poster* acknowledged Loïe Fuller's expertise at creating a familiar celebrity image and at managing her self-promotion in print. As the journalist's short introduction to the dancer noted:

> from the outset of her brilliant career, [Loïe Fuller] has been too shrewd to disdain the sweet uses of advertisement and she has remembered that artistic advertisement is of all the methods of publicity the most surely effective.[24]

Fuller's commitment to the 'sweet uses of advertisement' that were offered by the fin-de-siècle mass culture industries had – the interviewer argued – secured her status as 'far more than a popular favourite' amongst the numerous performers on the stage at the time. Rather, what she had achieved through her use of these technologies was the creation of a 'personality' that stood 'out vivid and distinct in an amazingly various aggregation of brilliant and fascinating personalities'.[25] As *The Poster*'s title suggests, this was a journal established in response to a wide interest in the medium. Its features and interviews were not only concerned with the aesthetics of the form, they also covered the advertising trade and commodity culture that the poster formed an intrinsic part of. In this 1899 interview, it is clear that Fuller was considered to be successful across these fused areas of modern entertainment advertising: shrewd and professional in both her aesthetics and her self-promotion.

The promotional images used by celebrities that were famous for their stage acts also needed to capture a sense of what it was that made their performance popular. Appearance and identity were crucial, but they were not substitutes for an individual on-stage style. The briefest of leafs through trade journals and reviews from the fin de siècle makes it clear that there were many conventionally attractive women on stage who failed to achieve celebrity status in the eyes of their audiences. Lithographers needed to capture and present a sense of what it was that made this particular dancer, singer or actress 'vivid and distinct' amongst the period's 'amazingly various aggregation of brilliant and fascinating personalities'.[26] Performers were not just presenting their image on these prints; they were also – wittingly or unwittingly – presenting a record of their practice.

Posters commissioned by, or designed for, individual celebrities (including Fuller) represent a distinct use of female corporeality in advertising. These images did not display anonymous or representative female forms. The female celebrity's presence on city walls, *colonnes Morris*, sandwich boards, omnibuses, in journals, and displayed in shop windows and exhibitions was a conscious and necessary choice. She appeared on posters in order to gain the essential exposure she needed to continue and extend a successful career. Unlike the Gaiety Theatre and the Palace Theatre of Varieties images discussed earlier, in these lithographs the central figure is simultaneously model and performer, object and subject. Offered to the spectator as a poster image, her visual identity existed in a space between these two roles.

Entertainment lithographs designed for fin-de-siècle female performers complicate approaches that locate objectified female corporeality as the keystone of advertising iconography. Artist and celebrity had a shared interest in the success of the promotional images that were produced for entertainment stars. This was a historically specific, reciprocal relationship. Popular poster artists had the techniques, talent and the following to place representations of female performers at the heart of modern urban spectacle, but this simply mirrored a position that they already held on the popular stage. Whilst the female celebrity was undeniably dependent on the advertising industry, she simultaneously supported it and shaped its remit and conventions. The expectation that the female celebrity should play an active role in her marketing is evinced in *The Poster*'s approbation of Loïe Fuller, and it was a role that offered her significant power.

In comparison to other contemporary visual art forms, a much wider audience viewed posters: effectively their potential spectatorship included anyone who had access to city streets. In the entertainment lithograph numerous and diverse metropolitan spectators were given access to images of their favourite celebrities, images that were often commissioned and controlled by the performers themselves. As Ruth E. Iskin has emphasised:

> posters which depicted urban women with agency participated in reshaping women's identities in the 1890s and early 1900s because they converged with a period in which the reception of such images was taking place in the midst of dynamic changes.[27]

In this context, the cultural icons of the popular stage possessed the potential to affect and to modify contemporary ideas about female representation, through the iconography they adopted and displayed in their promotional posters.

The lithograph's prominent cultural and social presence illustrates the significant role that the fin de siècle's new print industries and technologies played in establishing and maintaining the construct of female celebrity. However, it was not only the striking visual imagery made familiar by the work of poster artists that was central to the creation and dissemination of celebrity identity. Performers also employed the popular press and the contemporary fondness for the 'star' autobiography as powerful tools in the creation and recreation of on-stage and off-stage personas.

## The interview, the autobiography and celebrity image

During the 1880s and 1890s the content offered by an increasing array of newspapers, journals, novels and non-fiction works became more diverse. This choice indicates that, when it came to reading about the leisure industry, contemporary readers desired more than detailed accounts and reviews of the performances and on-stage appearances of their current celebrity favourites. Subscribers and buyers also wanted to know about stars' backgrounds, their opinions, their habits, their relationships and their aesthetic ideas. Consequently, many newspapers, journals and magazines were preoccupied with supplying their market with a steady stream of information, personal details, 'exclusives', gossip and speculation regarding the current celebrities of stage and society. From Paris' *Le Figaro* and *La Vie parisienne*, to London's *Era* and *The Times*, performers frequently supplied alluring headlines, and gossip-column material.

Whilst commentators raised concerned questions about the gossipy nature of the material that was regularly offered to this large reading public, editors and journalists continued to respond to the interests of their market. The popular press was – after all – a modern supply and demand industry.[28] Articles, interviews and images defined and distributed ideas of what celebrities looked like, how they behaved and what they did in their leisure time. Newspapers and journals guided their wide readerships' understanding of what a 'star' was. For the celebrities themselves, the readers of these widely available publications offered additional audiences that could be familiarised with their identities, and the opportunity to frame their images in different ways. Amongst the mixture of individuals who picked up their morning newspaper at home or in a café, or opened the latest copy of the journal that they had subscribed to, would be those who had already watched a performance by the subject of the article, interview or press release. The information in front of them would complement, or conflict with, that experience. For other readers who had not witnessed the performer on stage, the descriptions, images and approach expressed in print on the page in front of them would supply their entire understanding and impression of the celebrity figure in question. Like the lithograph, the relationship between the press and the personality was two-way.

The majority of articles and interviews from this period were accompanied by a selection of publicity shots: generally a mixture of photographs of performers in costume, frozen images of moments from their act, reproductions of popular poster representations of the star and shots of women in their off-stage clothing, looking like 'respectable' and fashionable society women. It is crucial that these images did not appear in isolation. Like the poster image in the context of the modern city, their location is vital in understanding their meanings. The words, the stories and the opinions that were printed alongside them guided the reader's response to the images themselves and, particularly in the case of the interview, the star's expression of their 'self' acted as a means of imposing a reading on the visual representations. The pages of newspapers and journals supplied a blueprint for contemporary celebrity, but it was a blueprint with two co-creators: the star and the publicity industry.

Successful performers engaged with the modern press. Extensive column space enabled celebrities to maintain the high-profile presence that was necessary in a competitive and rapidly changing entertainment industry. It also allowed them to shape and reshape the ways in which their audiences viewed them. They utilised the industry's techniques and technologies to foster the interest of their fans and to establish 'a set of commodified images by which they were "known" '.[29] Publicity was performance, a powerful performance. Whilst the entertainment lithograph formed part of the metropolitan spectacle of London and Paris, newspapers, journals and books regularly infiltrated the domestic space. Rather than being glimpsed in passing as a part of the chaotic spectacle of the modern urban terrain, or studied more closely as an example of a modern art form, the contents of mass-printed material could be ingested slowly and discussed in detail.

Star interviews and advertisements for merchandise associated with current celebrities, or for lessons and publications that were dedicated to emulating the performance styles of popular stars, appeared across a wide breadth of publications. Captured on the pages of mass-produced literature modern professional women found their way into the sanctified space of the drawing room; there their presence necessarily affected and influenced ideas about femininity. The carefully created images promoted by female performers entered into discourses about gender, not only on the stage, but also in the home – the ideological site that was assigned to the 'weaker sex'. The representations of celebrities contained in newspapers and magazines may not have been as visible as those offered on the period's striking posters. Nonetheless, the opportunities of image creation offered by print culture were a significant force.

In addition to becoming proficient at the new art of the interview, and maximising the press coverage that was available to them, popular performers also catered to the current vogue for celebrity autobiography. Examples of these works from the 1890s and early 1900s reveal that they were, to a large extent, formulaic. They remain immensely readable today, with their characteristic offerings of highly fictionalised and romanticised accounts of performers' childhood, their developing stage careers and their struggles to achieve fame. Successful autobiographical works by Loïe Fuller, Yvette Guilbert and Maud Allan explicitly conform to this format, yet they also emphasise their individual personas and performance styles.

Fuller wrote the manuscript for *Fifteen Years of a Dancer's Life, with Some Account of her Distinguished Friends* in English, but it appeared first in a French translation in 1908. An English translation appeared in 1913, and was sold in both England and America. Later in her life she produced extensive notes and drafts for a second volume of memoirs, but this never appeared in print. Yvette Guilbert was a prolific writer, publishing both fictional and non-fictional works and writing numerous newspaper articles and columns during her career. Her first autobiographical work was a 1910 co-publication with the English writer Harold Simpson, entitled *Yvette Guilbert: Struggles and Victories.* Her sole-authored, more extensive autobiography *La Chanson de ma vie: mes mémoires* appeared first in French in 1927, and then in an English translation as *The Song of My Life: My Memories* in 1929. Again this second version was marketed in both England and America. Maud Allan's *My Life and Dancing* offers a rather different timescale, although it adheres to the same romanticised conventions: the work appeared early in her career at the height of her fame in 1908, rather than as a retrospective account.

The interview and the autobiography cannot be relied upon as sources of accurate historical documentation. Fictitious stories and fantastical creations pepper examples of the written works published by the celebrities of the fin de siècle. To make the most of the opportunities for marketing that were offered by the interview and the autobiography, female performers needed to construct strong, identifiable and appealing off-stage identities: personalities that mirrored the ideas evoked by their stage performances, or conflicted with any negative assumptions about their profession that may have been present at the time. As Mary Jean Corbett has noted, 'whatever sort of roles it may recount, an autobiography or memoir is less an originary act of self-expression than another formally constrained or determined mode of performance'.[30]

As performance acts, autobiographical writings act as evidence of the techniques and approaches that were employed by successful female celebrities to deal with the press and to manage their image. Untrustworthy though they may be on the details of education, penury and auditions, as Maggie B. Gale and Viv Gardner have explained, what 'these public selves, as constructed through autobiographical negotiations . . . can reveal [is] a great deal about women theatre workers' professional lives'.[31] In the case of the star, these writings contain a sense of the current ideal of celebrity that was held by modern metropolitan spectators. They flesh out the audiences and the dynamics of the entertainment industry, and in the case of Allan, Fuller and Guilbert they also document ideas about performance practice.

At the fin de siècle, professional female performers presented themselves to the public as semi-mythological figures. These representations were framed by their on-stage performances, but they were also shaped by the wider mythologies about gender, performance and identity that were present in the modern city. As *The Poster*'s account has already suggested, Loïe Fuller was particularly adept at this, but in the early twentieth century Maud Allan challenged the American dancer's recognised prowess at image creation.

## Loïe Fuller: fat ladies and dancing fairies

Contemporary photographs and descriptions of Fuller off stage reveal that it would be reasonably difficult to imagine a more unlikely fairy. The dancer was plump, generally dressed badly and was unapologetically business-like in her approach to performance and fame. Nonetheless, for her sell-out audiences of the fin de siècle la Loïe was 'the fairy of electricity'. Using the technologies of modern culture, those sweet forms of advertisement identified by *The Poster*, Fuller managed to perform and promote an off-stage identity that was so concrete and convincing it led both the mass audiences and the aesthetic communities of London, Paris and New York to invest in it.

Across Europe and America Fuller fascinated and intrigued the press and the public. The great number of interviews and articles dedicated to the dancer led one publication to comment that the,

> story of [her] début in New York, her wanderings among the lesser cities of the Continent, and her ultimate triumphant and unequivocal conquest of Paris are matters so generally known that it were impertinent to narrate them afresh.[32]

For journalists and readers alike Fuller was not only an interesting and personable interviewee and an articulate and witty writer, she was also an intriguing conundrum. The autobiographical accounts that she offered to newspapers and journals, as well as those that she included in her own writings, were deliberately whimsical. In print incessant inventions and reinventions of herself were offered. Fuller's autobiographical 'I' was fundamentally unreliable, but in its very inconsistency a playful and astute manipulation of the cultural associations and assumptions surrounding performance, fame and femininity is revealed.

The multiple selves that Fuller projected in print were the product of the moment in which they were invented: as Margaret Haile Harris has noted, 'Loïe Fuller was the creation of her own imagination and the fantasies of fin-de-siècle Paris'.[33] Her success at self-promotion was the result of the dynamic relationship that she invited and created between herself/selves, the press and the public. It becomes more interesting with the knowledge that she did not maintain this construct in her off-stage appearance. Indeed Fuller deliberately refused to present an appearance that conformed to the beauty and femininity of the fairy when she carried out her day-to-day engagements and life.

Amongst the unpublished material that was destined for the second volume of her memoirs, Fuller recalled an encounter with an American journalist. The tone of her account is one of gentle satire. It begins with her mocking the journalist's pretension and undermining his authority: a response to his opening comment that *he* had, of course, predicted her phenomenal fame. She then records how he changed tack, in order to express his ongoing concerns about her refusal to adopt a more glamorous off-stage image. '[Y] ou've got something in you anyhow,' he concluded:

> but you certainly ought to take off those flat shoes. No actress in the world should go about without heels on their shoes, and *you* most of all because you're undersized already. For heaven's sake fix yourself up, you're a sight.[34]

The journalist was not alone. Contemporary accounts make it clear that the 'fairy's' unprepossessing off-stage appearance regularly caused feelings of surprise and disappointment. What they all reveal is that Fuller was more amused than troubled by this. *Fifteen Years of a Dancer's Life, with Some Account of her Distinguished Friends* contains another short narrative that explicitly deals with this area of her role as a personality. Here she recalled how a famous Parisian architect had approached her and requested permission for his young daughter – a great Fuller fan – to visit her backstage at the Folies-Bergère after a matinee performance. Fuller agreed and in the account she spends some time establishing the great excitement that was experienced by the child in anticipation of her visit, explaining that this excitement was provoked 'not at the idea of seeing me, but of being in the presence of an extraordinary creature, a kind of fairy'.[35] After the matinee had finished the child was taken to wait in a dressing room whilst Fuller changed. When the dancer appeared, without her costume or the cosmetic enhancement of stage lighting and make-up, the child shrank away from her and exclaimed: 'No, no. That isn't her. I don't want to see her. This one here is a fat lady, and it was a fairy I saw dancing.'[36] Fuller was right; her young fan had wanted to see the 'extraordinary creature' that her movement and technologies created on stage, but that vision was not on offer off stage.

The level of amusement contained in Fuller's prose style connects these two detailed autobiographical narratives of the technologies involved in celebrity identity. Her third-person narration distances the performer from the events recorded: they read as objective accounts in which the dancer's gentle but definite superiority over the naïve spectator who expects the fairy to exist off stage as well as on stage is assured. In both, the overall impression is that the Fuller on the page is simply narrating yet another version of herself: defining another element of her performance identity. Autobiographically, in interviews, and on and off stage, Fuller maintained and managed a complex network of modes of performance that stressed her individuality and emphasised her status as a performer rather than a glamorous society personality.

Fuller was adept at playing the fin-de-siècle media, as is revealed by an interview she gave to the British journal *Black and White* whilst she was performing in London early in 1896. The journalist recorded that their meeting was unplanned:

> La Loïe Fuller, the dancer who has just taken flight to the Riviera, leaving the stage desolate, was sitting in a hansom cab when a *Black and White* Representative called at the Savoy Hotel. 'I am just about to drive to the Palace', said she, 'Come into this cab for a few minutes and I shall be delighted to tell you a few things about my life, if they interest you. Are you comfortable? Well, then, I'll begin.'[37]

Whether this unlikely encounter actually occurred in this way, or is a romanticised version of a planned interview that took place under less spontaneous circumstances, is an interesting question, but not one that is central to Fuller's use of the contemporary press. What the suggestion of this kind of 'moment' between the interviewer and the star suggests to the *Black and White* reader is that they are getting more from this interview than they would from any other. Regardless of the actual verity of the event, the journalist's tone reveals the warmth and support that Fuller won from the press as a result of their mutually reciprocal relationship.

The dancer gets a good press article; the journalist gets the dancer's time, willingly given; the public are offered another fabricated, appealing version of her life's events.

Contemporary readers accepted that famous female performers behaved in this gracious and open way because of the projections of celebrity identities publicised by the press. The self-promotion techniques on offer enabled Fuller to refuse and evade many dominant ideas concerning femininity and celebrity. In her limited and strategic appropriation of the conventions associated with contemporary constructions of the female celebrity, the 'fat lady' discovered an opportunity to mythologise herself as a dancing fairy. For celebrities like Fuller and Allan, phenomenal success and international fame were the combined result of the originality of their performances and a realistic understanding of the workings of celebrity in the late nineteenth century.

## 'Rusticating at Hampstead': performing 'Maud Allan' off stage[38]

Repeatedly selling out the Palace Theatre of Varieties, featuring as a recurrent subject of press interviews and gossip columns and being located at the centre of debates about aesthetics, censorship and performance made Maud Allan the talk of early Edwardian London's fashionable social set. Seeing the dancer perform formed a chic and approved social activity. In 1908 *The Times* carried an article discussing the general improvement in the standard of acts on the variety stage and the moral amelioration evident in popular entertainment. They singled out Allan as a representative of this trend, noting that 'the exquisite charm and delicacy of Miss Maud Allan have drawn all artistic and social London' to Alfred Butt's venue.[39] Amongst the audience members Allan's dancing attracted to the Palace were high-profile representatives from the worlds of culture, politics and society, including the Prince and Princess of Wales, Baron Rothschild, the Asquiths, W. T. Stead, a young Winston Churchill and Arthur Conan Doyle.[40]

By the end of 1908 Allan had notched up 250 performances at the Palace Theatre, and she continued to attract capacity audiences to the venue. Always the entrepreneur, Allan selected the matinee performance that had been programmed to celebrate this anniversary to launch her autobiography, *My Life and Dancing*. Each audience member was given a souvenir copy of this short work that documented her creative and aesthetic processes, framing them in a romanticised – and often entirely fictional – narrative of her childhood and a mythologised 'history' of the origins of dance as a performance medium.[41] In this work Allan presented a vision of herself that conformed to the delicate and sweet image of woman: 'my baby heart', she recalled, 'loved and lived in fairy tales. Even now I revel in them, and nothing is sweeter than to let myself be carried off to mystic lands and mingle with the dear fairies.'[42]

Producing an autobiographical work at this early stage of a celebrity career was an unusual move. Most of the comparable publications by stars of the periods form retrospective accounts of their fame. However, Allan found herself in a rather different position to Fuller and Guilbert; she had already been victim to the insinuations of the Manchester Watch Committee, and the subject of much debate in the press. For a performer whose programme had attracted so much attention, comment and judgement, the 1908 appearance of *My Life and Dancing* served to firmly shape and promote a celebrity identity. The book's publication formed one part of a much wider project of image creation and projection undertaken by the dancer at the height of her fame.

The members of London's fashionable set who followed Allan did not only watch her perform, their continuing enthusiastic support also gave her access to the city's social scene. In the early twentieth century, representatives and photographers from the popular press tracked the dancer on a seemingly endless round of engagements and appearances. Gossip columns, interviews, articles and photographs documented her presence at the capital's cycle of garden parties, evening receptions and charity occasions, mingling with the most fashionable figures of the day.[43] As a player in the theatrical life of metropolitan spectacle, Allan presented her celebrity body and identity in a very different way to her stage appearances. Unlike Fuller, her off-stage identity did not surprise spectators with its lack of conformity; instead it depended upon a carefully managed and balanced blend of constructs of the glamorous celebrity and the respectable woman. Amidst London's social spaces Allan played the philanthropic, respectable society lady.

In July 1908, three months after her debut at the Palace Theatre of Varieties and a month after her Manchester ban, Allan performed at a fete that had been organised to benefit Chelsea veterans. With the ongoing press interest in her Salome dance, it is unsurprising that *The Vision of Salome* did not feature in Allan's programme on this occasion. Indeed the whole performance seems to have been organised to offer an entirely different vision of the dancer. A flower-covered woodland bower was constructed for her performance, housing a small stage and a backdrop that was painted to suggest the charm and prettiness of a fairy world. The language employed by journalists who covered the occasion reveals that Allan's performance was considered charming, and that – off stage – she also charmed both the veterans and other attendees at the fete.[44]

Maud Allan's management of her identity, particularly during 1908 and 1909, suggests that she quickly realised that negative responses to her stage performances could be counteracted with representations of the acts and the imagery of her off-stage celebrity identity and her social appearances. Unlike Fuller, who took this element of her celebrity reasonably lightly, Allan needed to invest much more intensively in the projection of an off-stage celebrity persona. It proved a successful tactic, in 'Thinking of that Watch Committee?', the Bystander's account of the Chelsea veterans' fete, the journalist noted that Allan's 'charming smile and the attractiveness of her personality redeem her from [the] commonplaces' of her act. One 'act' was used to 'redeem' another; one performance of gender and identity could displace and supersede another.[45]

Existing photographs of Allan reinforce this idea. Those selected to accompany press interviews reveal a careful blend of shots featuring the dancer in stage costumes, and images where she appears as the representative Edwardian lady.[46] One particularly interesting photo shoot staged the dancer in the garden of Kate Greenaway's former home, a property that Allan was renting at the time (Figure 8). Greenaway was a popular illustrator of children's books, whose career had peaked in the 1870s and 1880s.[47] Her drawings represent idealised Victorian childhoods, lived out in idyllic pastoral worlds. Their popularity sparked a merchandise industry, and Greenaway wallpapers, plates and dolls quickly became popular products in mid-Victorian England.

Although Greenaway had died in 1901, her image and her drawings retained a strong presence in popular cultural memory, and the associations between the illustrator and ideals of purity are clearly drawn upon in this set of photographs. Reminiscent of a Pre-Raphaelite damsel, romantically dressed in a loose gown of virginal white, Allan appears against the backdrop of a traditional English garden: enjoying the simple pleasures of outdoor life, accompanied by her small lapdogs and pet cats. This was a carefully planned photo shoot, and its images align the dancer with visions of Britishness and femininity. Publicity shots located Allan's body and appearance as the subject of the viewer's gaze. In them the dancer may not be on stage, but she is undoubtedly putting on a show, a performance that offered her the 'odd blend of notoriety and respect' she attained in London at this time.[48]

8  Maud Allan in Kate Greenaway's garden, *The Sphere* (1911)

The extent to which Allan understood the need to extend her performances beyond the auditorium is evinced in the memoirs of Edward Michael, a theatrical manager who accompanied the dancer on an American tour. Cashing in on his associations with Allan in an article entitled 'Tramps of a Scamp: On Tour with Maud Allan' published in the late 1920s, Michael recalled the differences between Allan's responses to public attention when she was off stage but on display, and when she considered herself to be wholly off stage: occasions when she was neither performing, nor performing her celebrity identity. During one Atlantic crossing, Michael recollected that Allan attracted the unwelcome attention of a group of fellow travellers. From them she received many lunch and dinner invitations, offers that she repeatedly refused explaining that, 'I consider it highly impertinent of strangers to ask me to eat with them . . . I am not a rare-show . . . if people are curious to see me, they can satisfy their curiosity through the box office.'[49]

Deconstructing Allan's celebrity persona in print reveals numerous identities across multiple performance spaces. Even her attempt to guard a separate private life was viewed as a facet of her wider reputation and her personality. Michael's response to the dancer's reaction to the other passengers (cited above) was to note that, 'if she did not wear much clothing on the stage, in private life she was abundantly draped in dignity'.[50] The box office was never the only means for the public to access Allan: they could learn about her through the media industries of the period. Her celebrity identity was compounded from these different areas and projections of her personality, moral status and creative ideas.

## The collapse of celebrity identity: murder, Maud Allan and Pemberton Billing

Allan's success at harnessing the sweet uses of advertisement was to change dramatically after the outbreak of World War One and the consequent shift in the socio-cultural climate. Indeed, as a result of the propaganda created by the conflict, the dancer was to suffer personal attack at the hands of society and the mass press. This character assassination was grounded in a family scandal that Allan had managed to conceal at the height of her fame, as well as her associations with the character of Salome. In 1895, her brother Theodore (Theo) Durrant had been arrested, tried, convicted and hanged for the murder of two young women. At the time of the trial Allan was in Berlin, and this geographical distance, coupled with the period of time that had elapsed between Durrant's execution and her rise to fame, had enabled her to evade any negative publicity associated with the case.

In 1918, the British war effort appeared to be heading towards total disaster. Politicians, generals and the public were desperately searching for an explanation for this military failure; someone or something was needed to blame. In late January, a British political newspaper, *The Imperialist*, ran a story that claimed to expose the 'cause' of this seeming defeat. The work of Noel Pemberton Billing, editor, independent Member of Parliament, journalist, actor, singer and inventor, the article alleged that a contingency of more than 47,000 British men and women were responsible for the dire situation that the nation's troops found themselves in. The newspaper claimed that it had unearthed a black book compiled by a German prince. One thousand pages in length, its contents detailed the depraved behaviour of the wives of cabinet ministers, dancing girls, privy councillors and chorus girls.[51] It was a successful blackmail campaign against these 47,000 individuals – silence for secrets – that was the cause of such massive British failures and fatalities in the war.

At the time, Allan was in rehearsal with the theatre director J. T. Grein, on the Independent Theatre's production of Wilde's *Salome*. Fuelled by her connection with the dance, Wilde and the play, Pemberton Billing listed the dancer amongst the depraved individuals. Allan sued Pemberton Billing for libel, beginning what Philip Hoare has labelled 'the trial of the century'. Allan grounded her case in the artistic merit of Wilde's play, not a terribly successful strategy bearing in mind the playwright's fate at the hands of the British justice system. Pemberton Billing's defence was largely supplied by scientists and medical specialists, none of whom had seen the Grein production, but all of whom were prepared to state that simply being involved with it exposed a perverse element in Allan's character.[52]

Perhaps unsurprisingly, Allan lost her case against Pemberton Billing. She also effectively lost the reputation and identity that she had so effectively constructed during the height of her fame. In times of social and cultural crisis, gender ideology became a real threat to the high-profile celebrity. The mythical image of Allan as a performer aligned with fairy worlds and Greenaway's idyllic visions could not be sustained amidst the chaos caused by the international mechanised conflict of World War One. Moreover, once the Pemberton Billing trial had supported the claims against Allan, disassociating the dancer from its ideas and ideologies becomes problematic. In spite of the fact that several years had passed between the popularity of *The Vision of Salome* and the court case, and that Pemberton Billing's accusations were linked to Grein's production of Wilde's *Salome*, the trial has become conflated with existing images of *The Vision of Salome*. In retrospect the two roles have been compounded.

Allan's various presentations of her fin-de-siècle selves experimented with and challenged ideas about gender and physical stereotypes. At the height of her fame she was as adept at managing the tricks and techniques of marketing and self-promotion as Loïe Fuller. However, this similarity is not something that is suggested by histories of these two performers. Maud Allan's involvement in the Pemberton Billing affair has impaired and limited understandings of her as a performer and a celebrity. It has dominated ideas about her to the detriment of the years of fame that she managed successfully before the world conflict and the court case. Examining examples of her image creation and promotion that date from the height of her fame enables a more realistic appreciation of the dancer's role as a respected celebrity figure.

As Walter Lecky rightly noted, fin-de-siècle celebrity success relied on the combination of a strong image and tireless self-promotion. Current gender ideology supplied perfect raw material for the female star: a set of visual iconography that could be appropriated and manipulated to create an individual identity. This process was strengthened by the unsettled cultural climate of the fin de siècle, an environment within which many of the ideas celebrities engaged with were at an embryonic stage, or in a state of transition. This instability of image and iconography made personality an area that could be mined and managed by the female performer. Amidst the quagmire of blurred gender roles and images, clear and individual celebrity identities could be discovered and developed: identities that it would not have been possible to sustain at other moments in history.

## Notes

1 Walter Lecky, 'Downfall of Zolaism', *Catholic World* 61:363, 1895, pp. 357–60 (357).
2 *Ibid.*
3 *Ibid.*
4 Arsène Alexandre, 'French Posters and Book Covers', *Scribner's Magazine* 17:5, May 1895, pp. 603–14 (611).
5 Cited in Alan Weill, *The Poster: A Worldwide Survey and History,* trans. by Marilyn Myatt (London: Sotheby's Publications, 1985), p. 31. Maindron also wrote for journals on the subjects of the poster and publicity, see, 'L'Affiche illustrée', *La Plume* 110, November 1893, pp. 474–80, and 'La Publicité sculpturale', *La Plume* 115, February 1894, pp. 41–2.
6 *The Saturday Review,* 18 February 1893, p. 169.
7 James Laver (intro.) and Henry Davray (ed.), *XIXth Century French Posters* (London: Nicholson and Watson, 1944), p. 7.

8  Charles Hiatt, *Picture Posters* (London: George Bell and Sons, 1895), p. 30.

9  *New York Times,* 1 March 1896, p. 10.

10  Alexandre, 'French Posters and Book Covers', p. 613.

11  Brander Matthews, 'The Pictorial Poster', *The Century: A Popular Quarterly* 44:5, September 1892, pp. 748–56 (748).

12  Jules Claretie, cited in Jane Abdy, *The French Poster: Chéret to Cappiello* (London: Studio Vista, 1969), p. 9.

13  Ernest Maindron, *Les Affiches illustrées, 1886–1895* (Paris: G. Boudet, 1896), p. 11.

14  Hiatt, *Picture Posters,* p. 1.

15  *Ibid.,* p. 367.

16  *The Saturday Review,* 15 December 1894, p. 657.

17  Matthews, 'The Pictorial Poster', p. 748.

18  Catherine Ruth Robbins discusses the liminal nature of fin-de-siècle popular culture in her doctoral thesis, 'Decadence and Sexual Politics in Three *Fin-de-Siècle* Writers: Oscar Wilde, Arthur Symons and Vernon Lee' (University of Warwick, 1996).

19  'Posters as Living Pictures – A Charity Ball in Melbourne', *The Sphere,* 3 November 1900, p. 146. The ball was given on 28 August at the Town Hall; the pageant followed a week later on 4 September at the Exhibition buildings.

20  *Ibid.*

21  Maindron, *Les Affiches illustrées, 1886–1895,* p. 59. As a collector, Maindron was interested in popular entertainment and many different forms of fin-de-siècle ephemera: in addition to his published work on lithographs, he also published collections of theatre programmes, menus and an illustrated history of puppets.

22  John Hewitt, 'Poster Nasties: Censorship and the Victorian Theatre Poster', in Simon Popple and Vanessa Toulmin (eds), *Visual Delights: Essays on the Popular and Projected Image in the Nineteenth Century* (Trowbridge: Flicks Books, 2000), pp. 154–69. See also Lori Anne Loeb, *Consuming Angels: Advertising and Victorian Women* (Oxford: Oxford University Press, 1994).

23  'La Loïe Fuller and her Artistic Advertisements', *The Poster,* February 1899, pp. 69–74 (74).

24  *Ibid.*

25  *Ibid.,* p. 69.

26  *Ibid.*

27  Ruth E. Iskin, 'The Pan-European *Flaneuse* in *Fin-de-Siècle* Posters: Advertising Modern Women in the City', *Nineteenth-Century Contexts* 4, December 2003, pp. 333–56 (337).

28  See Mikulas Teich and Roy Porter (eds), *Fin de Siècle and its Legacy* (Cambridge: Cambridge University Press, 1990).

29  Mary Jean Corbett, 'Performing Identities: Actresses and Autobiography', *Biography* 24:1, 2001, pp. 15–23. See also Sidonie Smith and Julia Watson (eds),

*Women, Autobiography, Theory: A Reader* (Madison: University of Wisconsin Press, 1998); Maggie B. Gale and Vivien Gardner (eds), *Auto/Biography and Identity: Women, Theatre and Performance* (Manchester: Manchester University Press, 2004).

30  Corbett, 'Performing Identities: Actresses and Autobiography', p. 15.

31  'Introduction', in Gale and Gardner (eds), *Auto/Biography and Identity: Women, Theatre and Performance*, p. 3.

32  'La Loïe Fuller and her Artistic Achievements', p. 69.

33  Margaret Haile Harris, *Loïe Fuller: Magician of Light* (Richmond: Virginia Museum of Fine Arts, 1979), p. 13.

34  'Dead Ashes', unpublished autobiographical fragment, Loïe Fuller Papers, 1892-1913, New York Public Library, Performing Arts Division, Jerome Robbins Dance Collection.

35  Loïe Fuller, *Fifteen Years of a Dancer's Life, with Some Account of her Distinguished Friends* (London: Herbert Jenkins, 1913), pp. 140–1.

36  *Ibid.*, pp. 141-2.

37  *Black and White*, 25 January 1896, p. 118.

38  Unidentified press clipping, Maud Allan clippings file, Mander and Mitchenson Collection, London.

39  'The Coming Elevation of the Variety Theatre', *The Times*, 21 November 1908, p. 12.

40  *The Era*, 28 March 1908, p. 22.

41  Allan's 250th Palace Theatre of Varieties performance occurred on the afternoon of 14 October 1908.

42  Maud Allan, *My Life and Dancing* (London: Everett and Co., 1908), p. 27.

43  Gilson McCormanck, *The Dancing Times*, undated press clipping, Maud Allan clippings file, Mander and Mitchenson Collection, London.

44  *The Bystander*, 15 July 1908, Maud Allan clippings file, Mander and Mitchenson Collection, London.

45  *Ibid.*

46  It is interesting that Jacky Bratton's early research concerning the music-hall singer and impersonator Vesta Tilley (later Constance de Frece) has revealed similar mechanisms at play in her visual celebrity image.

47  See M. H. Spielmann and G. S. Layard, *The Life and Work of Kate Greenaway* (London: Bracken Books, 1986).

48  Amy Koritz, 'Dancing the Orient for England: Maud Allan's "The Vision of Salome"', *Theatre Journal* 46:1, 1994, pp. 63–78. Koritz argues that Allan's performance of this one work is particularly interesting because it encapsulated two transgressive positions, that of gender and that of the Orient.

49  Edward Michael, 'Tramps of a Scamp: On Tour with Maud Allan', unidentified press clipping, dated 27 June 1928 by hand. Maud Allan clippings file, Mander and Mitchenson Collection, London.

50  *Ibid.*

51 See Philip Hoare, *Oscar Wilde's Last Stand: Decadence, Conspiracy and the Most Outrageous Trial of the Century* (New York: Arcade Publishing, 1998).

52 *Ibid.*, pp. 65–88.

# 6

## THE ART OF IMITATION: STAGING THE CULT OF CELEBRITY

Fierce competition between venues, managers and stars made new performers or performance styles sought-after commodities at the fin de siècle. Frequently, the emergence of an act that proved a hit with metropolitan audiences prompted immediate responses from rival venues, where copies or versions of the performance were rapidly programmed and advertised. As *The Saturday Review* noted in 1892, 'if a "hit" is made at one theatre', then another 'five or six other houses [across the city] follow suit', offering their audiences 'works of a similar, but, in nine cases out of ten, inferior, quality'.[1] On many occasions it was not just the new popular stage act itself that audiences desired to see replicated by other venues. After all, the particular dance, acrobatic trick, song or other novelty formed only one part of the package that had secured the new performer's success with contemporary spectators. What audiences demanded from these 'similar' performers was an entire recreation of the original; a copy that was as close to their appearance, style and identity as was possible.

Amidst a cultural landscape that was dominated by image, mimicry was to become a successful, lucrative and individual performance style. Its widespread popularity formed one element of a more extensive pattern of 'contemporariness' on stage. As entertainment programmes reveal, audiences favoured amusements that integrated familiar figures and themes. In London and Paris the social commentaries, references and satire characteristic of musical comedy, farce and burlesque continued to attract and satisfy large numbers of spectators well into the twentieth century. The appeal is clear: by recognising these contemporary references and drawing attention to their awareness of current trends and star performers, audience members were identified as 'in the know'; they were cast as 'up-to-date', fashionable participants in the theatre of the city. The star system that continued to dominate the entertainment industry of the day further reflected and strengthened these on- and off-stage cultures of familiarity and imitation that had become international vogues. Merchandising, advertising and product placement enabled the fin-de-siècle spectator to imitate their favourite performers during their quotidian existence. Buying merchandise, dressing in similar clothes, or choosing the cough sweets, face powder or toothpaste that they endorsed in journals and newspapers, made a small part of celebrity identity available to the everyday consumer. Here was another opportunity to advertise one's status as in the know in the modern city.

Mimicry's techniques permeated the outputs of the popular stage, winning the imitator recognition as an artist in her or his own right. For the contemporary female performer, however, the widespread presence of impersonation across entertainment forms had a dual effect. Six years after *The Saturday Review* commented on the dynamics of the London stage's response to popular acts, the competitive nature of the city's entertainment had not changed. Writing for *The Theatre* in 1898, Sylvia Grey reinforced the earlier article's emphasis on the inferior nature of imitations of successful performers that continued to prove popular with audiences. But Grey took her argument further, for her status as a professional performer increased her concern over the perceived threat that imitation posed to creative expression and new performance forms. Rather than dismissing 'inferior' stage imitations lightly, she condemned them wholly:

> when once a strong tide of popular favour flows towards some particular branch of art, the rush from all sides to clamber to the top of the tree is quite bewildering. It is like the scramble of gold-diggers when a new field is discovered.[2]

In this view, the replication of popular acts across city stages formed more than a reflection of the current trend for contemporariness, and was responsible for more than an increasing level of competition between venues and performers. Imitation also devalued and undermined the aesthetic credibility and originality of the new performance styles that were emerging from any 'particular branch of art'. The metaphorical associations Grey employs to vocalise her argument are particularly interesting. By aligning the popular stage practice of imitation with the primal drive for wealth witnessed in the gold rush, Grey draws upon ideas of capitalism and greed. Through these connections imitation is distanced from any connection with art and grounded in economics.

In terms of performance practice and experimental ideas, Grey's take on imitation is interesting. However, the form was significantly more complicated than she indicates in this article. Rather than creative 'theft' that damaged developments in performance, many successful impersonations were largely founded on the affirmation of a performer or a style. It is an old adage that imitation is the greatest form of flattery, but for the celebrity it was true. Featuring as a burlesque character, appearing as a subject in a mimic's variety routine, or having one's act copied by other performers validated a performer. It acted as clear proof that they had achieved star status within contemporary culture. Moreover, the original was consistently invoked as the benchmark against which imitations were judged and, as *The Saturday Review* and Grey's accounts have already suggested, the copy was rarely considered to be superior to the actual subject.

### 'Little misses who can twirl a few yards of muslin': the performer and the impersonator[3]

The complex forces at play in the popularity of imitation, and their effects on the individual female performer, can be traced in the Skirt Dance craze that swept Europe and America in the early 1890s. At its American premiere in the autumn of 1891, Fuller claimed the *Serpentine Dance* as her own original creation. The New York press was in agreement: 'there is a new dance in town', one publication recorded; 'nobody ever saw before anything like what Miss Fuller calls the Serpentine'.[4] Within days of her well-received first performance, numerous Fuller imitators appeared on the city's stages.

Fuller's immediate reaction was to turn to the courts. Her desire to exert control over 'her creation' led her to attempt legal action against two uses of the *Serpentine Dance* in the city that she considered to be unauthorised. First she sued the manager of the Casino Theatre, Rudolph Aronson, for continuing to use her image on the venue's promotional posters after she had ceased to perform there. Then she took action against the dancer Minnie Renwood, who had been performing a version of the *Serpentine* at Madison Square Gardens. Although Fuller had filed a copyright description of her new style as a precaution against mimics, both of these court cases failed, leaving the dancer to pay high court costs.

Interestingly, Fuller's move to defend her performance style and creative rights attracted little sympathy from the press or the public. With few exceptions, responses to the Fuller/Aronson and Fuller/Renwood cases were negative. Popular publications mocked the dancer, criticising her extreme reaction to the culture of imitation that shaped the entertainment scene of the day. In one article tracking the ongoing legal action against Renwood, the purpose behind the dispute was clearly belittled by the author's description of the court case as a 'snarl' between two dancers.

The account went on to record that 'Loïe Fuller, or rather her lawyer has reduced the *Serpentine Dance* to legal verbiage', its tone revealing that in the view of the popular press this was neither an acceptable nor admirable course of action.[5]

Mimicry and imitation were accepted components of the contemporary entertainment industry: objecting to them did not win the performer popular approval or the support of the press. Instead it was necessary for the female performer to work with these forces and to manipulate them. By the mid-1890s Fuller, now secure in her celebrity status, had entirely changed her approach to the question of her imitators. Rather than suing the performers who copied her work, she used the high level of press exposure that her stardom offered to talk explicitly about their acts, and to negate them. In an 1896 interview with *The New York Times*, she publicly dismissed the contingency of 'Muslin-Twirling and Toe-Kicking Imitators' who were filling the stages of European and North American variety venues. These women were not performers, she explained, rather 'little misses', 'who can twirl a few yards of muslin and bob in and out of the focus of a limelight'.[6] The dancer's rejection of these performers is complete. Mirroring the practices of contemporary critics, she holds their work up against her own performance, emphasises its lack of talent and creativity, and rejects it.

Competition and imitation could be used for gain, and Fuller had realised by this stage of her career that any act that was based on her internationally recognisable style verified and furthered her own fame. As is illustrated by the *The Times*' description of the London-based dancer Marie Leyton as 'an evident and only moderately successful imitation of the performances of Miss Loïe Fuller', spectators were led to compare stage imitators with the 'original' Serpentine dancer.[7] Whilst featuring as the subject of imitation undoubtedly solidified the position of the established star in celebrity culture, acknowledgement and management of the culture of impersonation could also emphasise her status as an authorised creative figure. It was, after all, the new performance form that she had created that was being copied on stage. As Loïe Fuller learnt to her own financial cost, imitation was a fundamental part of the fin-de-siècle entertainment industry. It was not only necessary for the female celebrity to understand and utilise such forces and dynamics to cement their own performance identity, they could also work to their advantage.

At the same time, imitation added a new, intrinsically modern performance form to the popular variety repertoire. The immediacy of its material and products placed it in constant dialogue with ideas about identity and individuality; it was always in flux, unfixable. Succoured by celebrity culture, it also rapidly contributed to it, as successful impersonators became stars in their own right. Amongst them, the music-hall performer Little Tich's (Harry Relph) comic impersonations of Loïe Fuller's skirt dancing proved popular with audiences in London, Paris and America, and Monsieur Stiv Hall, a Parisian performer who specialised in impressions of the singer Yvette Guilbert, became successful both in his home city and across Europe.[8] However, in spite of the followings achieved by male mimics like Relph and Hall, it was female performers that quickly came to dominate the field of imitation.

As with so many of the other elements latent within the construct of female celebrity, the innate connection between women and imitation can be interpreted on several levels. At first glance, it may seem to suggest the absence of the original creative act from dominant ideas about the popular female performer. However, impersonation offered new opportunities and openings to female performers. Susan Glenn has noted that the form created a new 'comedy of personality', a humorous style that commented directly on the cultures and fashions of the day.[9] The majority of the programmes offered by female imitators were made up of impersonations of female stars, although the occasional cross-dressing imitation did make it into their programmes as well. These performers were interested in restaging original female performances: the popularity of stage 'caricatures' further entwined the female celebrity with the creation and manipulation of public image.[10]

Female mimics did not neglect the power that was offered to them by this quintessentially modern collision of forces. The repertoires offered by successful and enduring performers were more complex than a selection of straightforward imitations. Instead the most popular imitators deliberately used the form as a framework to contain their own complex and witty social and cultural commentaries, instigating a 'critical dialogue about its cultural significance': as Glenn concluded these, 'attempts to situate their comic practices within the cultural discourses of the day reveal an extraordinary degree of self-consciousness about their craft'.[11] As a self-conscious performance practice, acts of imitation demand to be understood in the context of celebrity culture and the entertainment industry.

## Mimicking celebrity: Cissie Loftus

Cissie, or Cecilia, Loftus was a British variety performer who worked as an actress, a singer and a mimic during her professional career, but it was as an impersonator – a 'mimetic musical genius' – that she was best known and loved by her audiences.[12] The composition of Loftus' programmes contributed to and reflected the entertainment industry of the day, featuring impersonations of famous figures 'drawn from the front ranks of our stage favourites' that included Allan, Lind, Sarah Bernhardt, George Formby, Harry Lauder, Caruso and Yvette Guilbert.[13] Their popularity is documented in reviews from the time, such as the piece in *The Penny Illustrated* that recorded Loftus' 1910 return to the Coliseum Theatre, London. On this occasion, the reviewer noted, the audience demanded so many encores that he really believed that 'had [they] had their way Miss Loftus would still be giving her impersonations' as the paper went to print.[14]

By the time of her death in 1943, Loftus' transatlantic appearances and celebrity had spanned five decades. As the daughter of the successful Scottish music-hall performer Marie Loftus, she had been raised in a theatrical family. Although she began performing on the provincial circuit at a young age, it was in 1893, when she was engaged by Charles Morton to perform at the Oxford Music Hall on London's Oxford Street, that her professional entertainment career began. Loftus was an immediate success with the Oxford's audiences, and later that same year she was offered a contract with the Gaiety Theatre. On Edwardes' chic stage she appeared in *In Town*, a hugely popular musical comedy, followed by the long-running burlesque *Don Juan*, in which she starred alongside Grey. One year after her London debut, Loftus had become an established figure on the capital's stage. 'Anyone who knows anything of London music halls and the variety stage has heard of Miss Cecilia Loftus,'[15] recorded one publication; whilst in June 1895 *The Stage* asserted that her presence provided a 'sure and certain draw' for any production.[16]

In imitation Loftus discovered levels of fame and identity and diverse performance styles that far outweighed those of her many competitors. Contemporary accounts capture a sense of the stage presence and the command of her audiences that provoked those endless demands for encores:

> The dwarf pugilists had disappeared, succeeded by an acrobatic performance, followed in its turn by a duet of Swiss mountaineers exhibiting their aimless wares. But, although they were aimless, so were not the airs that they sang, one of which was a keynote to the great feature, the feature presently to appear – Cissie Loftus . . . The drop curtain rolled back, and from within a crimson portiere at the rear of the stage directly facing the audience came a little figure in simple, unostentatious white.[17]

A palpable feeling of excitement and anticipation within the auditorium is still discernible in this response, over 100 years after it was penned. Loftus' performances held her audiences; as the same reviewer noted later in her account, 'I watched and watched her.'[18]

Loftus' performances set the standard against which the work of other mimics was appraised. In a bizarre web of identity and performance, other stage impersonators were critiqued not only against the subjects that their act offered, but also against Loftus' imitations of the same figures. Clearly Loftus' imitations were considered to be unique performances, and it seems that it was her take on the celebrities that she mimicked that accorded them this status. On stage, she did not offer direct copies of high-profile performers, but recognisable interpretations of them: her success was largely due to the 'exquisite sense of caricature with which she imbues her studies'.[19] One particular imitation, Loftus 'à la Maud' Allan, supplies a good model of the imitation, intervention and self-conscious comic practices that characterised the mimic's popular performances.

Taking into account Allan's fame in 1911, it would have been easy for Loftus to stage a straightforward imitation of one of the dancer's works. She did not. Instead, the Loftus-Allan compounded numerous elements of the dancer's popular stage appearances. The impersonation began before Loftus entered on stage. Audiences watched the curtain rise with 'a slow and stately pomp' – an effect from Allan's *The Vision of Salome* that was copied here with only 'the faintest exaggeration'. As Loftus' spotlighted arm crept around the curtain in a sinewy movement, music from Grieg's *Peer Gynt* filled the auditorium. When the curtain rose completely, it was to reveal a stage set that was 'almost exactly like' Allan's at the Coliseum.[20] Loftus took the key motifs from Allan's performances and brought them together in her short impersonation. Her audiences needed to understand and be familiar with all of them, which not only suggests how far Allan's fame outweighed that of her characterisation of Salome, it also reveals that impersonation was a performance form in constant dialogue with its spectators.

It was the replication of the performance act, as well as the identity, that became Loftus' trademark. Her practice made it clear that talented mimicry was something more than staging a series of convincing visual look-a-likes of familiar figures. Indeed interviews with the star and accounts and images of her performances reveal that this element of impersonation was of minimal importance to her act. Costume was not essential in Loftus' staging of mirror images of her subject: she frequently appeared in a pale muslin gown, ornamented only with a coloured sash. As her imitation of Maud Allan suggests, her imitations essayed to capture the essential experience of watching a performer, often by combining many performance elements that would be seen separately from each other in the original. Although simple props and small accessories were used in her routines, the emphasis was always on the convincing mimicry of the physical and vocal performances of her subjects.[21]

In the case of the singers and the actresses that she selected for her repertoire, she repeatedly claimed that what attracted her to them (in addition to their cultural familiarity) was their distinctive use of voice, rather than their appearance. In her memoirs, the music-hall singer Vesta Tilley recalled that Loftus had, to her knowledge, been to watch and hear her sing on just one occasion. Nonetheless, she noted, the next night, she 'gave the best imitation of my voice I have ever heard'. For Tilley what distinguished Loftus was not just the duplication of her performance style, but her 'wonderfully quick and clever [way of] picking out little peculiarities in the artiste she mimicked'.[22] This element was central to two of the most talked-about impersonations during Loftus' career: one short-lived, and one that was to remain in her repertoire for a significant period of time – Letty Lind and Yvette Guilbert.

## The Loftus-Lind and the Loftus-Guilbert

In March 1894, Letty Lind opened in *Go-Bang!*; a musical comedy at the Trafalgar Square Theatre. Having evolved out of the popular programmes offered by the Gaiety Theatre, the framework of 1890s' musical comedy was loose: scant narrative was employed to stage a combination of spectacle, variety entertainments and familiar star performances. *Go-Bang!* fitted this criteria: the show was, 'a modest trifle', in the view of *Pick-me-Up*. Its plot was flexible enough to 'accommodate itself to any amount of altered conditions, to be obliging'.[23] Lind played Di Dalrymple, a variety stage dancer courted by the Boojam (or leader) of the country Go-Bang.

*Go-Bang!* was a great success with London audiences, running for 166 performances. Its warm reception and high press profile reinforced Lind's status as one of the city's most popular female stars, identifying the dancer and actress as an ideal subject for Loftus who incorporated an imitation of the Skirt Dance Lind performed at the Trafalgar into her current programme at the Palace Theatre of Varieties. This was a familiar pattern: popular success leading to mimicry. What makes this one moment of trend and impersonation particularly interesting is Lind's retaliation. The flexible framework of musical comedy, with its audience expectations of changes to accommodate current references and social commentary, made it simple for Lind to work her own imitation – of Loftus imitating Lind – into her performance in *Go-Bang!* Loftus, in turn, was unperturbed; she merely added an impression of Lind imitating Loftus imitating Lind to her own act at the Palace.

The two performers communicated with each other and their fans via the stage and the press, offering imitations and counter-imitations at different venues in the city. As one spectator recollected in the later 1930s:

> Miss Lind saw the performance [Loftus' impression] and promptly gave an imitation of Cissie Loftus imitating Letty Lind. This was funnier than it looks on paper, for Miss Loftus was about twice the size of Miss Lind and lacked the soubrette's vocal skill and grace of limb. Miss Loftus retaliated with an imitation of Letty Lind imitating Cissie Loftus imitating Letty Lind.[24]

Reflecting her conviction that mimicry was more than visual look-a-like, Loftus was very much present as an individual performer in this impersonation: her physicality made it very clear that this was not Lind. Indeed much of the comedy of this performance moment came from this fact. For the original mimic, impersonation was a self-conscious performance form that offered intervention and critique.

The Loftus-Lind dancing wars of 1894 not only reinforce the strength of celebrity culture at the fin de siècle, they also indicate the complex and self-conscious system of looking that defined the period's audiences. It was not in the spectator's interest, or part of their function, to suspend their disbelief whilst they were watching Loftus (or to a lesser degree the musical comedy). Rather, it was necessary for them to remain acutely aware of themselves, of their cultural moment and of their knowledge about the performance on stage. These were the terms of engagement: Loftus' act depended on her audiences' contribution of their own social knowledge and cultural awareness, and their application of them to their interpretation of the material presented to them.

In *The Song of My Life: My Memories*, the *chansonneur* Yvette Guilbert recorded that Cissie Loftus was the first performer to attempt to imitate her distinctive performance style. Furthermore, she notes that the 'charming imitator' had approached her in person to seek her help with the 'parody', a request to which, she informs the reader, she 'was very obliging'.[25] By the mid-1890s, the combination of Guilbert's vocal style, unusual physical appearance and celebrated comic timing had won her international celebrity status. However, her journey from reasonably successful, though typecast, bit-part actress, to café-concert singer, to 'la diseuse fin de siècle' – a 'personality unrivalled in the music halls', 'a stage personality of ineffable resource' – had been a lengthy one.[26]

By the new year of 1885, Parisian-born Emma Guilbert was eighteen years old, and had already worked as a seamstress, a street hat-seller and a shop-model at Héntenarts and at the Magasins du Printemps, one of the city's new department stores. That January, Guilbert records, on a 'day set apart by fate', she was walking along the River Seine, when she was approached by an elderly man who turned out to be the entertainment entrepreneur Charles Zidler. Zidler had been struck by Guilbert's tallness and striking physical stature, and he offered her work as a bareback rider and acrobat in his circuses on the spot. It was the same offer he was to make to Jane Avril four years later, but, unlike Avril, Guilbert refused the opportunity because of the danger involved in performing as an *écuyère*. Unlike the memoirs of her contemporaries, Guilbert's autobiographical writings do not reveal a general tendency for complete invention. Rather, they frequently focus on the harsh realities of the entertainment industry. So whilst it is likely that the 'facts' of this tale were subjected to romanticisation, it seems unlikely that it is completely untrue.

In spite of her rejection of Zidler's offer, Guilbert was tempted by the idea of performing. The following year, she decided to train as an actress, taking classes with the actor turned tutor Landrol and exchanging Emma for the more glamorous stage name Yvette. In 1887 she debuted on the Parisian stage, her career beginning with small roles at the Variétés, where the company included the popular actresses Gabrielle Réjane and Anna Judic. Across Paris, and Europe, the Variétés was renowned as the haunt of Paris' main theatrical celebrities, and Guilbert welcomed the bit-parts that she was offered there, using her time with the company as 'splendid tuition free of charge'.[27] Her interest in scrutinising the people that surrounded her and her corresponding talent for the mimicry of human nature, were to prove central to her later success. Time passed and Guilbert's stage experience increased, but she continued to be offered only small roles and her salary remained minimal. Furthermore, her performances were repeatedly criticised by theatre managers for their mournful nature, a tendency that they attributed to her unconventional physique and range of expression.

Having endured two theatrical seasons' worth of low-paid, small roles, Guilbert accepted that her acting career was not going to improve. The stage opportunities she was offered were restricted by the same striking physicality that had attracted Zidler's attention by the Seine, but this was to come full circle. Ultimately, Guilbert's distinctive appearance was to become an essential element of her international celebrity, and to prove important in her recognition as a creative and experimental performer. A brief glimpse at the dynamics of the entertainment industry in Paris at the time would have sufficed to dictate her next move: it was clear that engagements in the city's café-concerts would provide a better income than the string of bit-parts that she was currently being offered. Guilbert was not 'recruited' to the variety stage; she made an active choice to turn to the chanson, a decision provoked by economics and professional frustration.[28]

## 'I was horrified at the thought of having to entertain an audience like that'[29]

Aiming high, Guilbert approached the manager of the Eldorado café-concert to request an engagement as a singer.[30] The choice of venue was informed: in the late 1880s and the 1890s the fashionable Eldorado was a 'sort of comédie française of song',[31] a venue associated with the chanson's 'celebrities'.[32] Guilbert framed the way that she would be viewed and how her act would be interpreted from the outset of her career as a solo performer. After an audition and (as she documents in her autobiography) a fair amount of persuasion, Guilbert negotiated an Eldorado contract. Up until this point she claimed that she had never entered a café-concert as a spectator; after accepting the position she attended the venue nightly in order to study the performers, the programme and the audience.

The reality of the café-concert as a performance space came as a shock to Guilbert. In spite of the respected reputation that had drawn her to the Eldorado, the programmes offered by its favourite performers were shaped by current conventions. To Guilbert the songs these women offered seemed 'appallingly stupid – hopelessly idiotic'; banal material that led her to a definite decision about her own identity.[33] At this point, she concluded that neither her appearance, nor her performance style, would conform to those associated with the typical female singer of the day. From her earliest café-concert appearances, Guilbert was motivated by her desire to introduce something new, something strikingly different from established programmes and conventions. In her work she determined to challenge both the performance style and the visual spectacle that audiences expected from the female singer. But this was a problematic agenda, complicated by her choices of performance form and performance space.

Chanson was a definitive French form with a long cultural history. Its legacy in poetry, chivalry and revolution and its creative resurgence as an expressive art form at the fin de siècle were classified as masculine.[34] Whilst male *chansonneurs* like Aristide Bruant achieved respect and fame as autonomous performers, popular female singers were expected to offer their audiences a straightforward combination of beautiful appearance and sentimental melodies. At the other end of the spectrum, bawdy comic lyrics made more amusing by their performance by an overweight and unattractive woman also proved popular with audiences. What was clear to Guilbert at the outset of her career was that Paris' café-concert-goers were satisfied with this predictability and limited range. Indeed, she concluded, they were 'delighted with [their appalling stupidity], and seemed to find them highly amusing'.[35]

Intervening in and breaking down the dominant imagery of the female chanson performer demanded a strategic creative approach. Drawing on the 'freakish' element, or the *phénomène*, that defined both the beauty and the bawd, Guilbert created a striking on-stage visual appearance of her own.[36] The 'twisted silhouette' that appeared in front of audiences was grounded in its visual simplicity.[37] Tall, thin, mawkish and clothed in plain, low-cut dresses with elbow-length black gloves, she claimed that 'the effect I was aiming at was that of a poster, a poster drawn in sharp clear lines'.[38] Partly motivated by the costs of providing a stage wardrobe, there was clearly more to Guilbert's image construction than concern about rising costs. As her salary rose throughout her career her dresses remained plain and simply cut, and she continued to accessorise only with coloured sashes that were fashioned out of ribbons rescued from bouquets she received from her fans and with her 'legendary' pair of long black gloves.[39]

The simplicity of Guilbert's unique and successful image focused attention on her unfashionable tall, thin and flat-chested appearance. Audiences' gazes were directed on to a form that advertised the *chansonneur*'s desire for difference.[40] For the singer, this 'Yvette of the Black Gloves' formed a separate persona, a clear second identity that served as a functional tool. Not only did it stage a distinct contrast to contemporary ideas about beauty and femininity, it also enabled the development and acceptance of a new performance style. By appearing 'highly distinguished', Guilbert argued that she 'could risk anything, in a repertoire that I had decided would be a ribald one'.[41]

To win the audience's laughter, Guilbert selected and realised recent works composed by poets and writers from Paris' artistic cabarets.

Chansons and poems by Chat Noir regulars including Xanrof (Léon Fourneau), Jules Jouy, Aristide Bruant and Maurice MacNab featured in her programme. The adoption of the *chanson grivoise*, a daring form that tackled hard-hitting themes including death, sex and poverty, and relied heavily on sexual innuendo and double entendre, gave Guilbert her edge and allowed her to achieve her aim of assembling, 'an exhibition of humorous sketches in song, depicting all the indecencies, all the excesses, all the vices of my "contemporaries", and to enable them to laugh at themselves'. [42] In spite of the risqué nature of many of the works included in her programme, the censor took little exception, and audiences licensed them: by 1911 it was accepted that 'properly considered, Guilbert is a comedienne'. [43] As with mimicry, this was a comic practice that allowed her to comment on social conventions and dramatic ideas.

It is worth noting, however, that Guilbert's innovatory ideas did not meet with immediate approval from spectators, critics or managers. As she documents in her autobiographical writings, initially her new work was received in hostile silence, or met with overwhelming mockery and heckling. [44] This was certainly the case when she toured to London on the first occasion to perform at the Empire Theatre of Varieties. Straightaway it was clear that the city's audiences and its press were unconvinced by her repertoire and performances. It was essential that Guilbert discover a way of connecting with these new audiences: an aim made difficult by the language barriers in place. The answer was discovered in the successful introduction of a popular English song in her programme. The song was 'Linger, Longer, Loo', a work made famous by Loftus in her early stage appearances and still associated with the mimic. Her performance, more than slightly reminiscent of Loftus', offered this new set of spectators something that they could identify with. If Guilbert could perform this English song well then chances are her French works were of a high and entertaining standard as well. Whilst impersonations of Guilbert remained popular with audiences throughout Loftus' career, Guilbert's first well-received London performances were largely the outcome of her imitation of Loftus' success. Although Guilbert was not an impersonator, mimicry also formed an important element of her successful stage career.

The strikingly simple stage appearance of Guilbert, and her distinctive vocal style, made her an attractive subject for the fin-de-siècle stage mimic. By the 1930s, the Loftus-Guilbert had formed an appealing and popular part of Loftus' act for four decades. Nonetheless it still dominated adverts for the mimic's appearances, suggesting its continuing appeal for spectators. The simple silhouette created by Guilbert offered Loftus a

blank canvas that supported her performance style. Existing photographic spec sheets documenting the impersonation reveal in a series of
freeze-frames how Loftus reproduced each of Guilbert's movements and
facial expressions.[45] This impersonation was not about the visual appearance of costume – as *The Penny Illustrated* noted, initially Loftus did not
use any clothing or accessories related to Guilbert – this was an impersonation that was about performance, and reflected both performers'
rejections of the contemporary iconography of female celebrity.[46] Loftus
and Guilbert's identities were fused in the Loftus-Guilbert, and it was a
fusion that was accepted by audiences. Figure 9 shows 'Miss Cissie Loftus
as Mlle Yvette Guilbert': the mimic is clothed in a pale gown and sash that
reflects Guilbert's costume. She also imitates the physical stance Guilbert
adopted in her own promotional images. The appearance is both Loftus
and Guilbert; it simultaneously emphasises the individual identities of
both, by compounding them.

Loftus had a great deal of admiration for Guilbert as a performer. In
1895, when she was midway through a long run at the Palace Theatre of
Varieties, a journalist asked Loftus if she intended to carry on doing
impressions indefinitely. The mimic replied in the affirmative, but she
also noted that if she were to opt for a new performance form she would
be interested either in acting, or appearing in 'distinctly dramatic songs
dealing with phases of English life and character'. In these dramatic songs
she imagined that she would 'endeavour to reproduce on the English stage
a performance somewhat akin to that of Mdlle. Yvette Guilbert', for she
was 'perfectly certain . . . that the English music hall audience can appre-
ciate genuinely artistic work equally with the French'.[47]

## The 'success of girlish innocence and the absence of rouge'[48]

In Guilbert's eyes beauty and talent did not naturally co-exist. Instead,
many of the female performers that fulfilled the conventions of a beautiful stage appearance did so at the expense of stage personality, magnetism
and charm. They lacked 'soul', this being the 'compound of . . . intellectual faculties' that encompassed the heart, the brain, manners, taste and
art.[49] In opposition to the image of the attractive performer offering light
entertainment, Guilbert's practice and writing offered a system of rigor-
ous and practical training that was aimed at developing and maximising
magnetism and charm. Although they worked in different forms, Loftus
and Guilbert can be aligned in many ways. Not only did both performers

9  Cissie Loftus as Yvette Guilbert

discuss and document their creative process, they were also clearly connected by their expertise at the appropriation of celebrity culture to create
strong and utilitarian on- and off-stage identities.

Loftus' celebrity image reveals the combination of mass appeal and
creative practice that ensured her success. In the review cited earlier in this
chapter, a clear contrast was set up between Loftus the star as the 'great
feature' of the evening, and the simple 'little figure' in white that appeared
on stage and commanded the audience's attention. Figure 10, an Ogden's
collectible cigarette card featuring the mimic, shows her dressed in a loose
wide gown, her hair tumbling down over her shoulders. Her gaze is
directed at the photographer but the effect is simple and innocent. Ogden's
produced their popular tabs series between 1894 and 1907, favouring
trends, events and celebrities of the time. Like Lind, Grey and Guilbert,
simplicity formed the key motif of the strong on-stage and off-stage identities that were created and promoted by Loftus. It was a deliberate, self-
promotional move: against the backdrop of metropolitan spectacle, and
amidst the numerous familiar, glamorous and larger-than-life personalities on display in society and on stage, the adoption of a seeming 'non-
identity' became a powerful tool.

Like Guilbert's appearance, Loftus' image attracted attention because
it contravened the glamorous code associated with female stage performers at the time. Initially, its simplicity seemingly rejected the contemporary culture of spectacle, but as a carefully managed identity it became a
spectacle in its own right. The satirical critic Max Beerbohm drew attention to the fashion for Loftus' brand of unglamorous spectacle in his 1894
essay 'A Defence of Cosmetics', written for the first edition of the decadent journal *The Yellow Book*. Here he argued that the fact that 'a few
months past, the whole town went mad over Miss Cissie Loftus' indicated
the 'success of girlish innocence and the absence of rouge'. 'If such things
as these be outmoded' in the current cultural climate then why, Beerbohm
demanded, 'was she so wildly popular'?[50] Beerbohm was infatuated
with Loftus, which problematises his accounts of her to some extent.
Nonetheless, the rose-tinted visions of Loftus he offers centre her talent
both as a performer and as a capable manipulator of the period's entertainment industry.

Beerbohm's accounts acknowledge the strategy that governed Loftus'
identity. On and off stage her inversion of the iconography associated
with the popular performer allowed play with current conventions and
ideas about femininity. It interrogated images and stereotypes: for whilst
her identity conformed to reassuring ideals of the passive woman and the

10  Cissie Loftus, cigarette card

trappings of gentle and simple femininity, Loftus simultaneously performed a contrasting role as a modern female celebrity. An international star was contained within the simple, white-dressed, rouge-less form: a professional woman dependent on mass culture and the public spaces of modernity. As Beerbohm noted, in spite of first impressions, 'the little mimic was not a real old-fashioned girl after all'. She 'had none of that restless naturalness that would seem to have characterised the girl of the early Victorian days. She had no pretty ways – no smiles nor blushes nor tremors.'[51]

The iconography of girlish innocence Loftus adopted supplied her with a functional celebrity image. Superficially its codes suggested an inoffensive representation of 'the ladylike'; simultaneously, it offered space for social comment and a visual blank canvas. This was perfect material for her imitative art, which was, after all, concerned with displaying the characteristics and style of *other* famous figures of the day. Loftus' act demanded that other familiar identities be combined, temporarily, with her own. In this way her non-identity became a firm identity in its own right. It acted as an image that she played out visually and verbally; an image that shielded her from any assumptions or concerns raised by some of the other celebrity figures that she presented. On occasions, the construct of female celebrity can be deliberately distanced from its inherent connection with current conventions of glamour, or an aesthetically pleasing appearance. Instead, as in the cases of Loftus and Guilbert, visual image can be complicated. Both these performers continued to frame stage performances and images within the desires of their audiences, but they offered different versions of the image of female fame that in turn altered perceptions of it.

The extent of Loftus' fame, and Beerbohm's admiration of her stage persona, reflect her success at managing the technologies of fin-de-siècle celebrity. The identity that she adopted may have been rooted in simplicity, but it required as much press exposure as some of the more glamorous personalities projected by her contemporaries; perhaps more so. Interviews with Loftus reveal her skill at utilising the press to promote and publicise her performances and herself. On 8 May 1895 *The Sketch* published 'A Very Pleasant Little Chat with Cissie Loftus', a two-page spread comprised of an interview with the mimic and several photographic images.[52] Early summer 1895 marked an important moment in the mimic's career, as she was on the verge of returning to the Palace Theatre of Varieties after eloping with the novelist and playwright Justin Huntley McCarthy, and taking an extended honeymoon. The interview with *The Sketch* was designed to both announce and advertise her return.

The publication of the *Sketch*'s interview was in the interests both of the star and the journal. For the journal it represented a feature that should sell well, for not only was it with one of the capital's most popular performers, Loftus had also been temporarily absent from the social and entertainment scenes for a while as a result of the slight scandal caused by her impromptu marriage. For Loftus the press coverage offered an opportunity to heighten her public profile as a performer, it offered exposure that could help her to secure the large Palace audiences she was accustomed to. Rather than opening the article with a headline, or the interview itself, *The Sketch* began the feature with a page of photographs. These images represented Loftus in two of her most popular impersonations, 'as a Jap' and 'as Yvette Guilbert', and 'as Cissie Loftus', an acknowledgement that her celebrity identity was another role that she played on stage and for the media. This emphasis on performance was extended in the interview itself. Turning the page the first text offered to the reader took the form of a transcript of a note that had been 'sent' by Loftus to the *Sketch*'s correspondent: 'I have not written you sooner as I have been so rushed since my return to London', the celebrity apologetically explained, 'but if you care to call today at six, I should be able to see you . . . Mrs. Cecilia McCarthy.'[53]

There are two distinct personas at work here: two off-stage performances documented in print. The first is that of the journalist, who presents herself or himself as someone who has a relationship with the star that is close enough for her to apologise for not keeping in touch. By presenting the reader with this dialogue between journalist and performer that occurs outside the interview space, the indication is that what they read is something more than the result of a scheduled encounter between two professionals. The use of the note adds a level of assumed authority to the journalist's words about Loftus; it gives the interview a sense of exclusivity. The second performance is that of Cissie Loftus herself – or Mrs Cecilia McCarthy as she now presents herself to the interviewer and by extension her fans. Loftus is courting both the press and the public in this piece, playing the role of the female celebrity that she was renowned for imitating so effectively.

A symbiotic relationship existed between the talented female mimic and the female celebrity: a relationship that was inseparably linked to the fin de siècle's cult of personality. Audiences accepted, understood and embraced the complex web of identities that enmeshed the mimic and the celebrity. They demanded Cissie Loftus, Yvette Guilbert and Cissie Loftus as Yvette Guilbert, and could interpret each accordingly.

In their intersections, and in the dialogue between them, Loftus and Guilbert's performances demonstrate one way in which this specific cultural moment supplied a uniquely fertile environment for the female celebrity performer. In 1943 the *Times'* obituary for Loftus celebrated her popularity as an imitator, before affectionately dismissing the nature of her performances as 'delightful nonsense'.[54] By the mid-twentieth century, the historical moment and cultural context that had created Loftus' performance style had disappeared. Her success had formed a facet of a society whose members were preoccupied with watching each other. In the absence of the environment out of which it emerged, its meaning was lost.

The entertainment industry fostered self-creation as a by-product of its dependence on clear visual imagery and iconography. A new metropolitan space was created in its venues, audiences and publicity; a space where performances that rejected and interrogated popular stage conventions could occur, in front of an audience accustomed to new, complex modes of spectatorship and whose interpretations of the performances that they watched encompassed many forces and factors. The final two chapters of this study consider the ways in which the on-stage acts of female celebrities utilised this new space, simultaneously embodying the popular and the experimental.

## Notes

1  *The Saturday Review*, 23 January 1892, p. 96.
2  Sylvia Grey, 'Dancing', *The Theatre*, 1 January 1898, pp. 34–7 (34).
3  ' "La Loïe" Talks of her Art', *The New York Times*, 1 March 1896, p. 10.
4  'A New Dance in Town', press clipping, Maud Madison Scrapbooks, New York Public Library, Performing Arts Division, Jerome Robbins Dance Collection.
5  Press cutting, 19 May 1892, Maud Madison Scrapbooks, New York Public Library, Performing Arts Division, Jerome Robbins Dance Collection.
6  ' "La Loïe" Talks of her Art', *The New York Times*, 1 March 1896, p. 10.
7  *The Times*, 25 October 1901, p. 4. Leyton had also performed at the Gaiety Theatre during the 1880s and 1890s.
8  *The Times*, 20 January 1896, p. 8.
9  Susan A. Glenn, *Female Spectacle: The Theatrical Roots of Modern Feminism* (Cambridge, MA: Harvard University Press, 2000), p. 75.
10  'Caricature and the Mirror', *The Penny Illustrated*, 3 June 1911, p. 9.
11  Glenn, *Female Spectacle: The Theatrical Roots of Modern Feminism*, p. 75.
12  *The Penny Illustrated*, 16 October 1897, p. 3.
13  'Caricature and the Mirror', *The Penny Illustrated*, 3 June 1911, p. 9.

14 *The Penny Illustrated*, 21 May 1910, p. 14.

15 Unidentified clipping reporting Loftus' marriage to the politician and novelist Justin Huntley McCarthy in 1894, Cissie Loftus clippings file, Mander and Mitchenson Collection, London.

16 *The Stage*, 20 June 1895, p. 11.

17 Lucy Cleveland, 'For a Woman's Sake', *The Newark Daily Advocate*, 29 May 1893, p. 6.

18 *Ibid.*

19 'Caricature and the Mirror', *The Penny Illustrated*, 3 June 1911, p. 9.

20 *Ibid.*

21 'A Chat with Miss Cecilia Loftus', *The Playgoer*, June 1902, pp. 131–3 (131).

22 Lady de Frece, *Recollections of Vesta Tilley* (London: Hutchinson and Co., 1934), p. 53.

23 *Pick-me-Up*, 21 April 1894, p. 38.

24 *Oakland Tribune*, 10 February 1939, p. 14.

25 Yvette Guilbert, *The Song of My Life: My Memories*, trans. by Béatrice de Holthoir (London: G. Harrap and Co., 1929), p. 145.

26 Cited in Douglas Gilbert, *American Vaudeville: its Life and Times* (New York: Dover, 1963, first pub. Whittlesey House, 1940), p. 141. Guilbert adopted precise terminology when she identified herself as a 'diseuse', rather than referring to herself as a singer. The use of 'diseuse' defined her style as recitation – or speak-singing. Her self-alignment with the zeitgeist through the addition of 'fin de siècle' further honed this specific description of her act. This was a performance created from a moment, a performance distinct from that offered by other female singers of the time.

27 Guilbert, *The Song of My Life: My Memories*, p. 39.

28 Alison M. Kibler, *Rank Ladies: Gender and Cultural Hierarchy in American Vaudeville* (Chapel Hill: University of North Carolina Press, 1999), p. 2.

29 Yvette Guilbert and Harold Simpson, *Yvette Guilbert: Struggles and Victories* (London: Mills and Boon, 1910), p. 97.

30 Guilbert, *The Song of My Life: My Memories*, p. 41.

31 *Ibid.*, p. 43.

32 *Ibid.*, p. 44.

33 *Ibid.*, p. 97.

34 See Barry J. Faulk, *Music Hall and Modernity: The Late-Victorian Discovery of Popular Culture* (Athens: Ohio University Press, 2004) and Peter Hawkins, *Chanson: The French Singer-Songwriter from Aristide Bruant to the Present Day* (Burlington, VT: Ashgate, 2000).

35 Guilbert and Simpson, *Yvette Guilbert: Struggles and Victories*, p. 97.

36 G. Harris, 'But is it Art? Female Performers in the Café-Concert', *New Theatre Quarterly*, 1989, pp. 334–47. See also G. Harris, 'Regarding History: Some Narratives Concerning the Café-Concert, Le Music Hall and the Feminist Academic', *The Drama Review* 40:4, 1996, pp. 70–84.

37  Jules Claretie, *La Vie à Paris, 1890–1910* (Paris: G. Charpentier et E. Fasquelle, 1890–1911), p. 198.
38  Guilbert and Simpson, *Yvette Guilbert: Struggles and Victories*, p. 101.
39  *Ibid.*, p. 104.
40  Guilbert, *The Song of My Life: My Memories*, p. 61.
41  *Ibid.*, p. 47.
42  *Ibid.*
43  *The Penny Illustrated*, 29 July 1911, p. 26.
44  Guilbert, *The Song of My Life: My Memories*, p. 48.
45  These can be seen in the Cissie Loftus clippings file, Mander and Mitchenson Collection, London.
46  'Caricature and the Mirror', *The Penny Illustrated*, 3 June 1911, p. 9.
47  Unidentified press cutting, dated 1895, Cissie Loftus clippings file, Mander and Mitchenson Collection, London.
48  Max Beerbohm, 'A Defence of Cosmetics', *The Yellow Book I*, April 1894, pp. 65–82 (67). Beerbohm also wrote about Loftus in 'Lines Suggested by Miss Cissie Loftus', *The Sketch*, 9 May 1894, p. 71.
49  Yvette Guilbert, *How to Sing a Song: The Art of Dramatic and Lyric Interpretation*, (New York: Macmillan, 1918), p. 132.
50  Beerbohm, 'A Defence of Cosmetics', p. 68.
51  *Ibid.*
52  'Miss Cissie Loftus', *The Sketch*, May 1895, Cissie Loftus clippings file, Mander and Mitchenson Collection, London.
53  *Ibid.*
54  *The Times*, 13 July 1943, p. 6.

# Part IV

## INTERSECTIONS

'I want you to see, as *I* can.' (Maud Allan)

# 7

# MOVING AWAY FROM THE MUSE: ART NOUVEAU, NATURALIST AND SYMBOLIST PERFORMANCE PRACTICE ON THE POPULAR STAGE

As successful celebrity performers created, moulded and sustained by the entertainment industry of the fin de siècle, Maud Allan, Jane Avril, Loïe Fuller, Sylvia Grey, Yvette Guilbert, Letty Lind and Cissie Loftus were cultural products. Amidst a modern, competitive market, they owed their star statuses to the large metropolitan audiences that they attracted and commanded with their individual performance styles and the strong, international celebrity identities that they shaped and promoted. However, it would be overly simplistic and reductive to conclude that the female celebrity's necessary engagement with commodity culture precluded any potential for experiment in her performance. As we have seen, performers could offer their audiences experiences that worked on many levels: experimentations with innovative social and artistic ideas that were framed within the familiar conventions of the popular stage, and the construct of the female celebrity.

The intersections that occurred between the performance practices of individual contemporary celebrities and aesthetic innovations at the fin de siècle are documented in the writings of the performers themselves. They are also revealed by many extant representations of their work in print, on canvas and in sculptural forms. As the lithograph indicates, famous representatives of the entertainment industry provided stimulating subject matter for many artists, writers, poets and commentators. The figure of the female performer populates the work of Stéphane Mallarmé, Henri de Toulouse-Lautrec, Walter Sickert and Max Beerbohm amongst others. Comparisons between the work of star performers and the output and ideas of small experimental movements were common in popular print culture. The acceptance of these associations by writers for newspapers and journals meant that they were transmitted to a large readership, and thus became standard.

The identification of Loïe Fuller as the embodiment of the central tenets of Art Nouveau design offers a clear model of how dynamic relationships between artistic movements and popular performers were established at the fin de siècle. Emerging around the turn of the twentieth century, Art Nouveau was characterised by its use of whiplash curves, organic lines, and recurrent motifs of fecundity, mysticism and femininity.[1] For many, Fuller's dances seemed to both prefigure and to fulfil the movement's aesthetics; a celebration of the shapes, colours and technology of her performances can be traced in numerous Art Nouveau works.

Commentaries on the connections between Fuller and Art Nouveau did not only occur within the specialist discourses of art and cultural criticism. Newspapers and journals also reveal an interest in the emergence of the modern style and its connection with the international dance celebrity. The accepted link between the two was humorously immortalised in the words of one disgruntled letter writer to *The Times* in 1901. Prompted by a recent exhibition at the Victoria and Albert Museum of the new 'so called' art, the epistle expressed dismay at the status accorded to both the new form and the performer. The letter writer's impression was that the museum represented an authorised collection, and that this role meant that 'those who have some taste in art will feel that it was quite unnecessary to add specimens of the "Loïe Fuller style" '.[2]

Art Nouveau was, in the eyes of this commentator, the 'Loïe Fuller style'. The two terms are interchangeable: a conclusion that rather interestingly inverts the stance adopted by later critical works concerning the movement, where Fuller is repeatedly read as the 'muse of Art Nouveau'.[3] At the fin de siècle, Fuller was not anomalous in her location as the source of aesthetic debate and ideas. As Chapter three stated, the visual effects created by the Gaiety Theatre's first generation of Skirt Dancers were admired by John Ruskin, and by Pre-Raphaelite artists including the painter Edward Burne-Jones.[4] In Jane Avril's enigmatic, solipsistic performance style contemporaries discovered similar roots and ideas to the Symbolist movement. Yvette Guilbert's performance practice and her documentation of her creative processes engaged knowledgeably and articulately with the Naturalism of Emile Zola. Responses to her chanson programmes invariably turn to a vocabulary that is strikingly similar to that used to describe the performances of contemporary Naturalist actresses. Through active performance practice, female performers blurred the distinction between aesthetics and popular entertainment.

### The danger of the 'muse': repositioning the female celebrity in fin-de-siècle experimental performance practice

It is not the case that all records of the affiliations between female popular performers and experimental aesthetics have been completely omitted from histories of the late nineteenth- and early twentieth-century stage. Studies of innovative movements frequently offer information about individual celebrities, but these brief accounts of their work are framed within a rather different set of terms to those in which it was originally created and received. Endemic in early discussions of popular culture is a pattern of invoking the 'high' cultural connections of a performer, or a style, as a means of authorising the serious consideration of historical examples of entertainment that appealed to the mass audience. This pervasive argument loosely follows the logic that, if Loïe Fuller and Jane Avril appealed to the Symbolists then they must be of 'worth' – or of interest – to the performance scholar.

In the introduction to an important and productive article on Fuller, 'Poet and Dancer before Diaghilev' (1961), the critic Frank Kermode appears to have experienced this need to justify his position and material. 'It is a highflown way of talking about an affected music-hall dancer with an interest in stage lighting', he acknowledged almost apologetically, conceding further still that, 'we should hardly venture it without the authority of Mallarmé'.[5] Mallarmé had written about Fuller's work in his essay 'Crayonné au théâtre', celebrating its power to evoke metaphors on stage. In Kermode's 'we' an established academic community is invoked: a body with fixed value judgements about performance and cultural worth. For them, Mallarmé is turned to in order to endorse their interest: a poet, who knew virtually nothing about dance, but who has been historicised as an authorised aesthetic voice.

Popular entertainment's experimental connections are highlighted in this approach. However, they are raised to serve a purpose – celebrated as a means of validating mass cultural performance – and this function is prioritised over any exploration of the experimental nature of the popular act in its own right. For women, the omnipresent figure of the muse has been equally influential. In mid-twentieth-century studies of modernist artists and movements, actresses, dancers and singers, the female performer repeatedly appears as a source of inspiration: *watched* and *interpreted* by other, creatively superior and, often by implicit definition, male artists. In this way, significant amounts of space are devoted to Avril, Fuller and Guilbert in scholarly and mainstream works on Henri de

Toulouse-Lautrec. These limited accounts reveal little – if any – interest in the strong, individual performance styles that engaged the artist's interest. Instead anecdotal narratives and much speculation about the level of emotional and physical intimacy that existed between each woman and the painter dominate them.[6]

The muse's shaping influence on the ways that the female performers portrayed by fin-de-siècle artists have been understood can be attributed, at least in part, to the cultural terrain in which they emerged. As Julie Ann Springer has noted, a dominant feminine sensibility characterises visual art from the late nineteenth and early twentieth centuries. Across forms and styles, its iconography and products reveal a 'rarefied' feminine image, an ideal that had filtered down into culture from contemporary gender ideology.[7] In this rarefied vision of femininity, woman becomes a historically specific and loaded visual signifier. She has had enduring ramifications for the study of the female celebrity and questions of autonomous performance practice, for as Fuller, Allan and Guilbert have revealed, the female stars of the fin de siècle relied heavily on contemporary ideologies of femininity to frame their on- and off-stage identities.

Coupled with a reliance on high cultural associations to authorise popular performance, the dominance of the feminine muse makes the intersections between celebrity culture and experimental performance practice complex terrain that is difficult to map and negotiate. The tendency to represent individual celebrity performers as muses, cultural idols or aesthetic ideals (à la Mallarmé) has influenced their historicisation. This, in turn, has directed our understandings of the cultural landscape of the fin de siècle: a topography that turns out to be grounded on questionable methodology. Reinforcing, or constructing, a clear divide between the popular and the experimental performance spaces of the modern city neglects understandings of the agency available to the individual female performer. The potential to present large audiences with autonomous creative work becomes obsolete in these readings, and the diverse nature of the performance practices that occurred in the modern city is lost. Contemporary intersections between Avril and Symbolism, and Guilbert and Naturalism illustrate how this has occurred.

## Jane Avril and experimental performance

In the twenty-first century the name Jane Avril is equated with the Moulin Rouge cancan. Conversely, fin-de-siècle accounts recurrently represent the dancer as an individual performer. Descriptions and reviews focus on the distinct nature of her performance, and their distinctiveness from the frenetic cancan. Accounts emphasise the uniqueness of her dancing; discovering in her public appearances 'a strange flower, with a rare scent' that could be discovered amidst the other 'gaudily coloured blooms of the dance hall'.[8] Avril's individual and creative performance practice – the 'unique' style that the critics, artists and spectators of the fin de siècle evoked through references to 'whirlwinds' and 'phantoms',[9] 'feverishness'[10] and 'melancholia'[11] – has been subsumed by the enduring popular associations between the image of the dancer and cancan.

Recovering the significance of Avril's performance demands an acknowledgement that her dances appeared amidst an entertainment industry in which the experimental and the popular could and did intersect. Many members of the Parisian avant-garde communities were attracted by her idiosyncratic style, and the innovative use of colour, fabric and movement that characterised her performance practice that was detailed in Chapter four. Poems by Pierre Charron, Arthur Symons and Raoul Ponchon, sculptures by Antoine Bourdelle, drawings and paintings by Edouard Vuillard[12] and paintings by Jean Renoir and Henri de Toulouse-Lautrec were inspired by her dance. Although these numerous representations of the dancer can be interpreted as evidence of Avril as muse, they share an attempt, across diverse mediums and styles, to capture her movement. Painters, writers and sculptors were engaged by Avril's physical performance. Their responses do not locate her as a model, instead the sense is frequently evoked that she was a distant figure, whose performance was problematic to convey.

Avril did not only feature as a popular, if difficult subject for fin-de-siècle writers, painters and artists. She also mixed with and worked alongside several of the key creative innovators who were involved in the city's experimental communities. During the 1880s and 1890s she was an active member of the Café Vachette circle: a group closely affiliated with Symbolism.[13] During this period, the artistic café, like the artistic cabaret, offered an experimental community. A space in which, as Grand-Carteret has stated, 'young people could meet, mix freely [and] speak openly of politics and literature'.[14] As the small number of women involved in the Chat Noir cabaret has already indicated, there are few documented examples of women entering these environments as creative figures, although they did frequent them in the role of models, and of muses for the artists amongst the clientele. Nonetheless, at the Café Vachette Avril engaged with an artistic and social community that included the poet Jean Moréas (1856–1910); the director of the Symbolist Théâtre d'Art Paul Fort

(1872–1960); the novelist Villiers de l'Isle-Adam (1838–89); Oscar Wilde (1854–1900), and the movement's figurehead, the poet Stéphane Mallarmé (1842–98).

After her evening performance at the Moulin Rouge, Avril regularly left the venue to spend the remainder of the evening at the Chat Noir. There, she recorded, she spent 'happy' and 'unforgettable' periods of time watching the venue's renowned shadow-theatre shows. But she was not just a spectator at the cabaret, she also performed, offering improvised dances to the piano accompaniment of cabaret regulars Charles de Sivry and Martinetti.[15] Histories do not record Avril as a member of the Chat Noir circle. However, the spontaneous, low-key performances in its artistic, counter-cultural space indicate her status within Paris' experimental environments. They also raise the question of how many other performances have not been accounted for in the cabaret space because they were unscripted performance events.

At the fin de siècle Avril's performance career had a more extensive and diverse narrative than that which remains familiar today: a narrative that interwove the constructs of the celebrity, the cancan dancer, the muse and the active experimental performer. Details of her engagement with Paris' experimental communities should not be used as a means of authorising interest in her performance; what they emphasise is the complex cultural terrain that female celebrities engaged with during this period. On the dance floor of the Moulin Rouge, Avril discovered an accessible urban space: a mass entertainment site in which improvisation, creativity and autonomous performance were possible. Reflecting and combining popular conventions, individual creative process and experimental ideas, Avril's performances were both well received and bewildering. They pleased, but they also raised questions.

As the list of regulars that attended the Café Vachette suggests, it is the Symbolist movement that supplies the clearest alignment between Jane Avril and the experimental aesthetics of the fin de siècle. In histories of the avant-garde, Symbolism is primarily affiliated with poetry, literature and the visual arts. The movement also played an important role in performance.[16] Largely driven by a rejection of the documentary, scientific representation of modern life propounded by Naturalism, the Symbolists turned to themes and motifs familiar from their predecessors the Romantics and the Pre-Raphaelites. Mythical figures, fairytale worlds, and mystical, nightmarish and occult images pepper works from the movement.

From its earliest manifestations in poetry and in art, Symbolism's followers organised themselves around the philosophical conviction that the purpose of art could be discovered in the expression of absolute truths. Reflecting the current popularity of Richard Wagner's concept of the *Gesamtkunstwerk*, they sought the fusion of all artistic mediums in their work, fostering an unprecedented level of 'interchange between painters, poets and musicians'.[17] Using a language of symbols, the movement's practitioners aimed to express their messages and meanings indirectly: transmitting them to the viewer or reader through the use of emblems and codes embedded in human consciousness. As Stéphane Mallarmé instructed, Symbolist work should 'paint not the thing but the effect it produces'.[18] Springer has identified a sense of 'solitude' 'necessary for creative introspection' at the core of the Symbolist product, an 'alienation of the artist from society'.[19] Moreover, introspection was also at the core of the specific receptive processes that the movement demanded of its viewers and readers.

Echoing historical emblems, the visual iconography that the Symbolist movement utilised recurrently relied upon the female body: women signified metaphors of truths, myths, mysteries and danger. Dominating this feminine code of symbols that enmeshed the ancient and the modern was the female dancer. On the fin-de-siècle stage, dance was the one form that fused movement, colour, rhythm and music.[20] It shifted performance away from language, and for many contemporary aestheticians and practitioners it supplied a figurative representation of the desired synthesis of the arts. It is unsurprising therefore that Avril was not the only dancer to be affiliated with, and embraced by, Symbolism. As Kermode's article reveals, the association between Loïe Fuller and the organic, feminine and fecund motifs of Art Nouveau had evolved out of the earlier connection between her performances and Symbolist aesthetics. Mallarmé and others viewed La Loïe's work as a visual and moving manifestation of synthetic fusion; the organic shapes and abstract forms she created the pinnacle of their aesthetic ideal.[21]

Fuller was a representative danseuse for many Symbolists: a metaphor for the on-stage realisation of a world of inner realities.[22] Nonetheless, she retained her status as an active performer. In 'Crayonné au théâtre', Mallarmé commented on the 'industrial achievement' of her performances. The effects of her dance may have been interpreted as poetry, but the poet simultaneously acknowledged that this was a meticulously planned and choreographed vision of mystical symbology.[23] The cultural prestige accorded to dance increased exponentially at the fin de siècle, a shift that was both important and problematic for female performers working in the form. Its improved status was founded in the conviction that dance 'represent[ed] art in an undisclosed and unspecialised form', 'a semi-abstract evocation of the abstract "art"'.[24] The dancer haunts many ideas and images related to modernist aesthetic innovation, but these repeated invocations present her as a vessel for a primitive or primeval force. Rarely is she offered as a practising performer whose work deliberately engaged with or contributed to the ideas that it is understood to mirror.

This then is the dancer of the Symbolists; the legacy handed down in the products and histories of experimental art, literature and, to a lesser extent, performance. But she did not represent widespread contemporary social ideas. In his 1898 publication *Paris dansant*, the social commentator and cultural critic Georges Montorgueil described a strikingly different vision of the female dancer when he noted that they were consulted about art and ideas in a similar way to musicians and composers.[25] There would be no purpose to consult a figure that merely acted as a vehicle for the unconscious transmission of an aesthetic ideal on aesthetic matters. What Montorgueil's statement conveys is the current conviction that the dancer's performance could be both autonomous and creative.

### *Anitra's Dance*: Jane Avril, Henrik Ibsen and Aurélien Lugné-Poe

The clear alignments between Avril's solipsistic performance style and Symbolist idealisations of the danseuse complicate her status as an active performer at the fin de siècle. Unlike Fuller, her work did not depend on modern technologies and advanced staging, forces that demanded that the self-conscious choreographer be considered alongside the representative danseuse. Rather, Avril's performances evoked the sense that her movement was, to some extent, unconscious. Following the Symbolist doctrine, if dance was the manifestation of an instinctive, pure artistic force, then Avril's solipsism supported the idea that the dancer was not an active presence. The mystical effect of her performance leant itself to an interpretation of the staging of a timeless force: a force that was responsible for conjuring up the on-stage movements and the visual effects witnessed by the spectator. The reflection of current aesthetics in Avril's performance practice distracted from its choreography, its control and the rehearsal that it involved. Against this reading of Avril's performance, her engagement with the Symbolists make it clear that she was more than a muse for the movement. The attention that the unique nature of her performance form attracted made this dancer more than a decorative representation of the movement's desired 'world of inner realities'.[26] She was dancer, not danseuse.

Having grounded their aesthetics in earlier experimentations in poetry, fiction and the visual arts, Symbolist practitioners from diverse artistic backgrounds turned to the theatre during the 1880s and 1890s. In the stage's fusion of forms they discovered an experimental medium that offered new opportunities and approaches. Most notably, complicated and often unsuccessful stagings of new plays by Paul Fort's Théâtre d'Art and Aurélien Lugné-Poe's Théâtre de l'Oeuvre aimed at achieving synthesis through the theatrical form.[27] The collaboration of performers and artists that were involved in these productions reflected not only the Symbolists' own driving aesthetics, it also reflected a wider focus on community and the exchange of ideas that had grown out of the artistic cabaret and artistic café environments of the late nineteenth century. Regardless of their success, or lack thereof, these experiments, and their engagement with and reflection of new ideas and the modern city, were to be central to modern theatre.

Aurélien Lugné-Poe's Théâtre de l'Oeuvre favoured new writing: staging 'unforgettable' 'refreshing and stimulating' productions that 'bewildered the Paris of 1893 and the years following'.[28] As identified by a recent exhibition at Paris' Musée d'Orsay, the company's productions signposted the emergence of modern European theatre.[29] Lugné-Poe had first worked with Paul Fort and the Théâtre d'Art. When the company disbanded, he established a new amateur theatre group Cercle des Escholiers. The work he chose to stage, Ibsen's *The Lady from the Sea*, suggests his interest in new writing and the transition between Naturalism and Symbolism. Encouraged by this production, he founded the Théâtre de l'Oeuvre in the summer of 1893, in conjunction with the critic and writer Camille Mauclair and the Nabis artist Edouard Vuillard.

Collaboration remained central to the programmes offered by Lugné-Poe's new company, as did the work of important new playwrights including Ibsen and the Belgian Symbolist Maurice Maeterlinck. In the company's third year, Lugné-Poe paid a visit to Joseph Oller, now the sole manager of the Moulin Rouge. His intent was to secure Avril a temporary release from her dance-hall contract. He had cast the dancer as Anitra in the company's forthcoming production of Ibsen's *Peer Gynt* (part of their fourth season of work), and he needed her time for rehearsals and performances.[30] The important opportunities and characters Ibsen's plays offered to actresses and managers have been a source of interest for both his contemporaries and later scholars, but on this occasion his work supplied the vehicle for one of Paris' most popular stars to appear on the experimental stage.[31]

Peer Gynt was staged by the Théâtre de l'Oeuvre on 11 and 12 November 1896, at the Nouveau Théâtre, Paris. Such short runs of experimental productions were standard; a practice that in itself represented a striking difference to the long runs that funded the spectacular productions of the mainstream stage. In comparison to much of the company's other work, relatively little has been written about the production of this early Ibsen play. Its location in their output explains this: Peer Gynt was sandwiched between two theatrical events that have attracted significant interest and commentary. In February 1896, Lugné-Poe had staged the first public performance of Oscar Wilde's Salome. One month after Peer Gynt, the company offered Alfred Jarry's iconoclastic Ubu Roi: a performance securely located in the annals of theatre history.[32] Records of attendance for Lugné-Poe's company reveal that Peer Gynt and Ubu Roi were equally successful productions in their day. They earned the company the same amount of money.[33] In an auditorium filled with the same number of spectators who heard Père Ubu's now mythological 'merde', Jane Avril performed her vision of Anitra's Dance to Edvard Grieg's score.

In his memoirs Lugné-Poe notes that Avril knew the entire script of the play by heart by the time the production opened. In spite of her small role, she had been a constant presence at the play's rehearsals, watching and following its development. Her performance as Anitra was, he concluded, inimitable. Nobody else could have performed the dance as powerfully.[34] Interestingly Avril's autobiographical writings do not discuss the amount of time that she devoted to Lugné-Poe's rehearsals. Instead she states that her Anitra's Dance was spontaneous, utterly unchoreographed.[35] Avril's own recollection connects her performance with the Symbolist's ideal of the dancer, in a Symbolist theatrical production. By subscribing to the aesthetic construct of the danseuse, experimental performance space could be discovered, and innovation and experiment acknowledged and approved.

The forces contained within, and propagated, by the fin de siècle's cultural moment were malleable: flexible enough to enable Avril to bridge the modern metropolitan spaces of the popular and the experimental. As an active performer, the dancer actively engaged with the Symbolist movement, employing and maintaining her complicated position within their aesthetics. Her significance has been overshadowed by the ways in which her performances evoked ideas about femininity and constructs of the dancer. However, to evoke is not necessarily to conform, a strategy that is also clear in the work of Yvette Guilbert.

## The 'tragic realism' of Yvette Guilbert[36]

Whilst Avril was dancing regularly at the Moulin Rouge and the Chat Noir, Yvette Guilbert's performances were popularising Naturalist stage practice with large audiences in Paris and London. Defined by the novelist, playwright and critic Emile Zola, Naturalism invested in the scientific presentation of human nature. Characters determined by their genetic inheritance and the environments in which they existed dominated Naturalist narratives. The movement permeated literature and the visual arts during the second half of the nineteenth century, as well as entering into theatrical experimentation with the work of André Antoine's company the Théâtre Libre.[37]

Naturalism's precepts were not universally popular with audiences, artists or critics. Indeed Symbolism's reflection of a world of mystical, inner realities is often classified as a response to the prescriptive nature of its empiricist approach. By the time Guilbert's fame peaked, many considered Naturalism to be outdated, inconsistent with the forces and tensions of the fin de siècle. Its critics included the writer Marcel Proust, who dismissed the work of both the *chansonneur* and the movement in an article written for *Le Mensuel*. In her performances 'she makes one think of naturalism', he explained, 'a naturalism that is already outdated and so very different in any case from the art of today'.[38] In spite of these examples of Naturalism's diminishing dominance of experimental aesthetics, the movement continued to be associated with the popular *chansons grivoises*: the form that connected Yvette Guilbert with Montmartre's fashionable cabaret scene, and the well-publicised antics of the Chat Noirists.

Guilbert's sell-out performances at Paris' mainstream café-concerts and at international variety venues, staged experimental language and new forms in popular venues, in much the same way as Bruant had done at Les Ambassadeurs and the Eldorado. Incongruous though it may seem, versions of Naturalism became accepted themes in a spectacular entertainment industry. In *Popular Theatre: A Sourcebook*, Joel Schechter has cited Guilbert's chansons amongst 'some of the most innovative and provocative performances in the twentieth century [which] began less glamorously in small cabarets, nightclubs and vaudeville houses'. The relatively short list also features Laurie Anderson, Edith Piaf, Tristan Tzara, Bertolt Brecht and the Marx Brothers.[39]

Accounts of Guilbert's work concur with this location: as *The Times* stated, her performances became 'the standard by which the work of the diseuse is to be judged'.[40] Although aided by the haunting, half-sung, half-spoken nature of her vocal performance that is captured in existing phonograph recordings, it remains difficult to reconstruct the impact that Guilbert's performances had on fin-de-siècle audiences. Standing almost completely still on stage, and relying on facial expression and vocal technique, the diseuse demanded her audiences' attention and focus. Following the tradition of the *chanteur* and the aesthetics of Naturalism, creation of character was prioritised over attractive vocal technique. Guilbert's success did not lie in her musicality, but depended upon her 'ability to put across a song through expression, timing, innuendo, and the knowing use of gesticulation'.[41]

Guilbert offered her audiences a new performance of the chanson: 'her art is in her expression, rather than the tone or quality of her voice', one reviewer concluded.[42] The term 'singing' seems inadequate to convey the innovative nature of Guilbert's vocal performance style: the distinctive cacophony of noises that pleasantly assault the ear is too diverse and at times too disorientating to be contained within the term. Contemporary responses consistently emphasise the impact of her unique approach. To hear her 'is to experience the gamut of the emotions', noted one American spectator; not to have heard her 'means that one has not witnessed the possibilities of dramatic interpretation'.[43] Chanson and theatre coalesced when Guilbert took to the stage; her spectators were engaged by her performance, not by her appearance or the beauty of her singing style.

In *How to Sing a Song: The Art of Dramatic and Lyric Interpretation*, published in 1918, Guilbert defined her understanding of the chanson as a performance form. She used the metaphor of painting. 'Singers of songs' should think of themselves as painters, she explained: their 'voices are there to color the story, the picture we exhibit' to the audience. Their aim should be to 'help the public to see with their eyes what they hear with their ears'.[44] As this advice suggests, *How to Sing a Song* is a practical manual that documents Guilbert's performance practice, defines her aesthetics and provides instruction in the art of chanson. In its pages, the art of the chanson is broken down, each element is described and set facial expressions that correspond with emotions are documented in photographs. Chapter seven is dedicated to the importance of characterisation, and emphasises the need for realistic material to produce a successful chanson. Entitled 'The Development of the Faculty of Observation', Guilbert stresses the need for the singer to study human nature, and to incorporate this knowledge into a directed performance. On stage the *chansonneur* must be both 'observer' and 'philosopher'.[45]

Léon Xanrof's 'Le Fiacre', one of Guilbert's 'universal hits', tells the tale of lovers who have arranged an assignation in a Paris cab.[46] Whilst they are together, the woman is recognised by her elderly husband who happens – rather fatefully – to have taken a walk along the same street. Enraged at his wife's infidelity, the husband runs after the carriage, only to fall. With the affair discovered, the cab moves on with the two lovers still inside, leaving the husband prone on the street. Guilbert's performance of the narrative interspersed her droll account of the mercenary behaviour of the lovers, with the amusing, lilting and infectious cries of the cab driver driving the horses forward: 'Hu' dia! Hop la!' The cries give the chanson a sense of rhythm, lighten its mood, evoke the atmosphere of a central Parisian street, and temporarily distract the audience's full attention from the immoral attitude to marriage documented by the song.

Exposing the flippant attitude to adultery that she witnessed in the fin-de-siècle city amidst a light comedic framework enabled Guilbert to achieve one of her main aims. The international popularity of chansons like 'Le Fiacre' reflected her aim to expose 'all the brazen impunities, all the excesses, all the vices of my contemporaries' in song, whilst still offering her audiences 'an exhibition of humorous sketches in song' and the 'opportunity of laughing at themselves'.[47] It was a successful combination, as one reviewer noted 'the parade of gaiety serves only to emphasise the quintessential tragedy of the chanson; one laughs, but one laughs, as it were, at one's own agony'.[48] Her chansons draw attention to the humour and the tragedy of quotidian life in the fin-de-siècle metropolis and to the audiences' culpability in these events. Where much of the output of the entertainment industry glossed over the realities of contemporary poverty and morality, Guilbert brought them right into the heart of her performances: a tendency identified by Laurence Senelick when he described her performances as 'naturalistic to the max'.[49] The brutal nature of much of Guilbert's material was central to the intense experience that her spectators record, but this was nonetheless a modified Naturalism: a Naturalism that was slightly sweetened by the light touch of comedy.

Jules Jouy's 'La Soûlarde', another of her audiences' favourites, was a much darker chanson. An overtly political songwriter and author, Jouy uses this chanson to expose the poverty and cruelty that defined modern metropolitan life for the social outcast. Its lyrics describe the life of a drunken old woman pursued by stray dogs and mocked by street children. Guilbert's interest in character worked well with this material; as Edmond de Goncourt noted in her performances of 'La Soûlarde', 'the diseuse reveal[ed] herself as a great, a very great tragic actress who can wring your very heartstrings'.[50] When the Charpentiers invited Guilbert to perform before Zola at their publishing house, the site of many evening functions and entertainments, she spent much time deliberating which chanson to perform. Eventually she decided on 'La Soûlarde'. For Guilbert, this was the work that epitomised her aim to present Naturalism in chanson. Recalling the performance, she noted that 'Zola's round, staring eyes followed my every gesture, and I could feel his very critical attitude.' Nonetheless, by the end of the chanson she was convinced that Zola had found her character as 'tragic' as she had 'hoped'.[51]

Naturalist aesthetics and the *chansonneurs* of the Chat Noir may have supplied Yvette Guilbert with the basis of her style and a significant proportion of her material. What contemporary responses evince, however, is that the performances she created from them were unique. As one reviewer noted, Guilbert has 'something new to say, and she has discovered a new way of saying it'.

> She sings, for instance, songs of Aristide Bruant, songs which he had sung before her, and sung admirably, in his brutal and elaborately careless way. But she has found meanings in them which Bruant, who wrote them, never discovered, or, certainly, could never interpret . . . she has invented new shades of expression, she has discovered a whole new method of suggestion.

Realism, the account concluded, is 'Yvette Guilbert's domain; she sings it as no one has ever sung it before [and brings it] into the sphere of art'.[52] Aligning her work with Naturalism, and using characterisation and facial expression, gave Guilbert access to this new performance style. Both the content of her programmes and her approach to singing were experimental and radical. They were based on a methodology, a self-conscious performance practice.

On stage, Yvette Guilbert's distinctive body, skilful characterisation and expression and striking new material developed and changed ideas about what female performers did, what they were expected to do and, eventually, what they could do. The new modes of expression recognised in her performance depended upon her physical individuality and her unconventionality as a female celebrity. Her fame forced reviewers, critics and managers to change their approach to female singers, and to extend the vocabulary they employed to describe female singers of this period. Physically and vocally challenging conventional images of conventional femininity 'she . . . invented new shades of expression' and 'discovered a whole new method of suggestion'. Guilbert's performances became the benchmark that other performances – in song and in acting – were compared with, and judged against.

## Art of an 'essentially modern kind'[53]

In a pattern that mirrored the disruption of the defined separate spheres of the public and private that had been systematically assigned to men and women, the rapid growth of the fin de siècle's commodity culture and leisure industries unsettled existing demarcations between the physical and conceptual spaces that were attributed to the entertainment industry and to artistic innovation. Current ideas about these two areas of expressive activity became more closely aligned, on occasions existing symbiotically and interconnecting in works of performance, literature and art. Examples of these intersections on the stage reveal crucial and historically specific practices and aesthetics that drove experimental modern performance forward, not only in cabaret culture and in small theatre companies, but also amidst the programmes offered by music halls, dance halls and variety theatres in the modern city.

The cultural products and the performances of Jane Avril, Symbolism, Yvette Guilbert and Naturalism illustrate this interweaving of popular conventions and experimental aesthetics. As celebrities with strong identities, the audiences that watched these internationally famous performers did not interpret their work as visually mirroring the aesthetics that it engaged. Neither were they understood to be muses: passive figures of an essential femininity that inspired the creation of other artistic products. Avril and Guilbert were recognised as creative practitioners, performers who were actively engaged with current experimental ideas, and who initiated new ways of thinking about their specific forms of the dance and the chanson.

Historical understandings and analyses of popular performance during the late nineteenth and early twentieth centuries have tended to focus on the cultural status of venues, the reclamation of individual performers, and the urban and economic geographies and spatial configurations of the entertainment industry. Within this historiographical context, retrospective approaches have neglected to tackle the fin de siècle's alignment of individual popular entertainments and experimental aesthetic ideas. But this connection *was* acknowledged and accepted by its contemporaries: celebrity performers document interactions between the popular and the experimental in their writings, and the links are also recorded in the works of practitioners associated with the period's new movements.

In the experimental performances of Jane Avril and Yvette Guilbert it becomes clear that the construct of female celebrity at the fin de siècle, like the ideologies it partially emerged out of, was complex and malleable. Both of these performers reshaped ideas about the form that they worked within, remoulding the figure of the dancer and the singer respectively. Due to the high-profile cultural presence of active and creative female performers on the popular stage, ideas about celebrity underwent a continuous process of modification at the fin de siècle: an interrogation brought about by performances that remodelled and extended what the construct could offer to the creative practitioner. As the popular and experimental became more closely aligned, a space opened out amidst celebrity culture for the creation and staging of new performance modes: new forms of 'art' that were acknowledged alike by the press, the public and artistic communities to be of an 'essentially modern kind'. Whilst this chapter has focused on the intersections between experimental artistic groups and individual celebrity performers, connections between the experimental and the popular can also be traced in specific roles and themes on the popular stage. It is possible to see this very clearly in the use of one of the most renowned of the roles on offer to the popular star at the time, the Judean princess and uber-femme fatale, Salome.

## Notes

1 See Debora L. Silverman, *Art Nouveau in Fin-de-Siècle France: Politics, Psychology, and Style* (Berkeley: University of California Press, 1992).
2 '"L'Art Nouveau" at South Kensington', *The Times*, 22 August 1901, p. 5.
3 Gabriele Fahr-Becker, *Art Nouveau* (Cologne: Könemann Verlagsgesellschaft, 1997), p. 100.
4 In his early twentieth-century history of dance, Reginald St Johnston refers to an anecdote contained in the recently published biography of Edward Burne-Jones written by his widow. She recounts the moment when her husband and Ruskin discussed the famous Skirt Dancer and fell, 'into each other's arms in rapture upon accidentally discovering that they both adored her'. Reginald St Johnston, *A History of Dancing* (London: Simpkin, Marshall, Hamilton, Kent), p. 171.
5 Frank Kermode, 'Poet and Dancer before Diaghilev', *Partisan Review* 28, 1961, pp. 48–75 (75).

6 This situation has improved over the past decade with the publication of David Sweetman's study *Toulouse-Lautrec and the Fin-de-Siècle* (London: Hodder Headline, 1999) and Julia Frey's cultural history *Toulouse-Lautrec: A Life* (London: Weidenfeld and Nicolson, 1994).

7 Julie Ann Springer, 'Art and the Feminine Muse: Women in Interiors by John Alexander White', *Women's Art Journal* 6:2, 1985–86, pp. 1–8 (1).

8 'Le Sourire de Jane Avril', *Comedia*, 24 April 1924, Jane Avril clippings file, Site Richelieu, Bibliothèque Nationale de France.

9 Raymond Escholier, 'La Mélinite chez Toulouse-Lautrec', *Journal*, 2 March 1938, Jane Avril clippings file, Site Richelieu, Bibliothèque Nationale de France.

10 'Le Sourire de Jane Avril', *Comedia*, 24 April 1924, Jane Avril clippings file, Bibliothèque Nationale de France.

11 'Jane Avril est morte', *Petit Parisien*, 3 February 1943, Jane Avril clippings file, Bibliothèque Nationale de France.

12 Vuillard, 'Jane Avril with an Umbrella' (c1890–91).

13 Jane Avril, *Mes mémoires* (Paris: Phébus, 2005), pp. 40–1.

14 Jean Grand-Carteret, cited in Mariel Oberthur, *Cafés and Cabarets of Montmartre* (Salt Lake City: Peregrine Smith, 1984), p. 12.

15 Avril, *Mes mémoires*, pp. 63–5.

16 See Gunter Berghaus, *Theatre, Performance and the Historical Avant-Garde* (Basingstoke: Palgrave Macmillan, 2003) and Frantisek Deak, *Symbolist Theatre: The Formation of an Avant Garde* (Baltimore: Johns Hopkins University Press, 1993).

17 Philippe Jullian, *The Symbolists* (London: Phaidon, 1973), p. 9.

18 This instruction first appeared in an 1864 letter to Henri Cazalis, cited in Wallace Fowlie, *Mallarmé* (London: Dennis Dobson, 1953), p. 125.

19 Springer, 'Art and the Feminine Muse: Women in Interiors by John Alexander White', p. 3.

20 See Sylvia Ellis, *The Plays of W. B. Yeats: Yeats and the Dancer* (Basingstoke: Macmillan, 1995); Dee Reynolds, 'The Dancer as Woman: Loïe Fuller and Stéphane Mallarmé', in Richard Hobbs (ed.), *Impressions of French Modernity* (Manchester: Manchester University Press, 1998).

21 Stéphane Mallarmé found Fuller's work inspirational, and used her as the central figure of his writing on dance in 'Crayonné au théâtre', in Betrand Marchal (ed.), *Stéphane Mallarmé: oeuvres complètes* (Paris: Gallimard, 1998), p. 307.

22 See Felicia McCarren, *Dance Pathologies: Performance, Poetics, Medicine* (Palo Alto, CA: Stanford University Press, 1998); Mary Ann Caws, 'Dancing with Mallarmé and Seurat (and Loïe Fuller, Hérodiade and La Goulue)', in Peter Collier and Robert Lethbridge (eds), *Artistic Relations: Literature and the Visual Arts in Nineteenth-Century France* (New Haven and London: Yale University Press, 1994), pp. 291–320.

23  Mallarmé, 'Crayonné au théâtre', p. 307.

24  *Ibid.*, p. 49.

25  Georges Montorgueil, *Paris dansant* (Paris: Libraire L. Conquet, 1897), p. vi.

26  Springer, 'Art and the Feminine Muse: Women in Interiors by John Alexander White', p. 1.

27  See Patricia Eckert Boyer, *Artists and the Avant-Garde Theatre in Paris* (Washington, DC: National Gallery of Art, 1998).

28  Gertrude R. Jasper, 'Lugné-Poe and the Oeuvre', *French Review* 15:2, December 1941, pp. 127–34 (an article written in response to the news of Lugné-Poe's death).

29  'Le Théâtre de l'oeuvre, 1893–1900: naissance du théâtre moderne', at the Musée d'Orsay, Paris, 12 April–3 July 2005.

30  Avril, *Mes mémoires*, pp. 83 and 96.

31  See Elizabeth Robins, *Ibsen and the Actress* (London: Hogarth Press, 1928); Sally Ledger, 'Ibsen, the Actress and the New Woman', in Angelique Richardson and Chris Willis (eds), *The New Woman in Fiction and in Fact: Fin-de-Siècle Feminisms* (Basingstoke: Palgrave, 2000), pp. 79–93.

32  See Henri Behar, 'Alfred Jarry et le théâtre français à la fin du XIXe siècle', in Hub Hermans, W. E. Krul and Hans van Maanen (eds), *1894: European Theatre in Turmoil, the Meaning and Significance of the Theatre a Hundred Years Ago* (Amsterdam: Rodopi, 1994), pp. 41–54; Martin Esslin, 'Theatre of the Absurd', *Tulane Drama Review* 4:4, May 1960, pp. 3–15; Roger Shattuck, *The Banquet Years: The Origins of the Avant Garde in France, 1885–1918* (New York: Vintage, 1968).

33  These records were on display at the Musée d'Orsay exhibition, 'Le Théâtre de l'oeuvre, 1893–1900: naissance du théâtre moderne'. They are generally available at the Archives de la Société des Auteurs et Compositeurs Dramatiques, Paris.

34  Aurélien Lugné-Poe, *La Parade*, vol. 2: *Acrobaties: souvenirs et impressions de théâtre, 1894–1902* (Paris: Gallimard, 1931), pp. 171–2.

35  Avril, *Mes mémoires*, p. 104.

36  'Yvette Guilbert', *The Saturday Review*, 16 May 1894, p. 21.

37  See C. Schumacher, *Naturalism and Symbolism in European Theatre, 1851–1918* (Cambridge: Cambridge University Press, 1996); C. D. Innes (ed.), *A Sourcebook on Naturalist Theatre* (London: Routledge, 2000).

38  Marcel Proust, 'Pendant le carême', *Le Mensuel* 5, February 1891, p. 9.

39  Joel Schechter (ed.), *Popular Theatre: A Sourcebook* (London: Routledge, 2003), p. 5.

40  *The Times*, 24 May 1938, p. 14.

41  Laurence Senelick, 'Text and Violence: Performance Practices of the Modernist Avant-Garde', in James M. Harding (ed.), *Contours of the Theatrical Avant-Garde: Performance and Textuality* (Ann Arbor: University of Michigan Press, 2000), pp. 15–42 (21).

42 *Centralia Enterprise and Tribune*, 21 December 1895, p. 10.

43 *The Chronicle*, 5 March 1920, p. 10.

44 Yvette Guilbert, *How to Sing a Song: The Art of Dramatic and Lyric Interpretation* (New York: Macmillan, 1918), p. 4.

45 *Ibid.*, p. 103.

46 Yvette Guilbert, *The Song of My Life: My Memories*, trans. by Béatrice de Holthoir (London: G. Harrap and Co., 1929), p. 175.

47 'Yvette Guilbert', *The Saturday Review*, p. 21.

48 Anon., *John Bull's Trip to Paris* (London: Favourite Publishing, 1900), pp. 36–7.

49 Senelick, 'Text and Violence: Performance Practices of the Modernist Avant-Garde', pp. 21–2.

50 Edmond de Goncourt, cited in Guilbert, *The Song of My Life: My Memories*, p. 164.

51 *Ibid.*, p. 159.

52 'Yvette Guilbert', *The Saturday Review*, p. 21.

53 *Ibid.*

# 8

# AVANT-GARDE SALOMANIA: 'THE MOST FAMOUS DANCING GIRL IN HISTORY'?[1]

In 1913, Frankfort Sommerville's *The Spirit of Paris* appeared on the shelves and in the mail order catalogues of bookstores in London and around the world. Part authoritative city-guide, part cultural commentary, the work affirmed that the French capital's dominance of the modern world's tourist and entertainment industries continued well into the twentieth century. After celebrating the city's architecture, bohemian atmosphere and popular sites, Sommerville devoted Chapter eleven of the book, 'The Artists', to a light-hearted discussion of the fin de siècle's most pervasive, seductive and enduring construct of femininity: Salome, 'the most famous dancing girl in history'.

Salome was a product of the social, cultural and aesthetic forces of the late nineteenth and early twentieth centuries. Her story can be found in the New Testament gospels of Matthew and Mark. Princess of Judea, the virginal daughter of Herodias and the stepdaughter of Herod, Salome was infatuated with the prophet John the Baptist, who had been captured and imprisoned in the palace grounds by her stepfather. Herod, in the meantime, was also infatuated; not with his wife, but with his stepdaughter. Consumed by his overpowering lust, he demanded that Salome dance for him: a demand that she initially refused, conceding only when she was offered anything that she desired in return for her performance. Fuelled by her own resentment of John the Baptist's repeated, humiliating rejections of her pledges of love, and encouraged by her mother, who had herself been insulted and enraged by the prophet's widespread accusations that she was an adulteress, Salome agreed to dance on the grounds that her reward was the head of the prophet. She danced, her demand was met, and she was presented with John the Baptist's bleeding head on a silver platter. In this short, biblical narrative, a tale that revolved around a myth of dangerous and erotic femininity, the fin de siècle discovered a new craze and a burgeoning industry: 'Salomania'.[2]

Framed as an extended discussion of the artistic creations of one of his friends, in 'The Artists' Sommerville tells the reader of a talented painter whose professional career was governed and impeded by his relentless obsession with Salome. Dating back to 1897, the artist's desire to realise the Judean princess on canvas had completely 'possessed his soul', driving him to produce endless images of her, and to neglect all other areas of his work. In 1913, over a decade and a half after his initial attempts at the project, he still had not achieved a perfect representation, and had finally admitted that he was unable to 'cease painting her until he reache[d] his ideal'.[3] In his fixation, Sommerville's painter spoke for many other artists, performers and spectators of the day. Salome entranced society and culture at the fin de siècle. Her power, beauty and danger were widespread obsessions that aligned the outputs of European and American entertainment, literature and art: as Rhonda K. Garelick has commented, 'Salomania touched virtually every aspect of popular and "High" culture, from Symbolist verse to theatrical parodies, from night club reviews to department store fashions for women.'[4]

Created by the forces of celebrity culture, and born out of the current discourses that surrounded performance, orientalism, sexuality and gender, Salome was a motif of the zeitgeist. In novels, on the stage, in the popular press and in the visual arts she became a fictional personality. She simultaneously figured as the idol and destroyer of painters, poets and playwrights – a modern role adopted by many female performers – and the source of a mass trend. Moving between myth, muse, performer and product, Salome's cultural position was inherently ambiguous. On her dancing body the multiple meanings signified by female corporeality in contemporary visual culture were inscribed.

Stage incarnations of the most famous dancing girl in history interwove, reinforced and undermined ways of thinking about the relationships between women, performance, eroticism, madness and celebrity. Choosing to take on the role of Salome meant opting to interpret and present a powerful myth of femininity. A myth that was both archaic and current; a myth ostensibly based on a powerful dancing woman with murderous intent, but one that also clearly reflected much more widespread anxieties concerning changing ideas about gender at the fin de siècle. Yet, in spite of this complicated and difficult context, many female performers did choose to play Salome, much to the consternation of some cultural commentators who queried why,

> the most gifted, the most famous, the most adorable of all the women the modern stage has known have vied with one another, quarreled and fought, studied and labored day and night, for the honor of reincarnating in their lissome forms the soul of that vanished Salome?[5]

Toni Bentley has recently suggested that the role's appeal lay in the power that it offered: that 'when men offered her [the female performer] the power – sexual power –' of Salome, the 'Salome woman simply said "I'll take it" ', 'wiggled onto the stage', 'made Salome their own' and proceeded to have a 'fine time'.[6] However, contemporary responses to the role by female performers suggest that the practicalities, practices and conventions of playing the Judean princess were somewhat more complex than this approach indicates.

Salome cannot be understood in isolation from the entertainment industry that made her a household name. On the stages of the modern city she was a complex and multivalent symbol of femininity: powerful, yes; sexual, definitely. Nonetheless making Salome one's own remained a difficult process for the female performer to negotiate. Playing this compound construct of famous dancing girl, dangerous biblical princess and threatening, independent modern woman necessarily involved more than staging a biblical tale, or offering audiences a performance of the dance of the seven veils. It formed an active decision to engage with the same discursive fields that were being explored and publicised by academics, scientists, anthropologists, physicians and psychologists. The world of popular science had made these areas of investigation familiar to wide audiences, and any characterisation of Salome was inevitably loaded with their meanings and conclusions.

This final chapter considers the representations of Salome that were created by Maud Allan and Loïe Fuller between 1895 and 1910. Working within the role, the two celebrity performers commented on, and intervened in, the ideas, iconographies and assumptions embodied by the Judean princess. Their appropriations met with varying degrees of success, but the choices that they made concerning this quintessentially fin-de-siècle character fleshed out Salome and transformed her from a mythical construct into an important role for the female performer.

## From the easel and the page to the boards: staging Salome

Across literature and drama, histories of Salome in performance have tended to begin with Oscar Wilde's one-act tragedy *Salome*. Thematically and compositionally this poetic drama, written in French during the autumn of 1891 whilst Wilde was based in Paris, is infused with the ideas and motifs of the bohemian communities that he mixed with in the city. One such influence that has been widely noted and commented on was that of the Symbolist circle of painters, artists, poets, playwrights, directors and performers Wilde became involved with. Dramaturgically, the movement's experimentations with the aesthetics and possibilities of performance can be traced in the short tragedy's lyrical and mystical structure, and in the specificities of its setting, staging and speech.[7] However, it is not solely in these areas that the legacy of Symbolism is evident; it is also present in *Salome*'s content and characterisation.

Symbolism's long-standing preoccupation with manifestations of the femme fatale supplies one clear source for Wilde's beautiful, seductive and deadly leading lady. Although it took until the late 1880s for Symbolism to be formalised as an aesthetic movement, Salome had been closely associated with the poetic and artistic products that reflected, and experimented with, the group's emerging ideas during the 1870s and early 1880s. The presence of the Judean princess haunts the work of the poet Stéphane Mallarmé, the writers Gustave Flaubert and Joris-Karl Huysmans, and the painter Gustave Moreau. Moreover, Sommerville's descriptions of his friend's (the artist) paintings draw on this connection: they are packed with recognisable Symbolist motifs. The numerous Salomes that populate the canvases are characterised by their 'fiendish, haunting beauty', a beauty that is 'sometimes languorous and sensual, sometimes devilish and cruel and vindictive'. Her body repeatedly appears enwrapped with flowers: mystical, Symbolist flowers. Blooms that evoke '[Charles Baudelaire's] *fleurs du mal*': 'great scarlet passion flowers, that glower like a crime; purple blooms that hang heavy with lust; huge moon-flowers like visions of evil'.[8] Semiotically, the fin de siècle's Salome was a Symbolist icon, omnipresent in the movement's own aesthetic development and in popular literature and entertainment.

Wilde's *Salome* was intended for the stage, but stringent British censorship meant that the play existed solely as a published script for a significant length of time. In June 1892, Sarah Bernhardt became the first performer to rehearse for Wilde's vision of the role, in preparation for a planned production at the Palace Theatre of Varieties in London. Although she was to remain closely associated with the Judean princess in the minds of her contemporaries, and in histories of the play and the character, Bernhardt was to become the most famous actress never to play Salome.[9] Whilst in rehearsal, the play was refused a licence by Edward Pigott, the current examiner of plays. Pigott justified his decision to censor the work on the grounds that Wilde's drama contravened an archaic dictate by staging biblical characters and narratives. It seems more likely, however, that his refusal was actually the result of the drama's seductive and radical content.

Whatever the motive behind Pigott's ban on *Salome*, it effectively called the London-Bernhardt production to a halt. It was to be nearly another four years before Wilde's script was staged, and then the production did not occur in England, but in France. Taking into account the play's genesis, it is perhaps more appropriate that Salome's first stage appearance occurred in Paris, in a small-scale production by Aurélien Lugné-Poe and the Théâtre de l'Oeuvre on 11 February 1896. Performed at the Comédie Parisienne, *Salome* featured in the company's programme nine months before their production of Ibsen's *Peer Gynt* in which Jane Avril was to appear, and reflected Lugné-Poe's growing interest in staging the new and diverse aesthetics associated with theatrical Symbolism. Nearly a decade later, in 1905, London witnessed a private performance of the play, but the city had to wait until 1931 for a public production of the work.

Wilde's *Salome* has attracted significant attention for many reasons. Its connection with Sarah Bernhardt, the timing of the play's appearance in relation to Wilde's trial, the censor's ban, Aubrey Beardsley's Art Nouveau illustrations designed to accompany the script, and its reading as a queer narrative have all appealed to historians, scholars and Wilde fans. 'Wildean' has become a common adjective against which to judge and describe performers playing Salome and images of the Judean princess. This close connection between Wilde and Salome is, however, largely the result of the processes of history. Amidst the entertainment industry of the fin de siècle, and in the cultural references and imaginations of its audiences, the short play had relatively little direct impact on the ideas that aligned femininity and Salome. Significantly more high profile and influential were the dancers, actresses and singers who took on the role on the mass stage.

As we already know, Sarah Bernhardt was the 'one woman in the world' whose performances and celebrity Maud Allan desired to rival.[10] Like Allan, Fuller had seen 'this wonderful fairy of the stage' early in her own career, when the famous actress had toured America. In *Fifteen Years of a Dancer's Life, with Some Account of her Distinguished Friends*, Fuller claimed the Divine Sarah as a friend, a fan and a collaborator. This was, to some extent, true, if characteristically a little embellished. Bernhardt had seen Fuller dance at the Folies-Bergère on several occasions during the 1890s, and later sought the dancer's advice on the lighting effects for a production of *La Belle au bois dormant* (*Sleeping Beauty*) in 1907.[11] Yet while Bernhardt opted to avoid the role of Salome after Pigott's ban, Allan and Fuller were attracted to the figure, in spite of the problems that it raised. Susan A. Glenn has noted that Bernhardt's decision not to play the Judean princess:

> remains something of a mystery, although one of her biographers [Taranow] speculates that the character of Salome was so blatantly lustful, decadent and unsympathetic – so incapable of generating pity – that in the end even an actress as brazen as Sarah Bernhardt ultimately found the role too risky for her career.[12]

Was Salome one step too far over the ideological frontiers of femininity; too risky a role for even the established and adored fin-de-siècle celebrity? For the popular performer, it appears not. Loïe Fuller offered two versions of the tale during her career and, although they did not achieve the same level of mass popularity as other works in her programme, neither did they provoke accusations of brazenness, or claims that with this creative subject matter she was experimenting on risky territory. In the same way, before the associations between Maud Allan, the Independent Theatre and Oscar Wilde's play were fuelled by the social and political climate of international conflict that led to the 1918 Pemberton Billing affair, Allan had danced Salome for many years. The role had brought her public and critical support and acclaim, and had not hampered her recognition as a 'dramatic artist', or her ability to perform in other works or styles.[13]

It is clear that Sarah Bernhardt was a master of self-promotion and image construction, and the conclusions that Taranow reaches for the actress' decision to distance herself from the role of Salome appear both logical and distinctly possible. However, this fin-de-siècle construct of dangerous femininity could also be used as a role that the female performer could work within, as it was by Allan, Fuller, Gertrude Hoffman, Ida Rubenstein and many of those other women vying and labouring to present Salome on stage. Their versions reflected the time, space and culture in which they were created; Glenn has emphasised the specific appropriations of Salome that occurred in America, where she served not only 'as an important vehicle of female expression and sexualized assertiveness', but also as a 'malleable tool for playing out the [period's] anxious comedies of gender and race'.[14]

Internationally, the most famous dancing girl in history was not consistently 'lustful, decadent and unsympathetic'; on stage, in the hands of celebrity performers, she could also be interrogative, imprisoned and sympathetic. In Salome new visions of femininity could be anchored, visions that contested and disrupted the ideas associated with the femme fatale.

## 'A vision of the theatre of the future': Loïe Fuller's Salome[15]

Fuller first staged the Salome myth in 1895 when her fame remained at its peak across Europe and America, and she returned to the tale over a decade later in 1907.[16] Whilst the two works based on the tale do not feature amongst the most popular of her creations, they contain the dancer's most explicit on-stage challenges to contemporary ideas about femininity, performance and sexuality. Although La Loïe had already achieved celebrity status, and had her performances received with widespread artistic and critical acclaim and approbation, she remained determined to create a convincing Salome on stage. But, even for an international superstar, this did not prove to be an easy task. Fuller's preoccupation with Salome required that she modify her performance practice, prompting a shift away from her established and celebrated domain as the fin-de-siècle's Fairy of Electricity.

Staging the Salome myth demanded that Fuller engage with theatrical dance – a choreographed performance that was explicitly framed by narrative and character. This was a marked change from her characteristic works that did not depend on a narrative structure to convey or explain the aesthetic experience that they offered to the spectator. At its most fundamental level, the theatrical language Fuller employed in the two Salome works differed from the characteristic abstract material that audiences expected from her. The experimental process that this involved raised critical and aesthetic questions from many who normally supported and promoted her work, yet Fuller persisted with her ideas about the mythological role.

It is not difficult to explain or contextualise Fuller's interest in the figure of Salome: the celebrity dancer's own ambiguous cultural location and her scholarly and creative interests in ancient dance forms coalesced in the conventions and ideas embodied in the role. Classical Terpsichore fascinated Fuller, and in interviews she repeatedly drew attention to the hours that she had spent ensconced in Paris' museums and libraries studying texts, images and artefacts that documented early dance styles. This research led her to the conclusion that her own modern performance style shared its roots with the ritualised series of movements performed by the women of ancient cultures.[17] Her creative practice had, she argued,

> only revived a forgotten art, for I have been able to trace some of my dances back to four thousand years ago: to the time when Miriam and the women of Israel – filled with religious fervour and rapture – celebrated their release from Egyptian captivity with timbrels and with dances.[18]

Part aesthetic conviction, part careful manipulation of a respectable celebrity identity, Fuller's publicised interest in biblical herstory is not the only discernible source for her attempts to create a Salome for herself. The two versions of the myth that she produced were also driven by an acute awareness of the currency of their subject matter. Fuller was intrigued by the ways in which the figure of Herodias' daughter had been adopted and transformed by her headlong encounters with contemporary anxieties about gender, performance and society at the fin de siècle. Salome existed for Fuller as a 'fascinating subject'; an unstable subject that 'inspite of its antiquity' was nonetheless 'a most fascinating novelty' of the day.[19] Contemporary incarnations of Salome as the representative fatal woman – particularly the products of the Symbolist and Art Nouveau movements with which her performances were aligned – existed at the core of Fuller's own interpretation of the role. Their cultural dominance rendered them powerful images that could be easily appropriated and employed as a backdrop against which the dancer could explore her own creative agenda. In Fuller's Salomes modern women and archaic figures from herstory were entwined to create a new vision of femininity.

Judged against the near universal popularity of her performance, Fuller's 1895 staging of the Salome tale was not a success. Indeed it could be classed as a relative failure. Although *The Era* argued that of all La Loïe's previous works this was the most 'vivid' or 'striking', overall the thirty-minute piece proved unpopular with the majority of critics, and many of those who generally celebrated her style were quick to speak out against the new direction that this production indicated.[20] Shortly before beginning this first version of *Salome*, Fuller had been working with Armand Silvestre (the main supplier of music-hall librettos for the Folies-Bergère) who had commented that – for him – her performances evoked visions of the Judean princess dancing before Herod. It was an idea that engaged Fuller, and she commissioned Silvestre, in collaboration with Charles H. Meltzer, an American writer, the popular composer Gabriel Pierné and the designer Georges Rochegrosse, to create a 'pantomimic dance-play' for her, based on the tale of Salome.[21] The result was a one-act, lyric pantomime, staged at the Comédie Parisienne between 4 March and 27 April 1895. Featuring as the second half of a double bill of entertainment, Salome combined narrative and mime with five completely new dances: *The Black Dance, The Sun Dance, The White Dance, The Rose Dance* and *The Lily Dance*.

In their pantomime Fuller, Silvestre and Meltzer made important interventions into the tale of Salome. A year before the first stage appearance of

Wilde's lethal princess, La Loïe offered Paris a version of the fin de siècle's anti-heroine that was not motivated by obsession and revenge. Instead her 1895 Salome was a virginal figure who had converted to Christianity after hearing John the Baptist's message. At the Comédie Parisienne Herod alone ordered the prophet's death: his act provoked by his anger at John the Baptist, and his frustrated lust for his stepdaughter. After fruitlessly pleading for Herod's mercy, Salome danced in a final attempt to save John the Baptist's life. Her sacrificial act failed, and the prophet was beheaded. The dance concluded with the Judean princess falling into a state of unconsciousness at the sight of the prophet's head being brought to the King on a silver platter. Fuller's first Salome was patently not a femme fatale: she was portrayed as a victim of ideas about women in patriarchal societies, a victim of her own corporeality, and a victim of the power of her motion.

## Sweating and fleshy Salomes

*Salome* (1895) did not only draw on Fuller's skills as an actress, it featured other actors. In another radical move, the dancer was not the only performer on stage shaping and dominating the performance. Also missing was the standard black-draped box space that she generally installed to perform within. For *Salome* she decided upon a more conventional staging, selecting a realistic and colourful panorama of the city of Jerusalem as the play's backdrop. In keeping with this turn to more conventionally theatrical devices, she also swapped her usual diaphanous gowns and veils for stylised versions of biblical dress.[22] Part of Fuller's motivation in the creation of this work was to reveal her talents as an actress to her new fan base: it was, after all, an area in which she had much experience and ability, but not an area that formed part of her 1890s' star identity.[23] Visually *Salome* was an entirely different experience for Fuller's spectators. Parisian audiences were not accustomed to La Loïe as an actress. La Loïe the international celebrity was a dancer, and this new work confused her spectators' expectations.

This experiment with the fusion of acting and dancing in dance-pantomime proved to be a problematic change of approach for Fuller. But in many ways these problems can all be traced back to the ways in which the role and the production disrupted her established on-stage celebrity identity. In addition to the unexpected form taken by the material, the Comédie Parisienne was a far smaller venue than the Folies-Bergère. This difference in the spatial dynamics of the venue, and the relative lack of distance between the audience and the performer, made it significantly more difficult for Fuller to affect her renowned self-transformation on the stage. The on-stage fairy that Parisian audiences anticipated when they went to see Fuller proved difficult to invoke in this biblical pantomime. As Davinia Caddy has rightly noted, 'Salome was all flesh and hungry for blood, a woman – not a butterfly or the sun – in close up, in the here and now.'[24]

Ethereal fairies and fleshy Salomes do not sit comfortably together: a tension that goes some way to explaining the critic and self-appointed theatrical expert Jean Lorrain's negative response to the work. Fuller's previous dances had enraptured and fascinated Lorrain, yet in his response to the 1895 *Salome* he condemned her as, 'heavy, ungraceful, sweating'. The exertion of the performance, and the closeness of the performer to the spectator left him able to see 'her makeup running, at the end of ten minutes of little exercises'. For Lorrain this was a case of far too much woman, far too much in the 'here and now'.[25] The corporeality that Fuller's physically gruelling performances all depended on was too close for comfort in this work.

Lorrain's reaction is frequently cited as an example of a more general Parisian response to Fuller's first *Salome*, but the pantomime was not completely rejected by its audiences. Frustratingly for Fuller, it was not her characterisation of the Judean princess that proved popular; it was the five new dances that she had integrated into the mimed narrative that attracted spectators to the Comédie Parisienne. Indeed two of the works that she had devised for the production – *The Lily Dance* and *The Sun Dance* (later to become known as *The Fire Dance*) – were to become the most popular and most frequently represented of the many dances that she choreographed during her career. Out of the context of the original narrative and the dance-pantomime, however, they became rather different works.

The stunning visual effects of *The Fire Dance* continued to thrill Fuller's audiences well into the twentieth century. The work depended on the dancer's own patented under-lighting techniques to stage a vision of the performer amidst a conflagration. Red and orange tongues of flame gradually licked upwards before the spectators' eyes and eventually consumed the dancer entirely. As Fuller noted, on more than one occasion the dance provoked a real sense of panic in some audience members, who became convinced that the on-stage inferno was real and demanded that the act was stopped in the interests of safety.[26] Within *Salome* the sight of the consumption of the dancer by flames was intended to act as more than a spectacular diversion in its own right. But this conflagration of lust, this hellish inferno, was not appreciated as a symbolic element of a larger work by most of those who saw it, it was simply Fuller performing in a way that was familiar to her audiences, and it was welcomed by them.

The 1895 *Salome* ran for just eight weeks, and was not revived. Even during this short run the pantomime itself was completely cut on several occasions, and instead Fuller simply performed her five new dances in succession. Shortly after *Salome* closed at the Comédie Parisienne, she toured to America and to Europe. In both countries she again only presented the dances, with no attempt to stage the framing dance-pantomime. When Armand Silvestre had said that Fuller's dancing reminded him of Salome's dancing for Herod he was referring to her characteristic performance style. Her intervention into the role, and representation of Salome as a chaste version of the femme fatale whose power came from her lack of power was not what he had in mind. In this performance Fuller collided with her celebrity identity, and with contemporary ideas about the dangerous woman and, on this occasion, her audiences remained unconvinced.

## Loïe Fuller as Salome: take two

In 1907 Fuller returned to the character of Salome, staging a production of Robert d'Humières' *La Tragédie de Salomé* in November. This work was not only warmly received by the critic Jules Claretie, who described the performance as offering 'a vision of the theatre of the future', it was also embraced by the Parisian feminist journal, *Femina*, which welcomed a new interpretation of the figure that had rapidly become an iconic representation of the period's threatening femininity. With this early twentieth-century Salome, Fuller achieved something more than with her mid-1890s' version. The main reason for this difference seems to be that in the *Tragédie de Salomé* the chaste virgin had gone: this Judean princess was unquestionably a femme fatale. In commissioning the score from Florent Schmitt her direction was that his composition must mirror the 'demonic phantasmagoria' that were occurring on the stage.[27]

For this second attempt at staging the tale of Salome Fuller had selected the Théâtre des Arts, again a relatively small venue in Paris. On the production's opening night the theatre was filled with figures from the city's artistic and literary communities; it seems that the experience of withdrawing her first Salome pantomime from her repertoire had caused Fuller to realise that new work of this nature demanded a different kind of audience, at least for its first influential performances. In the 1907 interpretation of the role Fuller used more elaborate costumes than she had in 1895, ornamented with feathers and designed in brightly coloured fabrics. Nonetheless her dresses in this production again differed from the voluminuous silks that swathed her body during her characteristic dance performances. These costumes emphasised Fuller's corporeal presence on stage in another presentation of a fleshy Salome. The lighting effects were spectacular, requiring the use of over 600 individual lamps and numerous projectors, and again new dances formed an important part of the work. *The Dance of Pearls, The Snake Dance* (performed to an accompaniment of the dancer reciting wild incantations), *The Steel Dance, The Peacock Dance, The Silver Dance* and *The Dance of Fear* were all built into the narrative.

Fuller's 1907 return to Salome was simultaneously more controversial and more conventional. Her performance actively engaged with the female dancer as an exotic, erotic, corporeal and threatening signifier in order to invert this familiar representation. Audience members reportedly shrieked with terror at sections of the performance; but it was also interpreted as a new form of dance theatre.[28] Performed after the first staging of Wilde's play in Paris, and amidst the continuing cultural high profile of Salome, this second version was, in part, a response to the increasing number of artistic, musical and theatrical visions of the figure. Aged forty-five, Fuller charged the role of Salome with fatality and sexuality, but controversially. At the conclusion of the piece the shadow of the older dancer's naked, and plump, form was framed on a screen at the back of the stage: *La Tragédie de Salomé* confronted many of the ideas of eroticism and objectification that we associate with the image of the Judean princess.

Presenting a version of Salome that conformed to prevailing concepts and images of eroticism and exoticism would have been simple for Fuller. Lorrain's description of one of her dance performances illustrates how these works were founded on the visual spectacle and motifs of veiling, covering and uncovering.

> Loïe Fuller does not burn; she oozes brightness, she is flame itself. Standing in a fire of coals, she smiles and her smile is like a grinning mask under the red veil in which she wraps herself, the veil which she waves and causes to ripple like the smoke of a fire over her lava-like nudity . . . this motionless and yet smiling nakedness among the coals and the fire of heaven and hell for a veil. I have already talked elsewhere of the morbid voluptuousness of the Dance of the Lily . . . In a sea of shadows a grey, indistinct form floats like a phantom and then, suddenly, under a beam

of light, a spectral whiteness, a terrifying apparition. Is this a dead woman who has been crucified, hovering above a charnel-house, her arms still held out under the folds of her shroud, some huge, pale bird of the polar seas . . . how poignant, how superb, how overwhelming and frightening, like a nightmare induced by morphine or ether.[29]

In many of Fuller's works audiences were presented with images that reflected many of the ideas associated with the construct of Salome at the fin de siècle, perhaps more so than the works she dedicated to the figure. With Fuller's fame and the popularity of her performance style in mind, it seems logical to conclude that the use of motifs of organicism and exoticism to invoke the essential and threatening sexuality that was encapsulated in the figure of Salome would have increased the popularity of her stagings of the myth.

### 'Loïe Fuller's Salomé is destined to add a Salomé unforeseen of all the Salomés that we have been privileged to see'[30]

Fuller's radical decision to reject the accepted vision of Salome through the eradication of the visual associations between her performance style, the mystical and the dance of the seven veils represents a development of her staging of ideas surrounding gender and performance. Rather than present a conventional incarnation of Salome, Fuller offered a definite female corporeal presence on stage. Both her versions of the myth drew attention to the embodied humanity of Salome; chaste or evil, they interrogated the image of the femme fatale as an untenable mélange of sexuality and fatalness in a spiritual, disembodied form. In the construct of Salome the dancer's creative agenda, personal aesthetics and celebrity status intersected. She seems to have understood the role to be the culmination of her solo work, choosing to conclude *Fifteen Years of a Dancer's Life, with Some Account of her Distinguished Friends* with Jules Claretie's glowing account of the final rehearsal of her 1907 production of the *Tragédie de Salomé* (excerpts from which were cited earlier in this section).

Claretie's description is of the dancer in the moment of creating a performance; rather than the dancer framed in the trappings of the performance itself. Fuller appeared without costume and without make-up, he noted. Before him 'it was Salomé dancing, but a Salomé in a short skirt, a Salomé with a jacket over her shoulders, a Salomé in a tailor-made dress'.[31] Other descriptions of Fuller's work are more adulatory, and more flattering; but it was this account that Fuller chose to leave with her readers. An account of the female performer, actively and explicitly engaged in the creative process and the deconstruction of a mythical construct.

The disruption and reinterpretation of the Salome myth offered by Fuller in 1907 – thirteen years after she had begun regularly performing on the Parisian popular stage – revealed how dance within the arena of mass culture offered an opportunity for the female performer to actively engage with and modify contemporary female archetypes. The malleability of visual icons within the popular culture of the time is supported by Jules Claretie's conviction that, 'I can well believe that Loïe Fuller's Salomé is destined to add a Salomé unforeseen of all the Salomés that we have been privileged to see.' [32] Salome acted as a vessel for ideas and anxieties: Loïe Fuller had as much power to change the meaning(s) of this vessel as Gustave Moreau, Stéphane Mallarmé or Oscar Wilde. The show may not have lasted past the 1907–8 season, but that does not undermine its importance as a commentary on contemporary ideas about sexuality, performance and women.

## 'I want you to see, as I can': Maud Allan's vision of Salome [33]

As Chapter two briefly explored, Maud Allan's *The Vision of Salome* became such a familiar product in the international culture of the early twentieth century that the celebrity, the performance and the role were inseparable from each other. [34] For her audiences, Allan owned Salome. In the contemporary press her performances of the role were offered as a benchmark against which other versions were judged. Moreover, throughout history Allan has continued to own Salome. Or perhaps Salome has owned Allan? There is, undoubtedly, something about the 'most famous dancing girl in history' that maps neatly on to our historicised understandings of Maud Allan. The extant imagery of her dance reveals iconography that is undeniably both appealing and 'fin de siècle'; iconography that has shaped visualisations of gender, fame and popular performance practice at the time. Whilst Fuller's celebrity identity caused her problems in creating versions of the role, Allan's can be seen to have trapped her in a slightly different way.

Whilst the role of Salome secured Maud Allan's phenomenal celebrity, her belief that her audiences and critics repeatedly misunderstood the meaning of *The Vision of Salome* troubled her throughout her career. The final chapter of Allan's autobiography, *My Life and Dancing* (1908), is devoted to an extensive discussion of her most renowned work, *The Vision of Salome*. It is a piece, she opens by stating, that she was 'glad' to have been asked to write, as it 'gave an opportunity to explain what is the meaning that I wish to convey' in the dance. The 'meaning' of the work she argued has 'been dimly guessed at by some, hinted at by others, and perhaps more widely misunderstood by what in Jacobean times were called "the groundlings" than any dance in my collection'.[35]

Like Fuller's 1895 stage version of the Salome tale, Allan's *The Vision of Salome* departed from the biblical narrative and from other contemporary representations of the uber-lethal woman. Allan's autobiography fills in Salome's history – the Judean princess is given an in-depth backstory, a story that Allan claims to know from imagination, or perhaps memory. The action takes place amidst the 'sombre splendour' of 'pillared halls' hung with 'rare draperies'. Salome, just fourteen years of age, has been summoned by Herod to attire herself in 'jewelled robes' and 'delicate fabrics' to dance for his dinner guests, an order that 'half terrifies and half enchants her'. She dances, and then is offered anything she desires by Herod, but is afraid of the lust in his eyes and runs to her mother. Comforted in Herodias' arms, she is then instructed by her to ask for the head of John the Baptist as her prize. She obeys, and the head is brought in on the platter; Salome is overwhelmed with guilt and flees back to her apartments.

This is the point at which Allan's *The Vision of Salome* begins. The dance is based on 'the awful moments of joy and of horror which she has just passed through. Alone in the gloom the poor child's fancy assumes dominion over her.'[36] The dance itself was a return to the action of the biblical tale, its haunting of Salome's mind: *The Vision of Salome* was a dreamscape. Allan's description of the dance in *My Life and Dancing* is lengthy, but its meticulous detail makes it worth citing in full:

> Slowly to the strains of the distant music, reminiscently she raises her willowy arms. The movement thrills her whole slender frame and she glides as if in a dream. A voice whispers 'Your duty – your duty! Does not the child owe obedience to its mother?' On, on – wilder and more reckless than ever before! She sees once more the greedy glittering eyes of her stepfather – she hears again the whispered praises and encouraging words of her mother, and Salomé, child that she is, realises a power within her and exults. She sees again her triumph approach, her swaying limbs are in readiness to give way, when suddenly from out of the sombre death-still hall the wail of muffled distress – and a pale, sublime face with its mass of long black hair arises before her – the head of John the Baptist! There is a sudden crash. She is horror stricken.

Salome then takes hold of the head, embraces it and breaks into a 'mad whirl' of childish dancing that ends with her collapsing exhausted prone on to the 'cold grey marble'.[37] She may have convinced her audiences, but some critics complained that this reclamation of the Judean princess marked 'about the limit of female interpretation of the motives of fiendish little Salome'.[38] But even this gentle mockery in the press is not without an element of admiration. Allan's chapter is structured as a carefully devised, and articulately expressed, theatrical scenario. One that she hopes will enable her readers to see the work 'as I can', and for the most part it seems that this is what she achieved.[39]

That Allan appeared on stage 'almost naked' and 'kissed the waxen mouth of the severed head and caused a scandal' is, and was, only a small part of a much bigger narrative concerning women, performance and the entertainment industry.[40] Maud Allan's celebrity, and particularly her role as Salome, locates her as an extreme example of the tension caused by considering fin-de-siècle examples of female corporeality in the entertainment industry. But, as we have discovered, although the twenty-minute *The Vision of Salome* was a popular element of her programme, Allan's dancing was more varied and influential than the attention that has been devoted to this one work suggests. Historically the concern raised by what the *Times*' reviewer labelled as feminism of a more agreeable order has been influential. In the reductive understanding of Allan as Salome, an example of Grosz's feminist somatophobia can be seen in action.

The theatrical nature emphasised by Allan in this rationale and synopsis was also acknowledged by contemporary reviewers. 'Languorous' and 'seductive'[41] Allan's performance may have been but, as *The Times* stated, it was also a performance that contained great 'dramatic force', a 'dance of many passions . . . allurement, exultation, rage, fear, despair, even exhaustion'. There was 'no extravagance or sensationalism' about the piece; 'even when crouching over the head of her victim, caressing it or shrinking from it in horror, she subordinated every gesture and attitude to the conditions of her art'.[42] Audiences believed and invested in Allan's sympathetic staging of Salome.

## Is Salome in all of us?

The basic narrative that Allan employed to frame her detailed account of Salome's character and dance was that of the transition between girl and woman. Familiar conventions, mythological tropes and humanising elements are combined in this short piece of writing to produce what is, to a large extent, a coming of age story. Allan supplies an emotional narrative that women can empathise with; her vision of the dancing princess makes a fin-de-siècle 'every-woman' of Salome. This is a familiar and misled young woman, rather than a freakish and evil threat. On stage, Allan presented a controversial subversion of the role of the fatal woman that drew on many of the same questions and critiques as Fuller's 1895 presentation of the role. If 'Hedda is in all of us' was the cry of the matinee attendee of the mid-1890s, perhaps 'Salome is in all of us' was one representative sentiment that Allan desired to invoke in her female-dominated afternoon performances at the Palace Theatre of Varieties.[43] But she got away with it on the variety stage at this time; she shaped the role in a way that she could not when working with Wilde's heroine in a period that had undergone an extreme cultural shift.

The inherent problems raised by working within the fin de siècle's most explicit construct of dangerous femininity are made clear in responses to Loïe Fuller's and Maud Allan's performances, and reinforced by the other difficulties they encountered in their persistent engagements with the role. For the female performer these problems span the late nineteenth and the early twentieth centuries, affecting performances between 1895 and 1910: difficulties that predated and followed Wilde's *Salome*. Nonetheless their clear celebrity identities made Salome a role that they could approach and engage with. Elaine Showalter has stated that 'women who have performed the part have also had a difficult time, finding themselves conflated with Salome in the public mind and condemned for lasciviousness and perversity',[44] whilst Virginia Keft-Kennedy has noted that the Salome dancers of the late nineteenth and early twentieth centuries 'acted out an illicit femininity'.[45] But the clear image associated with the celebrity performer, an identity that remained present in the on-stage performance, frequently conflicted with the idea of 'lasciviousness' or 'illicit femininity'; it had, after all, been created to offer a respectable identity that played with the current conventions of femininity.

Gaps existed between the two powerful social and ideological constructs of Salome and the female celebrity. These images of femininity were not stable, and their fluctuating meanings opened up spaces in which performers could interrogate contemporary ideas. Sometimes these interventions were successful; sometimes they were not. However, the processes they involved, the attraction of the role of Salome that they reveal and their reception are enlightening regardless of their success as attractions. Fuller, Allan and Salome were images: icons that were the product of a specific historic moment that were interpreted by mass audiences, and aesthetic and avant-garde communities. Allan's and Fuller's performing celebrity bodies as Salome need to be read amidst this nexus of ideas and forces.

The practices of Allan's and Fuller's Salome performances conflicted with the cultural identity inscribed on the Judean princess by the fin de siècle. Neither performer reflected the mythological female image employed as a vessel to purge and contain ideas about dangerous femininity, instead both were engaged in a process of manipulating it. Their writings about the role document their struggle to vindicate and to authorise their own interpretations of Salome, revealing that the creative process was of as much interest to them as the products that it led to.

The cultural constructs of Salome and the female celebrity were inherently linked at the fin de siècle. They were facets of the same collation of anxieties, forces and ideas. The role offered female performers the opportunity to develop and present their own version of an archaic biblical woman, to stage a mythological figure that had been irreversibly integrated into the fabric of the cultural moment, but whose meaning there was still open to change. Salome's fluctuating meanings were complicated further still by the period's celebrity culture. For Fuller and Allan, playing 'the most famous dancing girl' in history as a performer who was in competition with her for that title moulded the unique terrain on which their performances – engagements of the two constructs – took place. The two dancers translated and changed the tale of Salome, staging versions of the myth that reflected their own cultural moment. The 1895 *Salome, La Tragédie de Salomé* and *The Vision of Salome* placed the fin de siècle's most famous dance and dancer amidst a new cultural narrative of gender and change: a cultural narrative that Allan's and Fuller's performances, fame and celebrity identities were instrumental in shaping.

## Notes

1 Frankfort Sommerville, *The Spirit of Paris* (London: Adam and Charles Black, 1913), pp. 106–7.
2 See Michael Kettle, *Salome's Last Veil: The Libel Case of the Century* (London: Hart-Davis, 1977).
3 Sommerville, *The Spirit of Paris*, pp. 106–7.
4 Rhonda K. Garelick, 'Electric Salome: Loie Fuller at the Exposition Universelle of 1900', in J. Ellen Gainor (ed.), *Imperialism and Theatre* (London: Routledge, 1995), pp. 264–98 (285).
5 *The Syracuse Herald*, 2 April 1911, p. 88.

6  Toni Bentley, *Sisters of Salome* (New Haven and London: Yale University Press, 2002), p. 34.

7  See J. L. Styan, *Modern Drama in Theory and Practice*, vol. 2: *Symbolism, Surrealism and the Absurd* (Cambridge: Cambridge University Press, 1983); K. E. Toepfer, *The Voice of Rapture: A Symbolist System of Ecstatic Speech in Oscar Wilde's Salome* (New York: P. Lang, 1991); Frantisek Deak, *Symbolist Theatre: The Formation of an Avant Garde* (Baltimore: Johns Hopkins University Press, 1993).

8  Sommerville, *The Spirit of Paris*, p. 107.

9  See Kerry Powell, *Oscar Wilde and the Theatre of the 1890s* (Cambridge: Cambridge University Press, 1990).

10  Maud Allan, *My Life and Dancing* (London: Everett and Co., 1908), p. 36.

11  Loïe Fuller, *Fifteen Years of a Dancer's Life, with Some Account of her Distinguished Friends* (London: Herbert Jenkins, 1913), pp. 84–100.

12  Susan A. Glenn, *Female Spectacle: The Theatrical Roots of Modern Feminism* (Cambridge, MA: Harvard University Press, 2000), p. 98.

13  *Weekly Dispatch*, 4 November 1917, p. 6.

14  Glenn, *Female Spectacle: The Theatrical Roots of Modern Feminism*, p. 99.

15  Jules Claretie, cited in Fuller, *Fifteen Years of a Dancer's Life, with Some Account of her Distinguished Friends*, p. 282.

16  For discussions of Fuller's two versions of Salome see: Bentley, *Sisters of Salome*; Rhonda K. Garelick, *Rising Star: Dandyism, Gender and Performance in the Fin de Siècle* (Princeton: Princeton University Press, 1998); Garelick, 'Electric Salome: Loie Fuller at the Exposition Universelle of 1900'; Felicia McCarren, 'The "Symptomatic Act" Circa 1900: Hysteria, Hypnosis, Electricity, Dance', *Critical Inquiry* 21:4, Summer 1995, pp. 748–74.

17  Unidentified press clipping, Maud Madison Scrapbooks, New York Public Library, Performing Arts Division, Jerome Robbins Dance Collection.

18  Loïe Fuller, cited in Mrs M. Griffith, 'Loïe Fuller – The Inventor of the Serpentine Dance', *Strand Magazine*, May 1894, pp. 540–5 (540).

19  'An Interview with Loïe Fuller', *Black and White*, 25 January 1896, pp. 118–20 (118).

20  *The Era*, 9 March 1895, p. 11.

21  'An Interview with Loïe Fuller', *Black and White*, p. 118; 'La Dompteuse des flammes: "Je sais tout" interviewe la Loïe Fuller', *Je sais tout*, February–July 1907, pp. 325–31 (330).

22  I am indebted to Richard Nelson Current and Marcia Ewing Current's, *Loïe Fuller: Goddess of Light* (Boston: Northeastern University Press, 1997) for its in-depth, well-researched discussions of both Fuller's versions of *Salome*.

23  *Ibid.*, p. 81.

24  Davinia Caddy, 'Variations on the Dance of the Seven Veils', *Cambridge Opera Journal* 17:1, 2005, pp. 137–58 (145).

25  Cited in Current and Current, *Loïe Fuller: Goddess of Light*, p. 83.

26 Autobiographical material, MS, The Loïe Fuller Collection, New York Public Library, Performing Arts Division, Jerome Robbins Dance Collection.

27 Jann Pasler, cited in Caddy, 'Variations on the Dance of the Seven Veils', p. 140.

28 Current and Current, *Loïe Fuller: Goddess of Light*, p. 180.

29 Jean Lorrain, cited in Philippe Jullian, *The Triumph of Art Nouveau: Paris Exhibition 1900* (London: Phaidon, 1974), pp. 89–90.

30 Jules Claretie, cited in Fuller, *Fifteen Years of a Dancer's Life, with Some Account of her Distinguished Friends*, p. 288.

31 *Ibid.*, p. 287.

32 *Ibid.*, p. 288.

33 Allan, *My Life and Dancing*, p. 120.

34 For discussions of Maud Allan's Salome see: Felix Cherniavsky, *The Salome Dancer: The Life and Times of Maud Allan* (Toronto: McClelland and Stewart Inc., 1991); Amy Koritz, 'Dancing the Orient for England: Maud Allan's "The Vision of Salome"', *Theatre Journal* 46:1, 1994, pp. 63–78; Judith R. Walkowitz, 'The Vision of Salome: Cosmopolitanism and Erotic Dancing in London, 1908–1918', *American Historical Review* 108:2, 2003, pp. 337–76; Kettle, *Salome's Last Veil: The Libel Case of the Century* (London: Hart-Davis, 1977).

35 Allan, *My Life and Dancing*, p. 120.

36 *Ibid.*, pp. 121–4.

37 *Ibid.*, pp. 125–6.

38 *The Syracuse Herald*, 2 April 1911, p. 88.

39 Allan, *My Life and Dancing*, p. 120.

40 Amanda Fernbach, 'Wilde's Salome and the Ambiguous Fetish', *Victorian Literature and Culture*, 2001, pp. 195–218.

41 *The Daily Telegraph*, press cutting, Maud Allan clippings file, Mander and Mitchenson Collection, London.

42 *The Times*, 10 March 1908, p. 5.

43 The actress Elizabeth Robins recalls this being one female spectator's response to Ibsen's *Hedda Gabler: Ibsen and the Actress* (London: Hogarth Press, 1928), p. 18.

44 Elaine Showalter, *Sexual Anarchy: Gender and Culture at the Fin-de-Siècle* (London: Virago, 1992), p. 159.

45 Virginia Keft-Kennedy, '"How Does She Do That?" Belly Dancing and the Horror of a Flexible Woman', *Women's Studies* 34, 2005, pp. 279–300.

# AFTERWORD

The on- and off-stage performances that have been considered in this volume occurred between the mid-1880s and 1910, concurrent with the emergence of the international female popular performer. In this context, Maud Allan, Jane Avril, Loïe Fuller, Sylvia Grey, Yvette Guilbert, Letty Lind and Cissie Loftus rapidly became visual representatives of metropolitan commodity culture: icons of their time. Simultaneously, they were creative, autonomous professional performers: products and active agents of the fin de siècle's burgeoning entertainment industry.

The fin de siècle's celebrity culture was established and fuelled by a rapid growth of metropolitan centres and the development of an international network of cultural communications. Its spaces supplied individual performers with access to varying levels of space, independence and creative freedom. Amidst city environments that were preoccupied with spectacle and display, the investigation of high-profile and unapologetic moments of female corporeality on stage is unarguably problematic. Nonetheless, to follow the assumption that an embodied act of performance that occurs in a specific cultural moment necessarily complies with and wholly reflects its constructs and ideologies is to align oneself, perhaps unwittingly, with Charles Zidler's statement that popular female performers were the 'women who bring us in money'.[1]

A consideration of the celebrity management, the performance practices and the diverse careers of these seven performers makes the unrealistic nature of Zidler's statement clear. His words formed the opening citation for this volume, because the simplistic position that they represent, and the implications concerning the objectification and disempowerment of the female performer that are inherent within them, remain more dominant than they should within the histories of performance of the late nineteenth and early twentieth centuries. The performances offered by Allan, Avril, Fuller, Grey, Guilbert, Lind and Loftus, and the celebrity images that they created and promoted, reveal that over the thirty years that spanned the end of the nineteenth century female celebrities presented important and innovative new ideas about performance, as well as remoulding the construct of the female performer.

The larger project that this book engages with is a work in progress: there is much more work to be done before we fully understand the richness of entertainment that was offered on the fin-de-siècle popular stage, and the space that it offered to experimental performers. With this in mind, I have chosen not to conclude this volume. It is my hope that the consideration of active, creative female performers within their professional context offered here will further open up the terrain of the popular stage for performance historians interested in practice and image; that it will shift interest and focus from biographical studies. Ultimately I hope that it will initiate the process of acknowledging the presence of the female celebrity, *non*-actress in the experimental performance of the late nineteenth and early twentieth centuries. A history from which she has been largely, and schematically, excluded.

## Note

1  Cited in Yvette Guilbert, *The Song of My Life: My Memories*, trans. by Béatrice de Holthoir (London: G. Harrap and Co., 1929), p. 35.

# BIBLIOGRAPHY

Abdy, Jane, *The French Poster: Chéret to Cappiello* (London: Studio Vista, 1969)

Adams, William Davenport, *A Book of Burlesque: Sketches of English Stage Travestie and Parody* (London: Henry and Co., 1891)

—— *A Dictionary of the Drama* (London: Chatto and Windus, 1904)

Alexandre, Arsène, 'French Posters and Book Covers', *Scribner's Magazine* 17:5, May 1895, pp. 603–14

—— 'Le Théâtre de la Loïe Fuller', *Le Théâtre*, 11 August 1900, pp. 23–5

Allan, Maud, *My Life and Dancing* (London: Everett and Co., 1908)

Anon., *The ABC Guide to London* (London: C. Baker and Co., 1900)

Anon., *The American Tourist in France* (New York: Tourist Publishing Company, 1900)

Anon., *Cook's Guide to Paris* (London: Thomas Cook and Son, 1900)

Anon., *The Crystal Palace Timetable and Guide to London Amusements* (London: Murray's Guides, 1895)

Anon., *The Handy Handbook of London* (London: G. Faulkner and Sons, 1903)

Anon., *John Bull's Trip to Paris* (London: Favourite Publishing, 1900)

Anon., *London: A Complete Guide to the Leading Hotels and Places of Amusement, etc* (1894)

Anon., *Tit-Bits Guide to London* (London: Tit-Bits, 1895)

Apollinaire, Guillame, *Chroniques d'art, 1902–1918* (Paris: Editions Gallimard, 1960)

Appiganesi, Lisa, *The Cabaret* (London: Cassell and Collier Macmillan, 1975)

Ash, Russell, *Toulouse-Lautrec: The Complete Posters* (London: BCA Publications, 1991)

Avril, Jane, *Mes mémoires* (Paris: Phébus, 2005)

Bac, Ferdinand, *Femmes de théâtre*, preface by Yvette Guilbert (Paris: H. Simonis Empis, 1896)

Backer, Noèmia, 'Reconfiguring Annabelle's *Serpentine* and *Butterfly* dance films', in Simon Popple and Vanessa Toulim (eds), *Visual Delights: Essays on the Popular and Projected Image in the Nineteenth Century* (Trowbridge: Flicks Books, 2000), pp. 93–104

Baedeker and Co., *Paris and Environs: Handbook for Travellers* (Leipsic: Karl Baedeker, 1900)

Bailey, Peter, *Popular Culture and Performance in the Victorian City* (Cambridge: Cambridge University Press, 1998)

Banes, Sally, *Dancing Women: Female Bodies on Stage* (London: Routledge, 1998)

Barnicoat, John, *Posters: A Concise History* (London: Thames and Hudson, 1972)

Bascou, Marc, Ted Gott *et al.* (eds), *Paris in the Late Nineteenth Century* (Canberra: National Gallery of Australia Press, 1996)

Beauroy, Jacques, Marc Bertrand and E. T. Gargan (eds), *The Wolf and the Lamb: Popular Culture in France from the Old Regime to the Twentieth Century* (Saratoga: Amni Libri, 1978)

Beckson, Karl, *Arthur Symons: A Life* (Oxford: Clarendon Press, 1987)

—— (ed.), *The Memoirs of Arthur Symons: Life and Art in the 1890s* (University Park and London: Pennsylvania State University Press, 1977)

Beerbohm, Max, 'A Defence of Cosmetics', *The Yellow Book I*, April 1894, pp. 65–82

—— *The Works of Max Beerbohm* (New York: Dodd, 1922)

Beizer, Janet, *Ventriloquized Bodies: Narratives of Hysteria in Nineteenth-Century France* (Ithaca: Cornell University Press, 1994)

Benjamin, Walter, *The Arcades Project*, trans. by Howard Eiland and Kevin McLaughlin (Cambridge, MA: Belknapp Press, 1999)

Benstock, Shari, *Women of the Left Bank, Paris 1900–1940* (London: Virago, 1987)

Bentley, Toni, *Sisters of Salome* (New Haven: Yale University Press, 2002)

Bergman, Gosta M., *Lighting in the Theatre* (Totowa, NJ: Rowman and Littlefield, 1977)

Berlanstein, Lenard R., *Daughters of Eve: A Cultural History of French Theater Women from the Old Regime to the Fin de Siècle* (Cambridge, MA: Harvard University Press, 2001)

—— 'Historicizing and Gendering Celebrity Culture: Famous Women in Nineteenth-Century France', *Journal of Woman's History* 16:4, 2004, pp. 65–91

Bessière, Emile, *Autour de la butte* (Paris: Joubert, 1899)

Bloom, Ursula, *Curtain Call for the Guv'nor* (London: Hutchinson, 1954)

Bonduelle, Michel and Toby Gelfand, 'Hysteria Behind the Scenes: Jane Avril at the Salpêtrière', *Journal of the History of the Neurosciences* 7:1, 1998, pp. 35–42

Bowlby, Rachel, *Just Looking: Consumer Culture in Dreiser, Gissing and Zola* (New York: Methuen, 1985)

Bradbury, Malcolm and James McFarlane (eds), *Modernism: A Guide to European Literature 1890–1930* (London: Penguin, 1991)

Bratlinger, Patrick, *Bread and Circuses: Theories of Mass Culture as Social Decay* (Ithaca: Cornell University Press, 1983)

Bratton, Jacky, (ed.), *Music Hall: Performance and Style* (Milton Keynes: Open University Press, 1986)

—— *New Readings in Theatre History* (Cambridge: Cambridge University Press, 2003)

Brécourt-Villars, Claudine and Jean-Paul Morel (eds), *Jane Avril: mes mémoires* (Paris: Phébus, 2005)

Bronfen, Elisabeth, *The Knotted Subject: Hysteria and its Discontents* (Princeton: Princeton University Press, 1998)

—— 'The Language of Hysteria: A Misappropriation of the Master Narratives', *Women: A Cultural Review* 11:1/2, 2000, pp. 8–18

Broude, Norma and Mary D. Garrard (eds), *The Expanding Discourse: Feminism and Art History* (Boulder: Westview Press, 1992)

Buckley, Cheryl and Hilary Fawcett, *Fashioning the Feminine: Representation and Women's Fashion from the Fin de Siècle to the Present* (London and New York: I. B. Taurus, 2002)

Butler, Judith, *Bodies that Matter: On the Discursive Limits of Sex* (London: Routledge, 1993)

—— *Gender Trouble: Feminism and the Subversion of Identity* (London: Routledge, 1990)

Caddy, Davinia, 'Variations on the Dance of the Seven Veils', *Cambridge Opera Journal* 17:1, 2005, pp. 137–58

Caradec, François, *Jane Avril au Moulin-Rouge avec Toulouse-Lautrec* (Paris: Fayard, 2001)

Carey, John, *The Intellectuals and the Masses: Pride and Prejudice among the Literary Intelligentsia, 1880–1939* (London: Faber, 1992)

Carlson, Marvin, *The French Stage in the Nineteenth Century* (Metuchen, NJ: Scarecrow Press, 1972)

Cassell and Co., *Cassell's Guide to Paris and the Universal Exhibition of 1900* (London: Cassell, 1900)

Castle, Charles, *The Folies-Bergère* (London: Methuen, 1982)

Cate, Phillip Dennis (ed.), *The Graphic Arts and French Society, 1871–1914* (New Brunswick, NJ: Rutgers University Press co-published with the Jane Voorhees Zimmerli Art Museum, 1988)

Cate, Phillip Dennis and Mary Shaw (eds), *The Spirit of Montmartre:*

*Cabarets, Humor, and the Avant Garde, 1875–1905* (New Brunswick, NJ: Rutgers University Press, 1996)

Charney, Leo and Vanessa Schwartz (eds), *Cinema and the Invention of Modern Life* (Berkeley: University of California Press, 1995)

Charnow, Sally, *Theatre, Politics and Markets in Fin-de-Siècle Paris: Staging Modernity* (Basingstoke: Palgrave Macmillan, 2005)

Cherniavsky, Felix, 'Maud Allan, Part I: The Early Years, 1873–1903', *Dance Chronicle* 6:1, 1983, pp. 1–36

—— 'Maud Allan, Part II: First Steps to a Dancing Career, 1904–1907', *Dance Chronicle* 6:3, 1983, pp. 189–227

—— 'Maud Allan, Part III: Two Years of Triumph 1908–1909', *Dance Chronicle* 7:2, 1984, pp. 119–58

—— *The Salome Dancer: The Life and Times of Maud Allan* (Toronto: McClelland and Stewart Inc., 1991)

Coffman, Elizabeth, 'Women in Motion: Loïe Fuller and the "Interpenetration" of Art and Science', *Camera Obscura* 17:1, 2002, pp. 73–105.

Coleman, Bud, 'The Electric Fairy – the Apparition and the Woman – Loie Fuller', in Kim Marra and Robert A. Shanke (eds), *Passing Performances: Queer Readings of Leading Players in American Theatre History* (Ann Arbor: University of Michigan Press, 2001)

Coquiot, Gustave, *Les Cafés-concerts* (Paris: Librairie de l'Art, 1896)

Corbett, Mary Jean, 'Performing Identities: Actresses and Autobiography', *Biography* 24:1, 2001, pp. 15–23

Cormack, Bill, *A History of Holidays, 1812–1990* (London: Routledge co-published with the Thomas Cook Archives, 1998)

Crary, Jonathan, *Suspensions of Perception: Attention, Spectacle and Modern Culture* (Cambridge, MA: Harvard University Press, 1999)

——*Techniques of the Observer: On Vision and Modernity in the Nineteenth Century* (Cambridge, MA: MIT Press, 1992)

Cruickshank, Graeme (ed.), *The Palace Theatre, 1891–1991: A Chronology* (London: Palace Theatre Publications, 1981)

Current, Richard Nelson and Marcia Ewing Current, *Loïe Fuller: Goddess of Light* (Boston: Northeastern University Press, 1997)

Cutler, Anna, 'Abstract Body Language: Documenting Women's Bodies in Theatre', *New Theatre Quarterly* 54:2, 1998, pp. 111–18

Davis, Jim and Victor Emeljanow, '"Wistful Remembrancer": The Historiographical Problem of Macqueen-Popery', *New Theatre Quarterly* 17:4, November 2001, pp. 299–309.

Davis, Richard Harding, *About Paris* (New York: Harper Bros., 1895)

Davis, Richard Harding, *Adventures and Letters of Richard Harding Davis*, ed. Charles Belmont Davis (New York: Charles Scribner's Sons, 1918)

—— 'The Show-Places of Paris: Night', *Harper's New Monthly Magazine* 90, December 1894–May 1895, pp. 125–39

Davis, Tracy C., *Actresses as Working Women: Their Social Identity in Victorian Culture* (London: Routledge, 1991)

——'The Spectacle of Absent Costume: Nudity on the Victorian Stage', *New Theatre Quarterly*, 1989, pp. 321–33

Deak, Frantisek, 'Kaloprosopia: The Art of Personality: The Theatricalisation of Discourse in Avant-Garde Theatre', *Performance Art Journal* 13:2, 1991, pp. 6–21

—— *Symbolist Theatre: The Formation of an Avant Garde* (Baltimore: Johns Hopkins University Press, 1993)

Deare, Lilian, 'Trilby on the Stage', *Stevens Point Gazette*, 5 January 1895, p. 13

Desmond, Jane, *Meaning in Motion: New Cultural Studies of Dance* (Durham and London: Duke University Press, 1997)

Didi-Huberman, Georges, *Invention of Hysteria: Charcot and the Photographic Iconography of the Salpêtrière*, trans. by Alisa Hartz (Cambridge, MA: MIT Press, 2003)

Dijkstra, Bram, *Idols of Perversity: Fantasies of Feminine Evil in Fin-de-Siècle Culture* (Oxford: Oxford University Press, 1986)

Doane, Mary Ann, *Femmes Fatales: Feminism, Film Theory, Psychoanalysis* (London: Routledge, 1991)

Dolan, Jill, *The Discourse of Feminism: The Spectator and Representation* (Ann Arbor: University of Michigan Press, 1988)

Donnay, Maurice, *Autour du Chat Noir* (Paris: Grasset, 1926)

Donohue, Joseph, *Fantasies of Empire: The Empire Theatre of Varieties and the Licensing Controversy of 1894* (Iowa City: University of Iowa Press, 2005)

Du Maurier, George, *Trilby* (Ware: Wordsworth, 1995)

Ellis, Sylvia, *The Plays of W. B. Yeats: Yeats and the Dancer* (Basingstoke: Macmillan, 1995)

Erdman, Andrew L., *Blue Vaudeville: Sex, Morals and the Making of Mass Amusement, 1895–1915* (London: Eurospan, 2004)

Esslin, Martin, 'Theatre of the Absurd', *Tulane Drama Review* 4:4, May 1960, pp. 3–15

Evans, Martha Noel, *Fits and Starts: A Genealogy of Hysteria in Modern France* (Ithaca: Cornell University Press, 1991)

Faulk, Barry J., *Music Hall and Modernity: The Late-Victorian Discovery of Popular Culture* (Athens: Ohio University Press, 2004)

Felski, Rita, *The Gender of Modernism* (Cambridge, MA: Harvard University Press, 1995)

Fernbach, Amanda, 'Wilde's Salome and the Ambiguous Fetish', *Victorian Literature and Culture*, 2001, pp. 195–218

Ferris, Lesley, *Acting Women: Images of Women in Theatre* (London: Macmillan, 1990)

Finn, Margot C., 'Sex and the City: Metropolitan Modernities in English Histories', *Victorian Studies* 44:1, Autumn 2001, pp. 25–32

Flitch, J. E. Crawford, *Modern Dancing and Dancers* (London: Grant Richards Ltd, 1912)

Foreman, Mrs H. A., *Illustrated Portfolio of Artistic Dancing* (Portland, OR: Peaslee, 1894)

Forth, C. E., 'Moral Contagion and Will: The Crisis of Masculinity in Fin-de-Siècle France', in Alison Bashford and Claire Hooker (eds), *Contagion: Historical and Cultural Studies* (London: Routledge, 2001), pp. 61–75

Foster, Susan Leigh, *Corporealities: Dancing, Knowledge, Culture and Power* (London: Routledge, 1996)

Franko, Mark, *Dancing Modernism / Performing Politics* (Bloomington: Indianapolis University Press, 1995)

Frece, Lady de, *Recollections of Vesta Tilley* (London: Hutchinson and Co., 1934)

Frey, Julia, *Toulouse-Lautrec: A Life* (London: Weidenfeld and Nicolson, 1994)

Fuller, Loïe, *Fifteen Years of a Dancer's Life, with Some Account of her Distinguished Friends* (London: Herbert Jenkins, 1913)

Gale, Maggie B. and Vivien Gardner (eds), *Auto/Biography and Identity: Women, Theatre and Performance* (Manchester: Manchester University Press, 2004)

Gamman, Lorraine and Margaret Marshment (eds), *The Female Gaze: Women as Viewers of Popular Culture* (London: Women's Press, 1988)

Garb, Tamar, *Bodies of Modernity: Figure and Flesh in Fin-de-Siècle France* (London: Thames and Hudson, 1988)

Gardner, Vivien, 'The Invisible Spectatrice: Gender, Geography and Theatrical Space', in Maggie B. Gale and Vivien Gardner (eds), *Women, Theatre and Performance: New Histories, New Historiographies* (Manchester: Manchester University Press, 2001), pp. 25–45

Gardner, Vivien and Susan Rutherford (eds), *The New Woman and her Sisters: Feminism and Theatre, 1850–1914* (Brighton: Harvester Wheatsheaf, 1992)

Garelick, Rhonda K., 'Electric Salome: Loie Fuller at the Exposition Universelle of 1900', in J. Ellen Gainor (ed.), *Imperialism and Theatre* (London: Routledge, 1995), pp. 264–98

—— *Rising Star: Dandyism, Gender and Performance in the Fin de Siècle* (Princeton: Princeton University Press, 1998)

Geffroy, Gustave, *Yvette Guilbert* (Paris: André Marty, 1894)

Gendron, Bernard, *Between Montmartre and the Mudd Club: Popular Music and the Avant-Garde* (Chicago: University of Chicago Press, 2002)

Gilbert, Douglas, *American Vaudeville: Its Life and Times* (New York: Dover, 1963; first pub. Whittlesey House, 1940)

Gilman, Sander, Helen King, Roy Porter, G. S. Rousseau and Elaine Showalter (eds), *Hysteria Beyond Freud* (Berkeley: University of California Press, 1993)

Glenn, Susan A., *Female Spectacle: The Theatrical Roots of Modern Feminism* (Cambridge, MA: Harvard University Press, 2000)

Goellner, Ellen W. and Jacqueline Shea Murphy (eds), *Bodies of the Text: Dance as Theory, Literature as Dance* (New Brunswick, NJ: Rutgers University Press, 1995)

Goetz, Christopher G. (trans. and comm.), *Charcot the Clinician: The Tuesday Lessons* (New York: Raven Press, 1987)

Goetz, Christopher G., Michel Bonduelle and Toby Gelfand, *Charcot: Constructing Neurology* (Oxford: Oxford University Press, 1995)

Goodall, Jane R., *Performance and Evolution in the Age of Darwin* (London: Routledge, 2002)

Gordon, Rae Beth, 'From Charcot to Charlot: Unconscious Imitation and Spectatorship in French Cabaret and Early Cinema', *Critical Inquiry* 27:3, 2001, pp. 515–49

—— 'Natural Rhythm: La Parisienne Dances with Darwin: 1875–1910', *Modernism/Modernity* 10:4, 2003, pp. 617–56

—— *Why the French Love Jerry Lewis: From Cabaret to Early Cinema* (Palo Alto, CA: Stanford University Press, 2001)

Gosling, Nigel, *The Adventurous World of Paris, 1900–1914* (New York: William Morrow, 1978)

Grau, Robert, *Forty Years' Observation of Music and Drama* (New York: Broadway Publishing Company, 1909)

Greenhalgh, Paul, *Ephemeral Vistas: The Expositions Universelles, Great Exhibitions and World's Fairs, 1851–1939* (Manchester: Manchester University Press, 1988)

Grey, Sylvia, 'Dancing', *The Theatre*, 1 January 1898, pp. 34–7

Griffith, Mrs M., 'Loïe Fuller – the Inventor of the Serpentine Dance', *The Strand Magazine*, May 1894, pp. 540–5

Grosz, Elizabeth, *Volatile Bodies: Towards a Corporeal Feminism* (Bloomington, IN: Indiana University Press, 1994)

Guérin, Jean, 'Rue (la) Caire à l'Exposition', *Magasin pittoresque*, 1889, pp. 215–19

Guilbert, Yvette, *How to Sing a Song: The Art of Dramatic and Lyric Interpretation* (New York: Macmillan, 1918)

—— *The Song of My Life: My Memories*, trans. by Béatrice de Holthoir (London: G. Harrap and Co., 1929)

Guilbert, Yvette and Harold Simpson, *Yvette Guilbert: Struggles and Victories* (London: Mills and Boon, 1910)

Gunster, Shane, 'Revisiting the Culture Industry Thesis: Mass Culture and the Commodity Form', *Cultural Critique* 45, Spring 2000, pp. 40–70

Haddon, Archibald, *The Story of the Music Hall* (London: Fleetway Press, 1930)

Hall, Thornton, *Love Romances of the Aristocracy* (London: T. Werner Laurie, 1911)

Harding, James M. (ed.), *Contours of the Theatrical Avant-Garde: Performance and Textuality* (Ann Arbor: University of Michigan Press, 2000)

Harrington, Lenore A., *Trilbyana: The Rise and Progress of a Popular Novel* (New York: Critic Co., 1895)

Harris, G., 'But is it Art? Female Performers in the Café-Concert', *New Theatre Quarterly*, 1989, pp. 334–47

—— '"A Great Bath of Stupidity": Audience and Class in the Café-Concert', *TheatrePhile* 2:6, Spring 1985, pp. 29–31

—— 'Regarding History: Some Narratives Concerning the Café-Concert, Le Music Hall and the Feminist Academic', *The Drama Review* 40:4, 1996, pp. 70–84

Harris, Margaret Haile, *Loïe Fuller: Magician of Light* (Richmond: Virginia Museum of Fine Arts, 1979)

—— 'Loïe Fuller: The Myth, the Woman and the Artist', *Arts in Virginia* 20, 1979, pp. 16–29

Hawkins, Peter, *Chanson: The French Singer-Songwriter from Aristide Bruant to the Present Day* (Burlington, VT: Ashgate, 2000)

Hayman, Philip, 'The Magic of Dancing is Sorcery Sweet', *The Theatre*, 1 May 1891, pp. 237–9

Hemmings, F. W., *The Theatre Industry in Nineteenth-Century France* (Cambridge: Cambridge University Press, 1993)

Henderson, John, *The First Avant-Garde 1887–1894: Sources of the Modern French Theatre* (London: Harrap, 1971)

Hermans, Hub, W. E. Krul and Hans van Maanen (eds), *1894: European Theatre in Turmoil, the Meaning and Significance of the Theatre a Hundred Years Ago* (Amsterdam: Rodopi, 1994)

Hiatt, Charles, *Picture Posters* (London: George Bell and Sons, 1895)

Hoare, Philip, *Oscar Wilde's Last Stand: Decadence, Conspiracy and the Most Outrageous Trial of the Century* (New York: Arcade Publishing, 1998)

Hobbs, Richard (ed.), *Impressions of French Modernity* (Manchester: Manchester University Press, 1998)

Holdsworth, R. V. (ed.), *Arthur Symons: Poetry and Prose* (Cheadle: Carcanet Press, 1974)

Hollingshead, John, *Gaiety Chronicles* (London: Archibald Constable, 1898)

Hopkins, Albert A., *Magic: Stage Illusions and Scientific Diversions (Including Trick Photography)* (London: Sampson Low, Marston and Co., 1897)

Horrall, *Popular Culture in London c1890–1918: The Transformation of Entertainment* (Manchester: Manchester University Press, 2001)

Houchin, John, 'The Origins of the Cabaret Artistique', *The Drama Review* 28:1, 1984, pp. 5–14

Hunter, Dianne, *The Makings of Dr Charcot's Hysteria Shows: Research through Performance* (Lampeter: Edwin Mellen Press, 1998)

Hutton, Patrick H. (ed.), *Historical Dictionary of the Third French Republic, 1870–1940* (Westport, CT: Greenwood Press, 1986)

Innes, C. D. (ed.), *Avant Garde Theatre: 1892–1992* (London: Routledge, 2000)

—— *A Sourcebook on Naturalist Theatre* (London: Routledge, 2000)

Iskin, Ruth E., 'The Pan-European *Flaneuse* in *Fin-de-Siècle* Posters: Advertising Modern Women in the City', *Nineteenth-Century Contexts* 4, December 2003, pp. 333–56

Jarrett, Lucinda, *Stripping in Time: A History of Erotic Dancing* (London: HarperCollins, 1997)

Jasper, Gertrude R., 'Lugné-Poe and the Oeuvre', *French Review* 15:2, December 1941, pp. 127–34

Jenkins, Emily, 'Trilby: Fads, Photographers and "Over-Perfect Feet"', *Book History* 1, 1998, pp. 261–7

John, Juliet and Alice Jenkins (eds), *Rethinking Victorian Culture* (Basingstoke: Macmillan Press, 2000)

Jullian, Philippe, *Montmartre* (Oxford: Phaidon, 1977)

—— *The Symbolists* (London: Phaidon, 1973)

—— *The Triumph of Art Nouveau: Paris Exhibition 1900* (London: Phaidon, 1974)

Keft-Kennedy, Virginia, ' "How Does She Do That?" Belly Dancing and the Horror of a Flexible Woman', *Women's Studies* 34, 2005, pp. 279–300

Kelly, Veronica, 'Beauty and the Market: Actress Postcards and their Senders in Early Twentieth-Century Australia', *New Theatre Quarterly* 78, May 2004, pp. 99–116

Kératry, Viscomte de, *Paris Exposition, 1900: How to See Paris Alone* (London: Simpkin, Marshall, 1900)

Kermode, Frank, 'Poet and Dancer before Diaghilev', *Partisan Review* 28, 1961, pp. 48–75

—— *The Romantic Image* (London: Routledge and Kegan Paul, 1957)

Kettle, Michael, *Salome's Last Veil: The Libel Case of the Century* (London: Hart-Davis, 1977)

Kibler, Alison M., *Rank Ladies: Gender and Cultural Hierarchy in American Vaudeville* (Chapel Hill: University of North Carolina Press, 1999)

Kift, Dagmar, *The Victorian Music Hall: Culture, Class and Conflict* (Cambridge: Cambridge University Press, 1996)

Knapp, Bettina and Myra Chipman, *That Was Yvette: The Biography of a Great Diseuse* (London: Frederick Muller, 1964)

Knepler, Henry (trans. and ed.), *Man about Paris: The Confessions of Arsène Houssaye* (London: Victor Gollancz, 1972)

Koritz, Amy, 'Dancing the Orient for England: Maud Allan's "The Vision of Salome" ', *Theatre Journal* 46:1, 1994, pp. 63–78

—— *Gendering Bodies/Performing Art: Dance and Literature in Early Twentieth-Century British Culture* (Ann Arbor: University of Michigan Press, 1995)

—— 'Moving Violations: Dance in the London Music Hall, 1890–1910', *Theatre Journal* 42:4, 1990, pp. 419–31

Kuppers, Petra, 'Moving in the Cityscape: Performance and the Embodied Experience of the *Flâneur*', *New Theatre Quarterly* 60, 1999, pp. 308–17

Lapauze, H., Max de Nansouty, A. da Cunha, H. Jarzuel, G. Vitoux and L. Guillet, *Le Guide de l'Exposition de 1900* (Paris: Ernest Flammarion, 1900)

Laquer, Thomas, *Making Sex: Body and Gender from the Greeks to Freud* (Cambridge, MA: Harvard University Press, 1994)

Laquer, Walter, 'Fin de Siècle: Once More with Feeling', *Journal of Contemporary History* 31:1, January 1996, pp. 5–47

Lauter, Estella, *Women as Mythmakers: Poetry and Visual Art by Twentieth-Century Women* (Bloomington: Indiana University Press, 1984)

Laver, James (intro.) and Henry Davray (ed.), *XIXth Century French Posters* (London: Nicholson and Watson, 1944)

Lecky, Walter, 'Downfall of Zolaism', *Catholic World* 61:363, 1895, pp. 357–60

Ledger, Sally and Scott McCracken (eds), *Cultural Politics at the Fin de Siècle* (Cambridge: Cambridge University, 1995)

Lehmann, A. G., *The Symbolist Aesthetic in France, 1885–1895* (Oxford: Blackwell, 1968)

Lejeune, Dominique, *La Belle Epoque, 1896–1914* (Paris: Armand Collin, 1991)

Léon-Martin, Louis, *Le Music Hall et ses figures* (Paris: Editions de France, 1928)

Loeb, Lori Anne, *Consuming Angels: Advertising and Victorian Women* (Oxford: Oxford University Press, 1994)

Loftus, Peter, 'The Loftus Line', *Variety Fare*, February 1947, pp. 14–15

Luckhurst, Mary and Jane Moody (eds), *Theatre and Celebrity in Britain, 1660–2000* (Basingstoke: Palgrave Macmillan, 2005)

Lugné-Poe, Aurélien, *La Parade*, vol. 2: *Acrobaties: souvenirs et impressions de théâtre, 1894–1902* (Paris: Gallimard, 1931)

McCarren, Felicia, *Dance Pathologies: Performance, Poetics, Medicine* (Palo Alto, CA: Stanford University Press, 1998)

—— 'The "Symptomatic Act" Circa 1900: Hysteria, Hypnosis, Electricity, Dance', *Critical Inquiry* 21:4, Summer 1995, pp. 748–74

McCormick, John, *Popular Theatres of Nineteenth-Century France* (London: Routledge, 1993)

Maindron, Ernest, *Les Affiches illustrées, 1886–1895* (Paris: G. Boudet, 1896)

Mallarmé, Stéphane, 'Crayonné au théâtre', in Betrand Marchal (ed.), *Stéphane Mallarmé: oeuvres complètes* (Paris: Gallimard, 1998)

Marks, P., *Bicycles, Bangs and Bloomers: The New Woman in the Popular Press* (Lexington: University Press of Kentucky, 1990)

Marshall, Gail, *Actresses on the Victorian Stage: Feminine Performance and the Galatea Myth* (Cambridge: Cambridge University Press, 1998)

Masini, Lara, *Art Nouveau* (London: Thames and Hudson, 1984)

Matthews, Brander, 'The Pictorial Poster', *The Century: A Popular Quarterly* 44:5, September 1892, pp. 748–56

—— *The Theaters of Paris* (New York: Charles Scribner and Sons, 1880)

Mayer, Jean-Marie and Madeleine Rebérioux, *The Third Republic from its Origins to the Great War, 1871–1914* (Cambridge: Cambridge University Press, 1981)

Mayne, Jonathan (trans. and ed.), *Charles Baudelaire: The Painter of Modern Life and Other Essays* (London: Phaidon, 1964)

Medina, Nadia and Sarah Stanbury (eds), *Writing on the Body: Female Embodiment and Feminist Theory* (New York: Columbia University Press, 1997)

Melrose, Susan, 'My Body, Your Body, Her-His Body: Is/Does Some-Body (Live) There?', *New Theatre Quarterly* 54:2, 1998, pp. 119–24

Micale, Mark, *Approaching Hysteria: Disease and Its Interpretations* (Princeton: Princeton University Press, 1995)

Miller, Michael B., *The Bon Marché: Bourgeois Culture and the Department Store* (Princeton: Princeton University Press, 1981)

Milling, Jane and Martin Banham (eds), *Extraordinary Actors: Essays on Popular Performers* (Exeter: University of Exeter Press, 2004)

Mizejewski, Linda, *Ziegfeld Girl: Image and Icon in Culture and Cinema* (Durham, NC: Duke University Press, 1999)

Mistinguett, *Mistinguett: Queen of the Paris Night*, trans. by Lucienne Hill (London: Elek Books, 1954)

Morinni, Clare de, 'Loïe Fuller: The Fairy of Light', *Dance Index* 1, 1942, pp. 40–51

Morton, William H., *Sixty Years Stage Service* (London: Gale and Polden, 1905)

Moynet, Georges, *Trucs et décors: la machinerie théâtrale* (Paris: Libraire Illustrée, 1900)

Musée d'Orsay, *Le Théâtre de l'oeuvre, 1893–1900: naissance du théâtre moderne* (Paris: Musée d'Orsay, 2005)

Muskerry, William, *Thrillby: A Shocker in One Scene and Several Spasms, etc. (Being a parody on Paul M. Potter's dramatised version of George du Maurier's novel, Trilby)* (London: Lacy's, 1897)

Naremore, James and Patrick Bratlinger (eds), *Modernity and Mass Culture* (Bloomington: Indiana University Press, 1991)

Naylor, Stanley (ed.), *Gaiety and George Grossmith: Random Reflections on the Serious Business of Enjoyment* (London: Stanley Paul, 1913)

Nead, Lynda, *Myths of Sexuality: Representations of Women in Victorian Britain* (Oxford: Blackwells, 1988)

—— *Victorian Babylon: People, Streets and Images in Nineteenth-Century London* (New Haven and London: Yale University Press, 2000)

Nord, Deborah Epstein, 'The Urban Peripatetic: Spectator, Streetwalker, Women Writer', *Nineteenth-Century Literature* 46:3, 1991, pp. 351–75

—— *Walking the Victorian Streets: Women, Representation and the City* (Ithaca: Cornell University Press, 1995)

Nye, Robert A. (intro. and ed.), *Gustave le Bon: The Crowd, a Study of the Popular Mind* (New Brunswick and London: Transaction Press, 1995)

Oberthur, Mariel, *Cafés and Cabarets of Montmartre* (Salt Lake City: Peregrine Smith, 1984)

O'Monroy, Richard, *La Soirée parisienne* (Paris: P. Arould, 1890)

Pascoe, Charles E. (ed.), *Our Actors and Actresses: The Dramatic List* (London: Benjamin Blom, 1880)

Pedley-Hindson, Catherine, 'Jane Avril and the Entertainment Lithograph: The Female Celebrity and *Fin-de-Siècle* Questions of Corporeality and Performance', *Theatre Research International* 30:2, 2005, pp. 107–23

Perruchot, Henri, *Toulouse-Lautrec* (London: Constable, 1994)

Phillips, Ernest M. J., *How to Become a Journalist: A Practical Guide to Newspaper Work* (London: Sampson Low and Co., 1895)

Platt, Len, *Musical Comedy on the West End Stage, 1890–1939* (Basingstoke: Palgrave Macmillan, 2004)

Pollock, Griselda, *Differencing the Canon: Feminist Desire and the Writing of Art's Histories* (London: Routledge, 1999)

Pope, W. Macqueen, 'Gaiety Girls in Town Again', *The Sphere*, 28 January 1950, p. 130

—— *Gaiety: Theatre of Enchantment* (London: W. H. Allen, 1949)

Popple, Simon and Vanessa Toulmin (eds), *Visual Delights: Essays on the Popular and Projected Image in the Nineteenth Century* (Trowbridge: Flicks Books, 2000)

Postlewait, Thomas, 'Theatre Autobiographies: Some Preliminary Concerns for the Historian', *Assaph C* 16, 2000, pp. 157–72

Powell, Kerry, *Oscar Wilde and the Theatre of the 1890s* (Cambridge: Cambridge University Press, 1990)

—— *Women in the Victorian Theatre* (Cambridge: Cambridge University Press, 1997)

Prendergast, Christopher, *Paris and the Nineteenth Century* (Cambridge, MA and Oxford: Blackwell, 1992)

Pressly, Nancy L., *Salome: La Belle Dame sans Merci* (San Antonio: San Antonio Museum, 1983)

Price, David, *Cancan!* (London: Cygnus Arts, 1998)

Purcell, L. Edward, 'Trilby and Trilby Mania', *Journal of Popular Culture* 11:1 1977, p. 62

Rearick, Charles, *Pleasures of the Belle Epoque: Entertainment and Festivity in Turn-of-the-Century France* (New Haven: Yale University Press, 1985)

Reynolds, Nancy and Malcolm McCormick, *No Fixed Points: Dance in the Twentieth Century* (New Haven: Yale University Press, 2003)

Rheims, *The Age of Art Nouveau* (London: Thames and Hudson, 1966)

Richardson, Angelique and Chris Willis (eds), *The New Woman in Fiction and in Fact: Fin-de-Siècle Feminisms* (Basingstoke: Palgrave, 2000)

Ripa, Yannick, *Women and Madness: The Incarceration of Women in Nineteenth-Century France*, trans. by Catherine du Pelous Menagé (Cambridge: Polity, 1990)

Roberts, Mary Louise, *Disruptive Acts: The New Woman in Fin-de-Siècle France* (Chicago and London: University of Chicago Press, 2002)

Robins, Elizabeth, *Ibsen and the Actress* (London: Hogarth Press, 1928)

Rojek, Chris, *Celebrity* (London: Reaktion Books, 2001)

Ruskin, John, *Sesame and Lilies: Three Lectures* (Orpington: G. Allen, 1894)

Rydell, Robert W. and Nancy Gwinn (eds), *Fair Representations: World's Fairs and the Modern World* (Amsterdam: VU University Press, 1994)

Sadoff, Diane, 'Experiments made by Nature: Mapping the Nineteenth-Century Hysterical Body', *Victorian Newsletter* 81, 1992, pp. 41–4

St Johnston, Reginald, *A History of Dancing* (London: Simpkin, Marshall, Hamilton, Kent, 1906)

Samuels, Charles and Louise, *Once Upon a Stage: The Merry World of Vaudeville* (New York: Dodd Mead, 1974)

Savran, David, 'Towards a Historiography of the Popular', *Theatre Survey* 45:2, 2004, pp. 211–17

Schechner, Richard, *Performance Studies: An Introduction* (London: Routledge, 2002)

Schechter, Joel (ed.), *Popular Theatre: A Sourcebook* (London: Routledge, 2003)

Schumacher, C., *Naturalism and Symbolism in European Theatre, 1851–1918* (Cambridge: Cambridge University Press, 1996)

Schwartz, Vanessa, *Spectacular Realities: Early Mass Culture in Fin-de-Siècle Paris* (Berkeley: University of California Press, 1998)

Segel, Harold B., *Body Ascendant: Modernism and the Physical Imperative* (Baltimore: Johns Hopkins University Press, 1998)

—— *Turn of the Century Cabaret: Paris, Barcelona, Berlin, Munich, Vienna, Cracow, Moscow, St Petersburg, Zurich* (New York: Columbia University Press, 1987)

Senelick, Laurence, *Cabaret Performance: Europe 1890–1920* (New York: PAJ Publications, 1989)

Shattuck, Roger, *The Banquet Years: The Origins of the Avant Garde in France, 1885–1918* (New York: Vintage, 1968)

Shercliff, José, *Jane Avril of the Moulin Rouge* (London: Jarrolds, 1952)

Showalter, Elaine, *The Female Malady: Women, Madness and English Culture, 1830–1980* (London: Virago, 1987)

—— *Sexual Anarchy: Gender and Culture at the Fin-de-Siècle* (London: Virago, 1992)

Silverman, Debora L., *Art Nouveau in Fin-de-Siècle France: Politics, Psychology, and Style* (Berkeley: University of California Press, 1992)

Smith, Sidonie and Julia Watson (eds), *Women, Autobiography, Theory: A Reader* (Madison: University of Wisconsin Press, 1998)

Sommer, Sally R., 'Loïe Fuller's Art of Music and Light', *Dance Chronicle* 4, 1981, pp. 389–401

—— 'The Stage Apprenticeship of Loïe Fuller', *Dance Index* 12, 1977, pp. 23–34

Sommerville, Frankfort, *The Spirit of Paris* (London: Adam and Charles Black, 1913)

Spielmann, M. H. and G. S. Layard, *The Life and Work of Kate Greenaway* (London: Bracken Books, 1986)

Springer, Julie Ann, 'Art and the Feminine Muse: Women in Interiors by John Alexander White', *Women's Art Journal* 6:2, 1985–86, pp. 1–8

Stokes, John, *The French Actress and her English Audiences* (Cambridge: Cambridge University Press, 2005)

—— *In the Nineties* (Chicago: University of Chicago Press, 1989)

Stokes, John, Michael Booth and Susan Bassnet, *Bernhardt, Terry and Duse: The Actress in her Time* (Cambridge: Cambridge University Press, 1988)

Stuart, Charles Douglas and A. J. Park, *The Variety Stage: A History of the Music Halls from the Earliest Period to the Present Time* (London: T. Fisher Unwin, 1895)

Styan, J. L., *Modern Drama in Theory and Practice*, vol. 2: *Symbolism, Surrealism and the Absurd* (Cambridge: Cambridge University Press, 1983)

Sweetman, David, *Toulouse-Lautrec and the Fin-de-Siècle* (London: Hodder Headline, 1999)

Teich, Mikulas and Roy Porter (eds), *Fin de Siècle and its Legacy* (Cambridge: Cambridge University Press, 1990)

Thétard, Henry, *La Merveilleuse Histoire du cirque* (Paris: Prisma, 1947)

Thomas, Helen, *The Body, Dance and Cultural Theory* (Basingstoke: Palgrave Macmillan, 2003)

Thompson, Helen Bieri and Céline Eidenbenz (eds), *Salomé: danse et decadence* (Paris: Somogy Editions d'Art, 2003)

Tickner, Lisa, 'The Popular Culture of *Kermesse*: Lewis, Painting and Performance', *Modernism/Modernity* 4:2, 1997, pp. 67–120

—— *The Spectacle of Women: Imagery of the Suffrage Campaign* (Chicago: University of Chicago Press, 1988)

Timms, Edward and David Kelly (eds), *Unreal City: Urban Experience in Modern European Literature and Art* (Manchester: Manchester University Press, 1988)

Toepfer, K. E., *The Voice of Rapture: A Symbolist System of Ecstatic Speech in Oscar Wilde's Salome* (New York: P. Lang, 1991)

Vandam, Albert, *An Englishman in Paris: Notes and Recollections* (London: Chapman and Hall, 1892)

Van Vechten, Carl, *Interpreters and Interpretations* (New York: Alfred A. Knopf, 1927)

Victoria and Albert Publications, *Liberty's, 1875–1975* (London: V & A Publications, 1975)

Walkowitz, Judith R., *City of Dreadful Delight: Narratives of Sexual Danger in Late Victorian London* (London: Virago, 1992)

—— 'The Vision of Salome: Cosmopolitanism and Erotic Dancing in London, 1908–1918', *American Historical Review* 108:2, 2003, pp. 337–76

Weber, Adna Ferrin, *The Growth of Cities in the Nineteenth Century: A Study in Cities* (Ithaca: Cornell University Press, 1968)

Weber, Eugen, *France: Fin de Siècle* (Cambridge, MA: Harvard University Press, 1986)

Weill, Alan, *The Poster: A Worldwide Survey and History,* trans. by Marilyn Myatt (London: Sotheby's Publications, 1985)

Weisberg, Gabriel P. (ed.), *Montmartre and the Making of Mass Culture* (London: Rutgers University Press, 2001)

Whiteley, Derek Pepys, *George du Maurier: His Life and Work* (London: Art and Technics, 1948)

Williams, Rosalind, *Dream Worlds: Mass Consumption in Late Nineteenth-Century France* (Berkeley: University of California Press, 1982)

Wilson, Elizabeth, *The Sphinx in the City: Urban Life, the Control of Disorder and Women* (London: Virago, 1991)

Winter, Alison, *Mesmerized: Powers of Mind in Victorian Britain* (Chicago: University of Chicago Press, 2003)

Witkin, Robert W., *Adorno on Popular Culture* (London: Routledge, 2002)

# INDEX